VINES

Foreword by PAIGE PATTERSON

VINES

My Life *and* Ministry

JERRY VINES

Nashville, Tennessee

Contents

Foreword

Wen the sun makes its final escape beyond the cumulus formation in the west, leaving only the painted horizon against the silhouette of Acacias, there is not much that you can do in the African wilderness but gaze into the flickering fire and immerse yourself in your deepest thoughts. Swathed in a Navajo blanket and propped as close to the fire as I could get, my thoughts took flight on this particular evening to the question of the greatness of the leaders that God has given to Baptists during the last decades of the twentieth century. As I considered those leaders, I found myself wishing that somehow Adrian Rogers had told us the story of his life. Homer Lindsay's story could also have been mesmerizing. I remembered evangelists like Angel Martinez and great missionaries like Lottie Moon. To read these biographies is interesting, but to hear their actual words on what happened through the mercies of God in their own lives would have been an incomparable blessing. Then the thought occurred to me that perhaps Jerry Vines, the Georgia country boy, will favor us by writing his own autobiography.

VINES: My Life and Ministry is the answer to that fervent hope. I wish that I had actually suggested to him the task of writing his story, but this superb autobiography was well on the way to completion before Dr. Vines informed me of the work. While Dr. Vines suggests that writing one's autobiography is "either an exercise in narcissism or done in self-defense," and adds that perhaps this one is both, I would find it far more accurate to say that this biography is a gift. It is a gift to many, but particularly it is a gift to any young man who feels the call of God upon his life despite the fact that because of his circumstances, he does not have confidence to believe that God might greatly use him.

The early chapters of the book chronicle the life of a common Georgia boy growing up in a small town in America. The young man enjoyed some advantages that are normally given insufficient shrift. First, he grew up in a God-fearing family, and his parents were faithful to the church and faithful to the task of rearing the children God gave them. Second, Vines had the benefit of attending a faithful Baptist church where the Word of God was believed and practiced to the best of the ability of the parishioners. Finally, small-town Georgia should not be overlooked. Although replete with all the difficulties that sin brings to a community, nevertheless this community was one in which God's hand was recognized and one in which a deep patriotism and a profound recognition of the grace of God overshadowing the events that transpired in our country was foremost in the minds of the citizens. Finally, Vines had the opportunity for the best that education could offer and took advantage of every chance to study and learn.

Unfortunately, not all of his educational opportunities prepared him for the tasks that he was to face. Attending a Christian University in which many of the great truths of Christianity were already under attack, he also attended a seminary that was supposed by most to be the most conservative of the six Southern Baptist seminaries, even though infected with the invasion of neo-orthodoxy from Europe. Vines was doubtless stunned on more than one occasion by the unbelief that he encountered in professors. On the other hand, he met hundreds of men who would be friends for life and whose fellowship he would cherish until now. Furthermore, he proved to be one among the fifteen per cent who are not particularly intimidated by the siren song of unbelief. Quite to the contrary, his theology crystalized around the Word of God and the person of Jesus. When I first became acquainted with Dr. Vines, I could not help but marvel at the strength, together with humility, of his faithful witness.

The story herein recounts the various pastorates in which Vines faithfully ministered the Word of God. Some, like West Rome, while not free of difficulties, were stories of one triumph after another. At West Rome Baptist Church, Vines moved from being an insignificant Georgia preacher to become a Southern Baptist pastor of renown. Other pastorates, such as Dauphin Way in Mobile, were tall mountains for the young minister to climb; but even in the most difficult days, Vines proved in his own life the certainty of the promises of God. Finally, his friendship with Homer Lindsay, Jr., brought him to the pinnacle of his pastoral ministry first as co-pastor and then as the pastor of the First Baptist Church in Jacksonville, Florida.

Much of the book pictures the amazing developments associated with First Baptist, Jacksonville, which burgeoned to be one of the greatest churches in the Southern Baptist denomination. Now after retirement, Vines ends the book in the final half of his seventh decade. This monograph is the story of God's mercies and providence in a man totally committed to Christ.

This book that you hold in your hands, *VINES: My Life and Ministry,* is a book flowing with humility as in the life of the man who wrote it. You will not find boasting anywhere in the book. You will find much to admire and little to dislike. The reader will discover as consistent a witness to the Lord as a preacher could possibly give. Somehow as I read the pages of this book and consider Vines, I am drawn to the picture of Barnabas in the Scriptures. He was patient, longsuffering, doctrinally solid, and a comforter of all younger men. Jerry Vines has excelled in these tasks as few others. This autobiography makes no effort to obscure the controversies into which Vines occasionally found himself immersed. With candor, in the hope that others will profit from how these happened and how God once again demonstrated His grace in them all, Vines recounts the story of God's grace.

Janet and the children have added glow to the already bright ministry of Jerry Vines. His gratitude for the faithfulness of Janet and for the encouragement of their children injects itself at critical points in this narrative. In a day when so many homes are decimated and so many ministries are ruined by the failure of husband and wife to love one another deeply, this autobiography is a profound encouragement to all who seek an example of marital love and fidelity.

Jerry Vines finished preaching through the Bible at First Baptist Jacksonville, Florida. He completed his series through every book of the Bible by preaching through the book of Deuteronomy, farewell messages from Moses to the people of God. For his closing message at First Baptist, Jacksonville, he walked toward the back of the worship center in Jacksonville still preaching. The parishioners had heard another marvelous exposition characteristic of Vines. His ability to take a text, look at it for a few moments, and find the hand of God at work in it, take that text and lay it out for the people to understand is legendary. But on this night, the hearts of the congregation were also heavy because they knew that their pastor was walking into retirement. But even though the moment was sad, in a sense it was a happy moment for the rest of the evangelical world. For since that day, the far-famed Jacksonville pastor has expanded his ministry to our seminaries and significantly to the entire world. I for one am very grateful that Jerry Vines has given us *VINES: My Life and Ministry* so that we can visit all the places where he labored and see them through the eyes of a man of God.

—Paige Patterson, President Southwestern Baptist Theological Seminary Fort Worth, Texas

Prologue

To write one's autobiography is either an exercise in narcissism or done in self-defense! Perhaps mine is a mixture of both. I guess I'm writing for my own benefit more than anything else. Benjamin Franklin said, "That which resembles most living one's life over again, seems to be to recall all the circumstances of it; and, to render this remembrance more durable, to record them in writing." I must say that this has been a special time for me. I recalled events and experiences not unpacked from my memory PDFs in quite a while. Just the memory of them brought me mostly pleasure, some pain, whichever the case may be.

I certainly haven't written about all of the experiences of my life and ministry. I attempted to write about the pertinent facts. I tried to be honest with myself. Along the way, in a 50+ ministry as a gospel preacher, some high mountains of delight enthralled me. Low valleys of despair and defeat beset me. There isn't a book big enough to include them all. I include enough of the mountains and valleys to give an honest appraisal of this redeemed sinner. You who read will make your assessment. The Judge of all the earth will render His at the Judgment Seat.

My primary structure for this volume is chronological. Starting with some historical background of my place of origin, I move to the present time. I date many of the events; others I do not. The general structure of the book takes me from birth to the present day. At times I dip back into a previous segment of my life. This enables me to summarize some crucial details of my life and interactions with others.

I was privileged to be pastor of eight churches during my ministry. Through the years of those pastorates I met many people. Some were irregular. Some were ornery. Some were difficult. Some were sweet. Some were godly. The overwhelming majority were a blessing. Some were special. They were pretty much like the kind of people any pastor will encounter during his career as a minister of the gospel.

When dealing with church problems I encountered, I chose not to use any names. I do not feel it is proper nor necessary. I do mention some names of people who were especially helpful in my churches. Futile would be an attempt to name every staff member who assisted me through the years. To try to name all the laypeople with whom I served along the way would be even more futile.

In dealing with certain Southern Baptist Convention issues, I do use some names. I do not mention them with any sense of rancor. I can truthfully say there is not one person mentioned in a negative fashion I do not love. Some are so high profile and the events that transpired are so well known most would know the names regardless.

I present certain aspects of Convention events as best as I can recall them. Others involved may dispute the accuracy of what is written in this book. I would encourage them to write down their own recollections. Then people can make up their own minds.

My desire is that all who read my autobiography would understand, though not stated on every page, that I fully recognize the presence and power of the Lord in my entire life and ministry. To Him goes all the glory for victories accomplished. To me goes all the blame for the defeats.

I hope this recounting of my life and times will be especially helpful to young servants of God. Early on God gave me a great love and respect for preachers. At my boyhood home the biggest event of the year was the visit of our pastor to share a meal. I think I understand how preachers feel. I served as pastor of churches in rural settings, neighborhoods, mill villages, and large cities. I served churches with forty to ten thousand in attendance. I offer this book in an attempt to help young preachers in sermon preparation. Many of my conference messages were prepared with them in mind. If this book can encourage preachers, especially the young, I will be glad.

I write so that my children and grandchildren might understand their dad and Poppy. There were many times when my responsibilities of ministry carried me away from my family. Joy, Jodi, Jim, and Jon never seemed to mind it. They are so loving and supportive of their dad through these years. I love them dearly. I am Poppy to Brittney, Ashlyn, Jay, Caroline, Catherine, Jack, and Carson. I pray this book will call them to a life of total dedication to the Lord Jesus Christ. Tim Williams and Leslie Vines are superb son and daughter-in-laws. Tim is a very effective evangelist. Leslie is a very fine educator. I am so proud of both of them. There is never a cross word between us. I pray this autobiography will help them understand me on a deeper level.

I write this book as a tribute to my wife, Janet. Now married fifty-three years, she is the love of my life. She served alongside me as the ideal preacher's wife. God gave me the finest wife I could ever have imagined. Though most of this book will not be new to her, I pray it will help her understand just how much I love her and how much she means to me.

I appreciate encouragement from many to write an autobiography. Primarily there is Dr. Paige Patterson. Though I thoroughly enjoy our pranks, banter, and studied insults, most of all I deeply appreciate his love and friendship. I am privileged to know a man of his profound scholarship, love for the lost, and deep devotion to the Lord Jesus Christ.

I want to express my thanks to Dr. Thom Rainer, CEO of LifeWay, for his willingness to publish this volume. And I am grateful for the help of Selma Wilson, Devin Maddox, and Kim Stanford at B&H. Thanks to our daughter, Joy, our sweet neighbor, Ashley Russ, and our Jacksonville photographer, Bill Thompson, who helped with the pictures for the Photo Gallery.

Finally, I want to offer thanksgiving and praise to my wonderful Savior, my Guide and Friend through these seventy-five plus years of *VINES: My Life and Ministry.*

Chapter 1

Totsi Goes to Town

Totsi wiped the sweat off his brow, looked at the red Georgia clay and the stubborn mule. "This is not for me. I'm going to town and get me a job where I have to wear a shirt and tie!" Totsi was plowing in the fields with his father and four brothers. Ossie, his mother, and Carrie, his only sister, were doing all the necessary work at the house. And they were preparing three bountiful meals every day for their hungry, robust men. The land wasn't theirs. They were sharecroppers. They rented the house and land. They were engaged in what was called "subsistence agriculture." The rugged typography encouraged such farming. They grew enough food to feed the family and to give the owner a share of the crops in return. This kind of farming was in contrast to the plantations common to the eastern parts of Georgia. Some cotton was grown, but this was diminishing where Totsi lived.

Totsi had really wanted to go to the University of Georgia. He was an outstanding basketball player at Roopville High School. What an opportunity! Receive a free education and play the sport he loved. His father, Jim, regretted it, but he needed him in the field. He didn't go to college. He was stuck with this hard, red-clay field and a smelly mule! His best friend, Otis Copeland, went on to UGA and became the founder of the successful *Southern Living* magazine. Totsi often wondered what he might have become had he been able to take the offer. He would never know.

Indian Territory

What did he care that the land encompassing Carroll County, Georgia, was a part of Indian territory in earlier years? From time to time, along with squirming snakes and hard rocks, he uncovered arrowheads in the field. The land that is now Carroll County was originally inhabited by the Cherokee Indians to the north and the Creek Indians to the south. In his volume, *Georgia's Last Frontier: The Development of Carroll County,* James C. Bonner provides helpful information about the frontier years of Carroll County.[1] The Cherokees to the north achieved a fairly high degree of civilization. The capital of the Cherokee nation was located at New Echota, fifty miles north of Carroll County. Their civilization produced a printing press and a newspaper. Chief Sequoyah had created a writing system for the Cherokees. This system of eighty-five letters was unique among Indians in its day.

The Creeks to the south were less progressive. In contrast to the clothing worn by Cherokees, they were primarily clad in loincloths. Winter coldness found them wrapped in blankets made of animal skins, moccasins, and leggings made of leather. The Creeks loved ornaments. Feathers, bracelets, and armlets were common. Creeks would paint their bodies yellow, red, blue, or black.

Creeks were also divided into two groups: Upper and Lower Creeks. Upper Creeks lived primarily in northern Alabama and down into Georgia. The Lower Creeks lived from the southern part of what is now Carroll County and below. Both groups felt the pressure of white settlers intruding on the land where their tribes lived and hunted wild game. White settlers outnumbered the Indians four to one. Increasingly the U.S. government pressured the Indians to cede more and more land to them. The Upper Creeks were stubborn in their resistance. A Shawnee leader named Tecumseh and his brother, known as the Prophet, had met with the Upper Creeks. A prophecy was made saying that the white settlers would be exterminated and the Indians could maintain their old ways. The Upper Creeks' opposition to expansion led to the Red Stick War. The Upper Creeks were defeated at the Battle of Horseshoe Bend on the Tallapoosa River. There American General Andrew Jackson defeated the

Upper Creeks (Red Sticks, as they were known). This defeat, and the fact that Lower Creek Indians fought with the U.S. army, created a great deal of hostility.

The Lower Creeks were not as resistant as were the Upper Creeks. This was due to the leadership of one of the most remarkable Indian chiefs of that time. The famous Chief William McIntosh was the leader of the Lower Creeks. George Chapman shares invaluable information about Chief McIntosh in his excellent volume *Chief William McIntosh: A Man of Two Worlds*.[2] Called "White Warrior," McIntosh was part Irish and part Creek. His father was John McIntosh, who had come with General James E. Oglethorpe from the Scottish Highlands to Savannah, Georgia. John married Senoia, a Creek Indian of the prestigious Wind Clan, which produced many of the leaders of the Creek nation.

Tall and light skinned, William spoke English and Creek (Muscogee). He was born between two worlds. A man of many gifts, he started successful businesses. Among them was an Inn at Indian Springs, Georgia (near Flovilla), a trading post, and other business ventures. He also built a two-story home for his family on a small plantation known as Acorn Bluff. Nestled in lush grasses, trees, and flowers near the Chattahoochee River, tribal council meetings and games were sometimes held there. Located four miles west of Whitesburg in Carroll County, Georgia, it was to be the scene of his murder.

McIntosh was a successful soldier. Because he fought with the U. S. in the Red Stick War, he was elevated to the rank of General. This, of course, created a great deal of animosity between McIntosh and the Upper Creeks.

He stood out as a great leader and gifted statesman for the Creeks. Visiting Washington, D.C., on numerous occasions, the Chief met with several Presidents, including Thomas Jefferson. McIntosh seemed to understand that the supremacy of the white man was inevitable. He also saw there were many advantages to the Indians from learning the white man's ways. He favored the work of Christian missionaries among his people. Many of the Lower Creeks became Christians, most of them affiliating with Baptists. He urged the education of Indian children.

Increasingly, the U.S. government wanted the Indians of Georgia to move west. In a series of treaties, eight in all, McIntosh agreed to yield more and more lands to the white settlers in exchange for monetary payment and the promise of a land of their own in Oklahoma. He lobbied powerfully for his Creek people to move west of the Mississippi to the Indian Territory. The U.S. government promised them protection and security if they would cede the right to their land. McIntosh, who was not only a chief but the speaker of the Creek Nation, spoke often and persuasively urging that the offer be accepted. In one of his most powerful pleas, he said, "To love the land is mean; to love the people is noble."[3]

The matter came to a head with the signing of the Treaty of 1825. The Upper Creeks were becoming more and more hostile to Chief McIntosh. Increasingly suspicious of him, his integrity was attacked. They sent dire warnings that if he signed the treaty he would be killed. According to Indian law, traitors were to be killed on their property in the presence of their family. Courageously, McIntosh signed the treaty. The Creeks were to receive $400,000 for the land. Chief McIntosh was to receive $25,000 of that for his leadership in bringing the Creeks to the table.

The die was cast. The Treaty was signed on February 10, 1825. On the night of May 30, 1825, warriors from the Upper Creeks set fire to the McIntosh home. Billows of smoke clouded the night air. Shots rang out. McIntosh retreated to his upstairs bedroom. The attackers caught him there, shot him numerous times, and finally plunged a long dagger into his chest. His oldest son, Chilly, sleeping in another building, escaped out a window, ran for his life, and plunged into the rapid current of the Chattahoochee River. In 1828, nearly a decade before the infamous Trail of Tears, Chilly led 738 Creeks to the Indian Territory. There in Oklahoma the McIntosh name is often recorded in the history of the Creek (or Muscogee) Indians. To this day, progeny of the McIntosh family can be found in and around Carroll County.

"So what?" Totsi would have said. Totsi had little to no interest in Creek Indians and what they did on Carroll County soil. Certainly didn't make his work anymore pleasant. The noonday sun was now bearing down upon him. The fragrant smell of honeysuckles on the edge of the field was smothered by the stench of mule manure. Hank Williams said,

"You got to have smelt a lot of mule manure before you can sing like a hillbilly." Totsi was interested in singing gospel but not mule-inspired hillbilly.

His mom and sister were bringing food to the field. This gave him some respite from plowing but none from the hot sun, his sweat-drenched overalls, and his dirt-covered brogans. "I'm going to town and get me a job in a store where there is a fan and I can wear a white shirt and a tie."

Carroll County

The founding of Carroll County was of no interest to Totsi either. Carroll County has been correctly called by Dr. James C. Bonner, Georgia's Last Frontier. The sixty-sixth county of Georgia's 159, its western border was joined to the state of Alabama. And it was the last land where Indians were located in significant numbers. After the signing of the Treaty of 1825, the U.S. government surveyed the land and distributed it by lot to its citizens. The county was chartered in 1826. The name honored Charles Carroll of Maryland, one of the signers of the Declaration of Independence. By 1829 the population of the new county was 4,186.[4]

Agriculture became the main occupation of the county. There was also some mining. Gold mining in the village of Villa Rica (meaning, Rich Village) brought settlers to the county. Gold from the Bonner Gold Mine near Bethesda Baptist Church was used to support the war effort of the Confederacy.

The early settlers of Carroll County were people of faith. In the earlier years Methodists far outnumbered Baptists. In 1850 there were twenty Methodist churches and only eight Baptist congregations. Methodists were greatly assisted by the Methodist Seminary located in Mount Zion in Carroll County. Baptists were adversely affected by the schism that rent Baptists in those years. The dispute arose between churches that came to be known as Missionary Baptist and Primitive or "Hardshell" Baptists. Primitive Baptists opposed foreign missions and an educated ministry. Beneath these conflicts was the doctrine of Calvinism, known as the "doctrines of grace." The Georgia Baptist state paper said of that conflict, "It tore Baptist congregations apart, destroyed friendships, and broke asunder many long-standing associations."[5]

While Primitive Baptist congregations in the county declined, Missionary Baptist churches grew. Baptists became more numerous than Methodists. Totsi's family was Baptist in its church affiliation. In the various Baptist churches where they attended, Totsi developed a love for singing and demonstrated musical ability as a tenor. He was often called upon to lead a song in one of the periodic all-day singings held in the rural churches. He learned to read shaped notes at singing schools held by the Stamps-Baxter Music Company. He and his bass-singing brother, Cliff, were part of several gospel quartets.

The strong faith of Carroll County citizens gave them a keen sense of moral rectitude. In the earlier years of the County's life, a well-organized gang of horse thieves, renegades, and outlaws called "The Pony Club" terrorized the county. Honest citizens known as "Slicks" banded together and put the gangsters out of business.

There was also a keen interest in the education of its young people. Bowdon College was started in 1857 and continued until 1936. In 1934 West Georgia A&M College (now University of West Georgia) was begun in Carrollton. The educational enterprise was interrupted because of the Civil War. A Bowdon College cohort of students became a part of Cobb's Legion that fought in several Civil War battles. They fought at Fredricksburg, Gettysburg, Chickamauga, and Chattanooga.

The presence of these educational institutions perhaps contributed to the fact that racial antagonism in Carroll County was relatively insignificant. Also, the political influence of Thomas E. Watson, leader of the Populist movement in Georgia, newspaper editor, and United States senator, was a positive factor. Bonner summed up the attitude of Carroll Countians thusly: "There are no leading people. Every man in CarrollCounty thinks he's as good as anyone else, if not a damned sight better."[6]

The Civil War brought its share of misery to Carroll County. Though there was no fighting on Carroll County soil, the county did experience the ravages of Sherman's March to the Sea. Many buildings were set on fire. Soldiers returned to find their homes burned and their families in desperate conditions. Two plantation homes survived: the Hobbes Plantation house and the Mandeville house.

Totsi knew nothing of the founding and history of the county. Nor did he care. All he knew was that plowing the difficult soil of the county was not for him. "I'm headed to town."

Carrollton

Carrollton! The county seat and the hub of the county's economic life. The original county seat was located near Sandhill, Georgia, eight miles northeast of Carrollton. The county seat was moved and incorporated as Carrollton in 1829. The original intention was to name the town Troupville, in honor of Governor Troup. However, Troup was in disfavor at that time, so the county took its name from Charles Carroll of Maryland as well.

Typical of many southern towns, Carrollton was laid out around the central feature of the town square. Adamson Square was named for Judge/Congressman William C. Adamson. In the center of the square was a small park area. Central to the park was a tall, magnificent memorial to the Confederate soldier. Made of Georgia marble, the monument had a soldier on top, standing on a square with a marble ball at each corner. Town citizens and county farmers mingled together on the square. This was the social gathering and shopping place of the citizens. Many a young man and woman "tripped the light fantastic," not on the sidewalks of New York but on the Square of Carrollton. Totsi wanted to be one of those. The girls of Adamson Square sure beat that cockeyed mule he was following.

The coming of a railroad in 1874 brought economic prosperity to the town and the county. The railroad enabled the farmers to ship their crops to other places. Also, fertilizer and agricultural supplies were shipped into Carrollton by rail. In addition, the railroad precipitated the growth of other industrial ventures, including textile mills. This kind of commerce created many other economic opportunities for the town. On the square were department stores: The Hub, The Leader, and The Globe. Locally owned grocery stores sprang up: Bonner's and Copeland's. Chain stores followed: A&P, Kroger, Colonial. Food establishments were few: The Dinner Bell café and McGee's Bakery.

Totsi was certainly interested in all of that! And, to repeat, the Carrollton Square was where pretty town girls promenaded in the evenings. Their heavily rouged faces, fixed-up hair, and flowing dresses beat a brown mule with bit and bridle. The year was 1936. Totsi was nineteen and looking to find a wife and build a life. "Yep, Carrollton. That's for me!"

The town and the county felt the effects of the Great Depression of the 1930s. The years were difficult, and farmers eked out a meager living for their families. The townspeople struggled to survive. After the depression of the 1930s, farming experienced some decline while urban job opportunities blossomed. In Carrollton there were jobs to be had and money to be made. That's what Totsi was thinking.

So Totsi left the farm, acquired employment at one of the department stores, and moved to town. That fan in the store sure did feel good! He looked so sharp in his white dress shirt and new tie. It was Sunday-go-to-meeting clothes during the week!

Pretty soon Totsi made his way to the early evening gatherings on the Square. There were girls galore and he was eligible.

Ruby

Ruby Ophelia Johnson was the only daughter of W. O. and Katie Lee Johnson. Her mother, Katie Lee Tuggle, was a daughter of the rather prosperous Tuggle farmers on the road between Carrollton and nearby village Bowdon. Her father was one of the few men in the county with a college education, having graduated from Bowdon College. Though with farming roots himself, W. O. had become a businessman. At the time he ran a boarding house in Carrollton. His wife, Katie Lee, was known for the fine home-cooked meals she prepared for their boarders. Ruby learned to cook from her mother. As the saying goes, the way to a man's heart is through his stomach!

Very often Ruby would make it to the evening strolls on the Square. Thin, rouged cheeks, pretty black hair, she was barely twenty-one. Totsi was walking in one direction; Ruby in the other. They met. On the square! A few words and both were smitten. A brief courtship ensued. Totsi was a talker. Ruby was quiet. Suited Totsi just fine. He liked to talk. Both were ready for marriage. So on September 19, 1936, they were married. Preacher Bonner performed the wedding underneath the shade trees in front of his house on the Bethesda Baptist Church road.

Me

Soon there was a baby on the way! September 22, 1937, at the old Griffin home on the Bremen Road, near Beulah Baptist Church, Charles Jerry Vines was born. I like to say I was born at a very early age. I was born at home because I wanted to be close to my momma. And I was so surprised by my new surroundings that I didn't speak for months!

So Totsi went to town. His name wasn't Totsi. Totsi was an Indian name for a girl, meaning "moccasion." His family gave him that nickname because a girl named Totsi at an adjoining farm was sweet on him. The family was made up of people who enjoyed kidding one another, so they started calling him Totsi. His real name was Charles Clarence Vines. He was my father. Ruby was my mother. The story begins.

Chapter 2

Meeting at the Tabernacle

I f you'll lay a bigger foundation, I will pay the difference." So said J. M. Johnson, chairman of the committee to build the new building for Tabernacle Baptist Church in Carrollton, Georgia.

Central Baptist Church

Totsi wasn't my father's real name. Tabernacle Baptist wasn't the church's first name either. The church was constituted as Central Baptist Church on October 15, 1899.[7] The church was organized by seventeen people from First Baptist Church, Carrollton, Georgia. There festered a growing controversy involving the pastor and one of the ladies in the church choir. Efforts were made to get the leaders of First Baptist to take action against the pastor. Failure to do so precipitated the decision of these seventeen to withdraw and start their own church.[8]

Central Baptist immediately began to grow. The congregation's first building, seating four hundred people, was located on Tanner Street. Soon, however, the congregation outgrew this first structure. A committee was selected to make plans for a larger building. J. M. Johnson, a deacon of the church and a prosperous, well-respected member of Central, was selected to be the chairman of the building committee. The decision was soon made to relocate and build a building on Bradley Street. This would provide more space for anticipated growth.

The Tabernacle

The new building was first referred to as "Tabernacle" in the church minutes of May 1913. There was a definite reason for this change of name. At that time Tabernacle Baptist in Atlanta was under the dynamic leadership of Dr. Len Broughton. The large Atlanta congregation was the most well-known and most evangelistic church in the state of Georgia. Dr. Broughton came from First Baptist Church, Jacksonville, Florida. A most colorful preacher, his shoulder-length hair and unusual messages drew people in large numbers. His dynamic preaching, innovative programs, and evangelistic outreach had resulted in the church becoming the largest congregation in the South. Central Baptist was also innovative and evangelistic in its emphasis. So the decision was made to build a tabernacle. The roots of such a structure and name can be traced back to Atlanta Baptist Tabernacle, Moody's Tabernacle in Chicago, and Spurgeon's Tabernacle in London.

"But, we have already laid a foundation," replied the building supervisor. "It will be too expensive to tear up the foundation and start over," he continued. Deacon Johnson replied, "We aren't building for today. We are building for tomorrow. If you'll lay a bigger foundation, I will pay the difference." So it came to be. The Tabernacle was enlarged. The church was built upon two foundations. Three actually. Spiritually, the church was founded upon the solid rock, Christ Jesus.

The Tabernacle was completed in June 1914. Remarkable indeed was the building. At the time it was the largest building in actual size in the state of Georgia.[9] Seating fourteen hundred people, it could accommodate more people than any auditorium in Atlanta with the exception of the Atlanta Baptist Tabernacle. At the time the population of Carrollton was five thousand. This means one in four people of the town could be seated there. This is even more remarkable because it was built by a congregation that numbered only 210. The choir loft was large enough to hold the entire congregation![10]

This beautiful, large meeting place witnessed several notable events in the earlier years. The Georgia Baptist Convention held its annual meeting there in November, 1914. President Franklin D. Roosevelt (then governor of New York State) spoke there. On his way to Warm Springs, Georgia, Roosevelt was scheduled to speak at an outdoor meeting on the campus of West Georgia College. Due to an unexpected rainstorm, the meeting was moved to the Tabernacle, the largest building in town. The church was filled and running over. Some even pulled their buggies and cars up to the windows to be able to hear and see Roosevelt. Governor Roosevelt, because of paralysis, could not stand without some assistance. He stood, bracing himself by holding on to the rostrum. An aide stood behind to catch him, should he fall.

His speech was a real crowd pleaser. While he was speaking, a little child came running down the aisle, crying. With the calmness and skill which were his as a public speaker, Roosevelt departed from his speech, looked affectionately at the child, and surmised that the child "must have come over the same roads I have. I could cry, too." The crowd laughed and Roosevelt continued his speech.[11]

Headed for the Meeting

However, those were not the most notable events to take place in the Tabernacle, as far as my story is concerned. Though I was not born at the time, God had led a Baptist congregation to build an edifice and have a ministry that would fulfill the purpose God intended for the Tabernacle in the wilderness: "There I will meet with Thee" (Exod. 25:22).

I was born on a country road; I never actually lived in the country. My dad intended to make town folks out of his family! Nevertheless, he still loved the country music he had heard in the country churches the Vines family had attended. He was fond of the all-day singings held at various churches. And that's how I made my first visit to church. I was only five weeks old. There was to be an all-day singing at Beulah Baptist Church, where the Vines were attending church at the time. Contrary to the recommendations of some pediatricians today, I was taken out for my first visit to church. Some seventy-six plus years later I don't think the trip to church hurt me much!

Clarence took his wife, Ruby, and me to Tabernacle Baptist Church— in town! The church was well thought of by the rural people of Carroll County. Most of the members had come from the farm to town, as had Clarence. One of his singing friends, Bruce Cumbie, a prominent Carrollton businessman, was director of music at Tabernacle. He enlisted Clarence to be his assistant director. My dad did assist when there wasn't an all-day singing somewhere!

In the early years I was a part of all the activities at the church. And there were many. I was placed in the nursery. As I grew older, I attended Sunday school. I was a part of the Sunbeams, a Bible and missionary program for children ages two through grade three. I sang in the children's choirs. There were times when I would be taken to the all-day singings. I didn't care much for the singings. But I really did like the dinner on the ground. Fried chicken legs, mashed potatoes, and banana pudding were just what a young boy wanted. When I grew older, I would fill one plate, take it to the car for later consumption, then return for my first meal.

We lived in a number of houses in the early years. My dad moved from job to job. He would get a better offer and would take it. He worked as a Merita Bread deliveryman. He was a butcher in grocery stores. He worked in department and furniture stores. A natural-born salesman, his services were sought by many in the retail business. As he could afford it, we would move to a nicer house.

My elementary years were spent at College Street Grammar School. Within easy walking distance of where we currently lived, I went there from first through seventh grades. Along the way I would meet up with friends. We would laugh, cut up, and walk along together.

Some teachers took a real interest in me. My all-time favorite teacher was Ms. Lera Maxwell, my sixth-grade teacher. She and her husband, James, were active members of Tabernacle Baptist Church. In future years my father would manage their furniture store. What a delightful, pleasant teacher she was! Each day she met us with a smile and a twinkle in her eye. She convinced me I could do most anything. I went all-out to please her. The result was a year with straight As.

My seventh grade wasn't so pleasant. My teacher that year was also a member of Tabernacle. But she was rather stern and demanding. I didn't do quite as well. In those years I had a cowlick on each side of my forehead. For you moderns that is a section of hair that stands straight up or lies at an angle at odds with the rest of the hair. And for my smart-aleck friends, my head was covered in hair back then! As a result of the cowlicks, my hair wouldn't stay up but kept falling in my face. My teacher kept telling me to comb it out of my eyes. I tried, but it kept flopping down. So one day she took a hairpin and pinned my hair in place. I was embarrassed and humiliated.

The next day, to my surprise, the entire class came with hairpins in their hair! Talk about peer support! That night the Vines family attended a cottage prayer meeting at my teacher's home. For me there was no choice in the matter, but I was not interested in going to a prayer meeting at her house. She realized she did the wrong thing and apologized to my parents and to me. The year went much better from then on.

There was a special day in my grammar school years. The Gideons came to our school. A talk was given about the importance of reading the Bible. Each student who would commit to reading the New Testament all the way through was given a free copy. I made the commitment and headed home with great excitement, holding my small, red Gideon New Testament. Though unaware at the time, God was putting His Word in my heart in preparation for the "Meeting at the Tabernacle."

Interrupted by War

My grammar school years were interrupted by World War II. Dad's youngest brother, Dumas, had been in the army and was seriously wounded in France. I can still remember him gathering the family at his parents' home. With great emotion he would retell the horrors of being shot. To get back to friendly territory, he crawled several miles holding in his intestines. Hearing such horrible experiences caused my dad to enlist in the Merchant Marines. To be near him my mother and I followed him to Saint Petersburg, Florida. We rented one side of a duplex apartment, next to a sweet Russian couple.

I remember quite well my mom walking me to school every day. I also remember quite well the bigger boys beating up on me, the new boy in school. And I also remember trying to jump a chain-link fence at the school, tripping and cutting both sides of my chin, leaving scars I carry to this day.

Everything wasn't bad, however. Right across the street from our duplex was Al Lang Field, where the New York Yankees conducted their spring training. I would often go over there and watch them. I could just see myself playing for the Yankees one day. On a day I was outside the ballpark and saw a fleet of cars drive up amid great excitement. Photographers were everywhere, lights flashing. A car door opened, and out stepped Babe Ruth, one of my baseball heroes! He was in poor health (he would die in 1948) but even then was a massive, impressive man.

Back to Carrollton

When the war ended, my dad hastily carried us back to Carrollton, Georgia. The "Meeting at the Tabernacle" was drawing closer. He quickly found employment. I returned to my grammar school. Normal life resumed.

The years of my boyhood were filled with typical fun and activities in a small, county-seat town. I mentioned earlier the square in Carrollton. On each side of the square were businesses. Some of the buildings also had second floors. One of the town dentists, Dr. Brock, had a second-floor office. In those years there were few if any painkillers. Some of us would stand under the window of Dr. Brock's office and hear people yell as he filled or pulled teeth. I suppose it was our version of a horror show!

I did not avoid my share of narrow escapes. One that vividly stands out in my mind is falling while climbing a tree in the backyard. I was cut badly under my left armpit. My parents rushed me to the hospital. I was given ether, and the doctor sewed up the torn flesh. The doctor told my parents after the surgery that if the limb had gone any farther, I would have bled to death before they could have made it to the hospital. I still have the V-shaped scar in my armpit. Spared by inches. God's hand of protection was upon my young life. I was heading to my "Meeting at the Tabernacle."

I Am a Great Sinner

On Sunday mornings shoeshine boys would set up shop on a corner of the square. I would often go with my dad there. The men would get their shoes shined, smoke cigarettes, then wait to hear the church bells calling people to church. We would walk the brief distance down Bradley Street from the square to the tabernacle. Little did I realize I was walking ever closer to the "Meeting at the Tabernacle."

I learned very early that I was a sinner. One experience made it painfully apparent that I was a sinner boy who needed a Savior. Between school and our house there was the County Sale Barn. Farmers would bring their mules and cows there every Tuesday to trade and sell. This became a popular destination for young boys. I would drop by there on the way home from school. Joining in with other boys, we would ride the wild mules. There were ropes hanging from the rafters in the ceiling to grab and eject ourselves from the back of the mule in case things got too difficult.

My dad didn't like me going there, realizing it wasn't the safest place for me to be. "Don't go to the Sale Barn anymore, Jerry," my dad ordered. Well, one day the temptation of the wild mules was too great. I stopped by for my thrill ride. On the way home I realized I had mud from the Sale Barn lot all over my shoes. What to do? Within sight of my house was a mud puddle on the sidewalk. I would just tell my dad I got the mud on my shoes walking through the mud puddle. Just couldn't help myself! I gave my dad the explanation. He didn't buy it. "Let's go see the mud hole." Upon arriving, I quickly saw that the mud on the sidewalk was black. The mud on my shoes was mule-barn red! I had lied to my father. I was well aware that I deserved the spanking he administered. And I was aware that I was indeed a great sinner. I was getting in the proper frame of mind for my "Meeting at the Tabernacle."

Brother Ebb

Tabernacle Baptist Church had a long line of capable pastors. The church was deeply committed to sound Bible teaching and aggressive evangelism. The coming of Ebb G. Kilpatrick to be pastor in 1939 was a milestone event. The church had experienced a difficult time during the brief tenure of the pastor just before Brother Kilpatrick. Though well liked and a good preacher, the previous pastor suffered a complete physical and mental breakdown. There is speculation that a spinal injury in the war may have contributed to his illness.[12] In the providence of God, there was another man just ahead who would lead the church to its greatest period of progress and growth than in all of her previous years.

Ebb Kilpatrick became the pastor of Tabernacle in November 1938. Though not an outstanding preacher, he was more than adequate. He excelled as a motivator and builder. And as a pastor. He saw the need for the church to build Sunday school educational buildings to provide needed space to reach the people. He had the rare gift of balancing determination with patience. Leading the people slowly, his goals were systematically met. His pastoral work was his greatest strength. He was extremely good to visit the sick. This is always a congregation pleaser. He took strong stands against sinful activities in the town and county. The congregation valued a strong sense of morality and ethics. His leadership in this regard was greatly appreciated by his people.

In addition to leading the congregation in its building projects and being an exemplary pastor, Brother Kilpatrick also led in ministry projects. His emphasis on evangelism and deep spiritual growth kept the church in a constant state of revival. Strong lay leadership was developed in the church. Stewart Martin, a local undertaker and mayor of Carrollton, taught the largest men's Sunday school class. The Philadelphian Bible Class, as it was called, was broadcast live on radio every Sunday morning. The church became known for its emphasis on young people. A number of young men were called into the ministry during the Kilpatrick years.

My mom and dad were cultivated by "Brother Ebb," as the people loved to call him. They were involved in the Sunday school. My dad participated in the music program when there wasn't an all-day singing! I was enrolled in the nursery and spent my early years moving up through the Sunday school. I attended Training Union on Sunday night. There I learned to stand before the other children in the class and give my "part" (a part of the printed material for that Sunday evening). I also was involved in the mission programs of the church. I moved from the Sunbeams to the RAs (Royal Ambassadors). The "Meeting at the Tabernacle" was drawing nigh.

I Met Him at the Mercy Seat

For all their involvement in Tabernacle activities, my parents did not attend the Sunday evening services in the early years. We lived within easy walking distance of the church, so I could attend, going to Training Union and the evening service.

The afternoon of March 16, 1947, my best friend, Ray Riggs, came by the house. He was planning on joining the church that night and wanted me to join with him. I agreed to go with him to the services. I was nine at the time; I would be ten September 22. I recall quite well going by Brother Ebb's study that evening. We told him of our desire to join the church. He explained to us the plan of salvation. We went from his study to Training Union and then to the evening service.

I remember very little about the service. I do remember I was sitting on the second row from the front. No idea what kind of attendance there was for the service. Don't remember a song that was sung. No recollection about Brother Ebb's message. But this I do remember. As he preached that night, the lights in the building reflecting off his glasses showed tears streaming down his cheeks. He was pleading for people to receive Christ as their personal Savior.

I understood several basic truths: I was a great sinner; Jesus is a great Savior; I could receive a great salvation. When the invitation time came, I went forward, giving my hand to the preacher and my heart to the Lord Jesus. I repented of my sins and trusted Christ as my personal Savior. I was born again! I was converted! I was justified! I was redeemed! I was saved!

I went home and told my parents. I don't remember their response. I am sure they were glad. Shortly thereafter I was baptized as the Lord Jesus had commanded me to be. I really didn't understand a lot of what had taken place in my life. Had I been asked to give explanations of repentance, faith, regeneration, etc., I could not have done so. All I knew was that "I once was lost but now am found." There was "a new name written down in heaven, and it's mine." I could now sing, "Saved, by His power divine. Saved, to new life sublime. Life now is sweet and my joy is complete, for I'm saved, saved, saved!"

Old Testament believers in the wilderness gathered around a portable structure known as a tabernacle. In the holy of holies there was a mercy seat. Once a year before and upon the mercy seat, the high priest could sprinkle the blood of the lamb. This Old Testament ceremony pointed to the coming of the true Mercy Seat, the Lord Jesus. God promised, "There I will meet with thee, and I will commune with thee from above the mercy seat" (Exod. 25:22).

On a spring Sunday night in 1947 at Tabernacle Baptist Church, in Carrollton, Georgia, a small-town boy went for himself to the Mercy Seat, and I had a personal encounter with the Lord Jesus. And that was my "Meeting at the Tabernacle." In no way did I imagine that night what that meeting meant and where the ramifications of that meeting would take me. I have been learning about it now for over sixty-five years. I fully expect to continue learning about all that meeting entails throughout the countless ages of eternity. One unexpected result was soon to be revealed to me.

Chapter 3

My Chicken Funeral

I loved my pet chicken. I was given one for Easter. I kept it in its special place, fed it, and watched it grow from a tiny bitty to a beautiful grown chicken. Then one morning I went to see my chicken, and it was dead! I was crestfallen. My pet chicken must be given a proper burial. A cigar box sufficed for a casket. I informed my little friends of the sad development. They met me at the house, and we formed a somber funeral procession.

Chicken Heaven

There was a small Baptist church near the house. In those years all the churches were open. Often people would stop by to pray. On this particular day there was going to be a funeral. For my pet chicken. I led the procession into the church auditorium, my friends in solemn procession behind me. The cigar box casket was placed on the Communion table in front of the pulpit. My friends sat on the front row, carrying on like you never heard. I mounted the pulpit and proceeded to preach the funeral for my beloved chicken. I preached my pet chicken straight into chicken heaven!

Little did I know what the Lord was preparing for me. Someone said, "The Lord prepares us for what He is preparing for us." I was headed for a lifetime of preaching funerals, performing weddings, preaching the Word of God, and serving as a pastor. At my chicken funeral God was giving me dreams about my future.

God prepared Joseph by some dreams when he was a young man. The dreams of the sheaves and the stars were special to young Joseph. Hebrews 1:1 teaches that God used different ways to communicate His Word in Old Testament times. Hebrews 1:2 makes clear that today God speaks to us by His Son. We read about the revelation of the living Word, the Lord Jesus, in the pages of the written Word, the Bible.

God was arranging the circumstances of my life to bring me to the point of His call upon my life. I had received the Lord Jesus as my Savior at the age of nine; now I was on a track to experience the call to preach at age sixteen. Doesn't take too long to go from a chicken funeral to bigger responsibilities.

Boyhood Years

My boyhood in a small Georgia county seat town was fairly typical. Carrollton, Georgia, was a good place for a boy to grow to manhood. Those years were also fairly uneventful. Although, when I was eleven, something special happened at our house. For eleven years I had been an only child. That can have its perks but also its disadvantages. I got all the attention at my house, but there was no one to blame! I started noticing unusual activity at the house. My mom was knitting baby booties. And there were other unmistakable signs. Sure enough, my mother was going to have a baby! On February 1, 1949, my sister, Brenda, was born. What an exciting time. What a wonderful sister she would prove to be. More about her as the story unfolds.

During my young years a new technology was developed. Television. You could actually sit in your home and watch pictures on a small, black-and-white screen. There were programs like *Howdy Doody, Milton Berle,* and *Ed Sullivan*. We were one of the first families in our neighborhood to get one. Our screen was about twelve inches. The picture was like looking at something through a snowstorm. But each night neighbors would gather at our house. We even watched the test pattern before the programs came on the air. We were glued to that little screen. When others came, we never looked up. We just said, "Come in." None of us ever imagined where television technology would go in the years to come.

The schools were excellent. Carrollton funded its own school system, independent of the county system. There were no middle schools or junior high schools in those years. We went straight from seventh grade grammar school, as it was then called, to eighth grade and high school. I walked from home to school every day. The town was small, and so from just about anywhere in the town the walk wasn't far. Carrollton High didn't have a cafeteria. We got an hour for lunch. I walked back home for lunch, then returned to school. I made the transition from grammar to high school with no trauma. In those years we really didn't know about adolescence, so I guess I never went through it! I was not an outstanding student. Doing just enough to get by is about all I did. I had other things far more interesting.

Football

One of those interests was football. I desperately wanted to play football. My dad, who had been an outstanding basketball player, would have none of it. For one thing, I was small and skinny. Instead I joined the high school band and played the trumpet. I was certainly no Harry James (the premier trumpet player in those years). I did work myself up to first chair of the trumpet section. I was also elected captain of the band. We played during halftime at the football games. Also, we competed in the state band festivals. Our band director was Dr. John Dillard. Dr. Dillard started the band program in 1948. He was an outstanding trumpet player himself, having played with a number of bands in New York. Normally the band would receive a superior rating. One year we didn't do as well, one reason being that I went flat on a number. Fellow band members never let me forget it. Dr. Dillard was followed by Ernest McClendon.

I was fairly active in a number of high school activities as well. I was assistant editor of the Gold and Black, the school newspaper. My senior year I was elected one of six most outstanding seniors. I participated fully in the high school experience. But, none of this completely satisfied me.

I couldn't get my mind off football. I played on Sundays with a lot of my friends who were on the team. I competed well against them. The fire was burning. My junior year I could stand it no more. I ballooned up to 130 pounds. Without my father's knowledge I went out for the team. I can still see it now. During afternoon practice I saw my dad's car pull up to the practice field. He got out of the car and motioned for me. End of practice. End of promising football career. There would be a revival of that career sooner than I expected. Stay tuned.

Pranks

I was well known for my pranks at school. I could always find out some way to create havoc. My dad was a relentless kidder. I was much like him in that regard. I kept a great deal of mischief going on at school. I became an expert at starting something, getting my buddies neck-deep in it, then retreating to the background! There were two new lady teachers in high school. Recently graduated from college, they weren't much older than we were. When they stood in the hall between classes, we would whistle at them, causing them to rush back into their rooms. I became adept at changing my voice, making noises, and watching with glee when teachers blamed one of my friends!

The mischief wasn't confined to just the school building. In the middle of the square up town was the Confederate soldier monument made out of marble. At each of the base corners, there was a marble ball. A group of boys took the marble balls and baptized them into the Little Tallapoosa River. I've always wondered just who were the boys involved in such a deed?

In the corners of the square water could collect after rains. One night a group of boys (I'm not using names) took chunks of sodium nitrate from the high school chemistry lab and threw it into one of the puddles. Sounded like an atomic bomb going off. Police cars converged upon the square from all directions while the boys stealthily drove away. I know who did it, but I'm sworn to secrecy. I suppose a great deal will be revealed at the judgment seat of Christ!

Our family was nominally active at Tabernacle Baptist during my high school years. I had received Christ as my Savior, but I was growing little in my Christian life. Sunday morning Sunday school and church service was basically it. During all-day singing season my dad would take us to a singing.

John T. Tippett

In 1947 the pastor who led me to Christ, Brother Ebb, left our church. I thought that was the end of it for the church. There just could never be another pastor as good as he was. God has a way of surprising us. The pastor who followed him was John T. Tippett. Brother John or Preacher Tippett, as he became known, was that surprise. He was young, fiery, and energetic. His preaching was strong. His wife, Elise, though eleven years older than her husband, was charismatic and quite a people person. They moved to Carrollton with their sons, Tom and Jim.

Things began popping around the church. Though our family was on the periphery of the church's activities, we were drawn to Brother John's preaching. He preached right at you. He didn't cut corners with the Word of God. When he preached, the fires of Carmel burned in our church. He thundered like an Old Testament prophet. Some liked it; some did not. Our family liked it. We were always there on Sunday morning. When there was not an all-day singing!

Brother John was a Sunday school man. He quickly organized the Sunday school for evangelism and Bible study. His uncle, Tiny Tippett, served as the Georgia Baptist Sunday School Director. Though there was some grumbling when classes were divided, the Sunday school grew, and the people saw the wisdom of the process.

Preacher Tippett was also vitally interested in young people. He built the youth program around a youth camp emphasis. During the summer he would conduct a youth camp for children and for teenagers. He pulled no punches. He strongly emphasized the lordship of Christ and separation from the world. Many young people were saved and called into the ministry as a result of his strong preaching.

I was still only nominally active at the church. I was pretty much wrapped up in my activities at school. I was not close to the Lord. I wasn't into open sin. I never touched a drop of alcohol. I was morally clean. But I wasn't living for the Lord. I was actually afraid of Brother John. I admired him. I liked his preaching and his strong stand on moral issues. But I felt uneasy around him. When I saw him somewhere in town, I would go in the opposite direction. I knew I wasn't committed to the Lord and was afraid he would confront me about it.

Called to Preach

In my sixteenth year I became uneasy about my Christian life. I thought I had received Christ at age nine, but I had no assurance of it. I began to doubt my salvation. I reasoned: If I am really saved, why am I not living for the Lord? And I was involved in some worldly activities that caused me to doubt.

Though I was not into open sin, I became entangled in some activities that were not wholesome. I was pretty good on the trumpet. A few of us decided we would form a dance band. We started to rehearse and got pretty good. So much so that we were asked to play at a dance at the local VFW Club. I knew about the club. My favorite uncle started going there to drink and eventually lost his family. But I wasn't going to drink. I was going to play my trumpet. And make a little extra change to jingle in my pocket.

My parents knew I was playing in a band. They knew I was practicing at a friend's house. I dared not tell them I was scheduled to play for a dance at the VFW Club. The day of our commitment to play for the dance that night, I told them I was going to my friend's house to rehearse. The lie was bald-faced. And, to complicate matters, one of the band members came by the furniture store where my dad was manager. He bragged about our gig that night at the VFW Club. Even told him how much we were getting paid.

Later that afternoon my dad asked me again what I was doing that night. I lied again. Nighttime came. We played the first set. Pretty good sound. We were even discussing a record deal with some people!

Break time came. The bartender from downstairs came up. "Is there a boy named Vines in your band?"

"Yep, that's me," I said, waiting for a compliment on my fabulous trumpet playing.

"Well, there's some man on the phone downstairs who says he wants to talk to you."

My heart stopped. I went downstairs. The drinking and carousing and carrying on were loud. On the bar I saw the receiver off the hook, frowning at me. My heart revived, beating furiously! I picked up the phone, said, "Hello," and heard my dad's voice.

"You have five minutes to get home." Click. Dead silence.

I rushed upstairs telling the boys, "I've got to go home."

I had no car. I borrowed one from a band member. There were no shock absorbers on the flivver. I ran the jalopy full speed, bouncing up and down. I knew I would be dead on arrival. The hour was approaching midnight.

I arrived at the house. No lights. I opened the door, expecting the roof and walls to cave in around me. I knew this was judgment. My dad met me in the darkened hallway. I saw his barely visible form and heard his voice as he said, "Jerry, I want to remind you that your favorite uncle lost his family at the club where you were tonight." He turned around and went back to bed.

The words stabbed my soul like a thousand daggers. I went to bed. But I didn't go to sleep. The beginning of the end was upon me. No more playing for dances. No more band. No more peace.

I just knew I wasn't saved. "If I am saved, I wouldn't be going to a place like that," I reasoned. My nights became sleepless. Some nights I would get up in the middle of the night and just wander around town. Doubting my salvation. Wondering what was going on in my soul.

My pastor, Brother John, placed a strong emphasis on the lordship of Christ. His messages had been challenging me. For sure, Jesus was not Lord over every area of my life. I had pretty much made my own plans. I wanted to be a football coach. My dad wanted me to be a surgeon. I gave little to no thought about what the Lord Jesus wanted for my life. I am sure the preaching of the Bible truth of lordship was doing its work down inside me. Whatever, I was a troubled sixteen-year-old boy.

The moment of crisis came. We were living in a small, four-room, white-framed house on Carroll Street. I gave up. I remember distinctly kneeling down beside my bed. I don't remember the exact words. I do recall that I asked the Lord, if I was not saved, I wanted to be. His answer was clear as a bell. I didn't hear an audible voice. He was louder than that! Basically, what He said to my heart was, "You don't need to be saved. You already are. I want you to totally yield your life to My lordship and surrender to My plan for your life."

Then I prayed something like this: "Lord, here I am. I yield my all to You. I acknowledge Your lordship over every area of my life." Then, much to my own surprise, I prayed, "If You want me to, I will preach for You." Preach? Me? The boy who almost flunked junior English because I had to make a five-minute speech? I couldn't talk for laughing. I wasn't trying to be funny. I was so nervous and afraid, all I could do was laugh. The thought of standing before people and talking terrified me. But there seemed to come a deep, settled peace in my heart. I sensed the Lord was saying to me, "Yes, I want you to preach." I somehow understood God calls us to His service, then equips us for that place of service. Paul put it this way, "And I thank Christ Jesus our Lord, who hath enabled me, for that He counted me faithful, putting me into the ministry" (1 Tim. 1:12).

I was on fire to tell someone. The first person who came to mind was John Tippett, the preacher who frightened me. The man I avoided. I wanted to tell him. I headed to church. I found him in his study. I told him I had something I wanted to share with him. I don't know why, but instead of telling him in his study, I took him to a Sunday school room. He sat down in one chair, and I pulled a chair in front of him. I blurted out, "The Lord has called me to preach." I will never forget the look of astonishment and disbelief on his face. He blurted out, "Aaah naaah!?" He just couldn't believe it. He later told me I was the most unlikely boy in the church to be called to preach. He said I was so full of mischief and such a rabble-rouser that I surely wasn't called to preach. In succeeding months he never allowed me to preach. In later years I preached revivals for him. But he said he had been afraid of what I might say in the pulpit!

I told my parents. They were supportive. The next Sunday, from the back row in the church where the young people sat, I walked forward to publicly announce my call to preach. Brother Tippett told the people I was publicly announcing my call to preach. At the conclusion of the service, he placed me in front of the church. The people came by to give me words of encouragement. My mom and dad came. With tears my dad said, "You can count on me." And for all of the rest of the years, I could.

My junior year in high school I took the required aptitude test. They shared with me the results. I was told I should pursue a life's work in fields related to mathematics or science. By all means, I was to avoid any occupation that involved writing or public speaking. Think the Lord has a sense of humor? Probably quite a few people who have heard me preach or read my books through the years think the test results were spot-on!

At that point in time, my early preparation began. I started reading everything I could find in the church library. I read every study course book published by the Southern Baptist Sunday School Board's Convention Press. They were books on Baptist doctrine, building a Sunday school, alcohol, personal soul winning, etc. I volunteered to do anything around the church. I totally immersed myself in the life of the church. I was learning what church was all about.

I even entered the speakers' tournament! I won at the local associational level. Then I went to the state competition. I really don't remember how I did there. Probably not so well. Nor do I remember the subject of my speech. None of that really mattered. What mattered was that the Lord helped me get up before people and say anything! He was preparing me for what He had prepared for me.

My First Sermon

Soon I received my first invitation to preach at a church. I was invited to preach at the Wednesday night service at Shady Grove Baptist Church, Villa Rica, Georgia. The church was small, but I was wired and ready to go. I prepared a message. My friend, Charlie Vaughn, was going with me to lead the singing. The night arrived. As we Georgians say, it came a gully washer. There was such a hard rain, no more than eight or ten people showed up for the service. I was nervous. Charlie led the singing. When he finished the hymns he directed, I told him to sing some more!

Finally, my time came. I took as my text Philippians 3:13–14. My title was, "On to the Goal." I used everything I discovered in my meager preparation. I threw in everything I ever heard my pastor say. Then, in total exhaustion, I sat down. Twenty minutes total. I can imagine someone in the tiny audience heading home in the rain saying, "He'll never make a preacher." I really wasn't interested in audience response. I was just thrilled the Lord helped me stand before people and attempt to preach. Without fainting!

The Tent Revival

That summer Brother Tippett took a group to the Holy Land. His brother, Abner Tippett, our associate pastor, was left in charge. Tabernacle had started a mission church in a housing project. A tent was erected for a revival. Abner was to preach, and I was asked to lead the music. One night in the service I was attempting to lead "Amazing Grace." There was a good Pentecostal sister there. I guess it was the snuff in her mouth. She didn't sing the words in tandem with my leading. Her pace was more like: "Aaaaaaaaamaaaaaaazzzzzzzzinggggg Graaaaaaaceeeeee." Talk about messing up a young song leader!

In the afternoons Brother Abner took me visiting with him in the project apartments. I agreed to go but told him I couldn't witness to people and not to expect me to say anything. One afternoon we went into an apartment where two brothers, ages fifteen and thirteen lived. We sat down in the living room. Brother Abner looked over at me and nodded his head up and down. He wanted me to witness to them! No way. I nodded my head side to side. Nope. He just clammed up. I soon realized he wasn't going to say anything; it was up to me. I remembered a few verses Brother John had taught us to use about the way of salvation. I stumbled through those. Then, in a sense of desperation, I said, "You wouldn't want to get saved, would you?" To my utter astonishment, they both said, "Yes!" We bowed, they received Jesus into their heart as personal Savior. The next Sunday night at the Tabernacle, I saw both of them baptized. I can't explain it. But a fire started burning in my soul that has not gone out until this day. There have been times I needed to stir up the soul-winning fire, but it is always there. There is a desire and fire to tell people about the salvation that is available in the Lord Jesus Christ.

Beside my Bible there was only one religious book in my possession. The book consisted of a number of sermons of George W. Truett, pastor of First Baptist Church, Dallas, Texas. Titled *A Quest for Souls*, this book helped fan the flames of evangelism in my soul. From that day until this, I do not remember a time when I haven't wanted to see people come to Christ.

Poppa Johnson

My grandfather, W. O. Johnson, influenced my life greatly. He was converted in his buggy as he crossed the creek coming from a morning revival service at Indian Creek Baptist Church, near Bowdon, Georgia. Poppa Johnson was an entrepreneur. Later in life he became a country evangelist. He was a man of strong Bible belief and solid convictions. He taught me the premillennial return of Christ on his front porch. He had never read a book on the subject; he just used his Bible. He was a man with unshakeable convictions and bold courage. On one occasion he got an injunction to close the movie theaters on Sunday. Ebb Kilpatrick, a state legislator and father of one of my friends, owned the theaters. He was outraged. He came down to my grandfather's little three and a half-room, white-framed house. "Old man, I'll starve you to death."

"Ha!" said my grandfather, "you'll have to starve God Almighty first!"

He taught me to stand for my convictions without compromise, regardless of the consequences. This lesson served me well through the years.

A stroke caused his death at the age of eight-four. In the closing hours of his life, unable to speak, we saw him smiling and waving. I believe he was seeing the angels as they came to take him to heaven. Often the words of the old song remind me of his leaving: "O come, angel band. Come and around me stand. O bear me away on your snowy wings, to my eternal home."[13]

The Young Television Evangelist

There was another influence on my life soon after I was called to preach. There was a young evangelist on television. His youthful song leader was named Cliff Barrows. Another young man, George Beverly Shea, would sing just before the young evangelist would preach. Often he would sing "I'd Rather Have Jesus." This song was deeply moving to me. The words expressed my total commitment to Jesus as Savior and Lord. The song became my theme song. This young evangelist's crusades in major cities were being shown on television. Billy Graham was the fiery young preacher. His sermons were dramatic. He prefaced many of his remarks by the statement, "The Bible says, . . ." He preached against sin. He called people to repentance and salvation. I remember quite well a sermon he preached on the end of the world and the return of Christ. He said, "Keep your eyes on Israel. That's where it's all going to wind up."

A Sunday School Teacher

Mr. Thomas, my Sunday school teacher when I was fifteen, made an indelible impression on my life. One Sunday he told us he turned down a job offer to drive a beer truck, with a very good salary. He turned it down because he didn't want anything to hurt his influence with us. I never forgot it. When I was pastor in the Chattanooga area, Mr. Thomas was working in a clothing store there. I went to see him and thanked him. With tears he bowed his head. "Jerry, I resigned that class sometime later. I thought I was a failure." I was still learning lessons that would guide my ministry. You are never a failure when you are obediently serving the Lord.

I was well on the way from my chicken funeral to a life of preaching, winning people to Christ, and serving as pastor of Baptist churches.

A Career Revived

And, oh, there was an added bonus. As I approached my senior year in high school, I had grown to the mammoth size of 150 pounds! My dad relented and let me go out for football. When I stepped on the scales for my physical, the team doctor said, "You're one of the big ones." Our line averaged 150 pounds, and our backfield averaged 140 pounds. I played end, on offense and defense. I dreamed beyond my chicken funeral. I wanted to get a scholarship to play football and study for the ministry at Baylor University, considered the Mecca for preacher boys in those years. Turns out my football career was not that promising. I won a starting position and played fairly well. But the next Heisman Trophy winner I was not. I really did enjoy it though. My love for football has never diminished.

One weekend game stands out to me. Not because of my performance. But because of a decision I made. During the season there was a revival meeting held at the Tabernacle. In those years revivals would begin on Sunday and go through the next Sunday. Some might even go for two weeks or more. This particular week a big game with a major rival was scheduled on Friday night. I was torn. Should I play, or should I attend the Friday night revival service? I decided to play. But I was troubled by it. I promised the Lord I would never again let a game interfere with my commitment to Him. Looking back, perhaps I was unnecessarily torn. In today's atmosphere where anything and everything is allowed to come before God, my uneasiness seems rather legalistic. But I just knew Jesus must be absolutely first in my life.

I soon found out my senior year everyone was not thrilled I was going to be a preacher. Some of my teammates on the football team gave me a hard time. They used profanity in front of me just to see how I would react. When I went to the junior/senior banquet and dance, I left before the dance. Several teachers stood in the door and tried to talk me into staying. I respectfully refused. I remember driving from the country club to the square that night. The square was deserted. All the young people were at the dance. The devil seemed to say to me, "See there! You are making a fool of yourself, and you have lost all your friends." It certainly seemed that way.

Then the Lord seemed to say to me, "Jerry, I'll be your Friend."

"Lord," I replied, "I'd rather have You to be my Friend than anyone else."

Since that time, following Jesus has brought me thousands of friends.

Standing by My Convictions

After the football season I went back to the band. We were preparing for the band festival. The band director announced some special rehearsals for Wednesday night. I told him I couldn't make it.

"Why can't you?"

"Well," I said, "we have prayer meeting on Wednesday night."

The band director was also the music director for the First Methodist Church. He loudly informed me, "I'm willing to give up my church night for band, aren't you?"

I was unwilling. He really got upset with me. He went to the high school principal, Mr. McEntyre (I later was his pastor in Rome, Georgia), and told him I was refusing to come to Wednesday night rehearsals. He wanted to know what to do. "You'd better change your rehearsal night; that's what you'd better do!" I was learning early to stand by my convictions and not compromise. Sometimes you can make a difference when you dare to take your stand.

The senior year was soon to be over. The time had come to choose a college. That's when the story gets really, really interesting!

Chapter 4

"You've Got to Go to Mercer"

D o you want to preach and pastor in Georgia?"

"Yes, sir."

"Well, you've got to go to Mercer."

Thus went the conversation between my pastor, John Tippett, and myself. I was completing my senior year in high school and was getting ready to go to college. The previous summer two ministerial students from Wake Forest University and Howard College (now Samford University) came to Carrollton as door-to-door book salesmen. Talmadge Williams and Jimmy Auchmuty got involved in the activities of Tabernacle Baptist. We became good friends, and they started talking with me about going to their schools. I made a visit to Wake Forest on its brand-new campus. I really liked it. But it was a long way from Carrollton!

I also visited Howard at Birmingham, Alabama. I wasn't too thrilled by the barracks being used for mens' dormitories at the time, but I met some really neat people. And there was even an opportunity to play football! In addition some college students from my home church were attending Howard. I was inclined to go there.

Mercer

Brother John got wind of my plans to go to Howard. He called me to his study. And the above conversation ensued. I was only seventeen. I didn't know I could preach anywhere but Georgia. In my mind I would be the pastor of a country church in Carroll County. Or, if my ministry really took off, I might even get to one of the town churches. I didn't even know I needed to pray about where to go to school. No kidding.

Tippett was a Mercer graduate and very active in the Georgia Baptist Convention that supported the school. He correctly told me that to be a Mercer graduate was a distinct advantage for a Georgia Baptist pastor. My pastor told me what to do. I followed his counsel.

Looking back on the mandate from my pastor, I know he had my best interests in mind. I sometimes wonder the direction my life and ministry might have taken had I gone to Wake Forest or Howard. But there are no regrets. I believe, as I have previously stated, God was preparing me for what He was preparing for me. And William Cowper put it well when he wrote, "God moves in mysterious ways His wonders to perform."

In the fall of 1956, I made my preparations to go to Mercer in Macon, Georgia. The total cost for a year's tuition, room, and board was the outrageous amount of $750! I never even considered that my father would help me with that exorbitant amount. I heard that Warren Sewell, the owner of a suit factory in Bremen, Georgia, provided financial help for deserving students. I met with him and obtained a loan for my freshman year. The agreement was that I would work during the summer and pay back all I could. I did this for all four years of my college education. When I went to pay back my loan for my senior year, I was told that because I was so faithful to pay back the loans, they were giving me my senior year's amount as a gift!

Off to Macon, Georgia, I went. I couldn't have been more excited. Mercer University was founded in 1833 by Georgia Baptists, under the leadership of Baptist minister Adiel Sherwood. The school was named for Jesse Mercer, prominent Baptist leader and the first chair of the Mercer Board of Trustees. A strong school academically, Mercer was the sine qua non for aspiring young Georgia Baptist preachers such as myself.

I thought I was headed for a four-year revival. I was going to study the Bible, learn how to preach, and have a glorious time with the godly, scholarly professors who would teach me. And I would be there with other young men totally dedicated to the Lord Jesus and preparing for the ministry.

Shock and Awe

My first night at Mercer was not what I expected. Some of my new classmates suggested we go to a local drive-in restaurant and get a bite to eat. When we drove up, one of the guys said, "Let's get a beer." Before I realized it, I was out of the car.

"What are you doing, Vines?" one of them said.

"I'm walking back to school."

"Why?"

"Well, I'm down here to study for the ministry. I'm not going to start my college off by drinking alcohol."

"Ah, get back in the car. We won't get any beer then."

I was beginning to wonder what I was getting myself into at Mercer.

What transpired my first night in the Roberts Hall dorm was totally unexpected. The alcohol flowed freely. I had never heard such carousing and carrying on in my life. That's the way it was constantly. Each weekend the garbage cans filled with beer and liquor bottles. Surely the officials at Mercer didn't know this was going on. This couldn't be happening at a Baptist college! I was shell-shocked. Not all were participating, of course. Other young students were just as stunned as was I. But the greater shock was ahead.

I was going to do a major in Christianity. I would do a double minor in philosophy and Greek. I remember distinctly how I anticipated my first class. I was going to study the New Testament! I had my Bible before me, the textbook for the course of study, and open ears for the great truths I was about to hear. The New Testament professor, Dr. H. Lewis Batts, walked into the class. I waited for the opening prayer. There was none. His first words were (a direct quote), "Any man who says the New Testament is not filled with contradictions is a fool." I couldn't believe my ears. I seemed to bounce off the four walls of the classroom. He continued. "All that stuff you learned in your Southern Baptist Sunday school Literature is just not true." I'm bouncing off the walls some more.

A young Korean girl was in the classroom. She raised her hand. "If what is written in the Sunday school literature is not true, why do you send it to our people?," she asked. Our professor said nothing. He just glared at her. That was day one of my four-year education at a Baptist college, supported by the faithful giving of Georgia Baptist people.

I was totally unprepared for what I experienced. I did have the advantage of being brought up in a Bible-believing church. John Tippett faithfully preached the Word. My Sunday school teachers were good and godly people. But I was hearing things new and disturbing to my young ears. My church history professor, Dr. Harold Macmillan, said (a direct quote), "Christianity is on the way out. It will be replaced by something better." The Christianity department was liberal and neoorthodox to the core. There were some good men, of course. Dr. Ed Johnston, our Greek professor, seemed to be a Bible-believing man. And there were good and godly teachers in other schools in the university. I found my faith under attack the entire time I was at Mercer. I saw young men who had come to school to prepare for the ministry fall into the trap of liberalism, abandon their faith, and never pursue their calling. If they had indeed been called by God.

As I look back, I marvel at the grace of God that carried me through those years and kept my faith intact. I am actually grateful I was exposed to a thoroughly liberal education. In later years I was able to spot liberalism and neoorthodoxy immediately. I'm sure it's not original with me, but I explain neoorthodoxy this way: "It uses our vocabulary but not our dictionary." I mean that the neoorthodox can talk about the resurrection of the Lord Jesus, but they do not mean what Bible believers mean by it. They mean some kind of "spiritual" resurrection not a literal, bodily, time and space coming back to life that occurred when Jesus rose from the grave.

Conservative Influences

I am also grateful to God's grace that He placed influences around me to keep me strong in my faith. The Lord placed certain books in my hands. I don't really know how I came to have them. There was

E. J. Young's *Thy Word Is Truth* and B. B. Warfield's *The Inspiration and Authority of the Bible.* W. A. Criswell's *These Issues We Must Face* helped ground me. My liberal professors tried to indicate that any intelligent person would surely take a liberal view of the Bible. These books demonstrated to me there were scholarly men who believed the Bible to be without error.

There were men God used to help me get through those difficult years of exposure to liberalism. When I returned home, I would tell my pastor about what I was experiencing at Mercer. He would look at me in disbelief. And he seemed to indicate to me that I was just misunderstanding what the professors were saying. I think his great love for Mercer and involvement in the Georgia Baptist Convention gave him some blind spots, as we all seem to develop along the way.

Our minister of music at Tabernacle Baptist was John Atherton. Mr. Atherton was a very godly man, in addition to being a superb choir leader and concert pianist. He had graduated from Moody Bible Institute and Wheaton College. I would visit him and tell him what I was experiencing at Mercer. He encouraged me in my faith. He also placed in my hands *Archaeology and the Bible* by Joseph P. Free, archaeology professor at Wheaton. This book showed me that the Bible had been proven to be accurate over and over again by archaeological findings.

There was a pastor in Macon who helped me stay true to the faith. Around Mercer his name was mentioned only in derision and scorn. I thought he was some kind of hayseed country preacher who had stumbled into a city church pastorate. Being curious by nature, I decided one Wednesday night to visit Mikado Baptist Church, where Dr. E. Clint Sheehan was pastor. The service was being held in a sawdust-floor tabernacle. Yep, just what I thought. Country bumpkin come to town. There were five hundred plus people there. Uh-huh, just some country people come to town who were going to hear a rip-snorting, yelling preacher. Imagine my astonishment when Dr. Sheehan opened his Greek New Testament and began to teach! Being a Greek student myself, I was impressed to say the least! I later found out he had graduated from Mercer with honors. He was a thorn in Mercer's side. He never failed to point out their liberalism, the immorality on campus, and whatever else might be in his crosshairs. Dr. Sheehan helped me stay strong in my convictions.

Another man helped me. After my classes I would sometimes get in my car and just fret over the liberal things I had heard. One day I was scanning the radio stations hoping to find some Christian music to soothe my troubled heart. I ran across a radio preacher named Brother Maze Jackson. He called himself "the young man with the old message." He was a wide-open, preach-the-paint-off-the-wall evangelist from Atlanta, Georgia. I liked it! Every day after class I would get in the car, tune in, and hear Brother Maze. He preached topical sermons, shouted, talked about the drunks getting saved in his meetings. He was having a joyful, Holy Ghost good time preaching. He kept me anchored.

I received some help from an unexpected source. I had become somewhat enamored with Emil Brunner, the Swiss neoorthodox theologian. I suppose you can't be exposed to neoorthodoxy and liberalism daily and not be affected to some degree. I read his book, *Faith, Hope and Love*. There is much good in the book. I mentioned to Mrs. Smith, a Sunday school teacher at Tabernacle, that I liked the book. She asked to read it. She returned it with a note I still have. She pointed out that in the book Dr. Brunner said, "We should not worry so much about certain narrow-minded literalistic interpretations of the so-called Second Coming of Christ."[14] In her kindly note she wrote, "We cannot receive part of the Word and reject other portions and be pleasing to God." That counsel has served me well through these years.

There was a lot of intimidation. My freshman year I was initiated into Phi Kappa Phi, a society for academic achievement. I attended the dinner for new members. Dr. Malcolm Lester, dean of the school, was sitting next to me.

"Vines, what are you studying to be?"

"I'm going to be a preacher."

The dean looked at me and with a sneer said, "A preacher? I thought better of you than that."

Wow. I went to Mercer thinking it existed to help prepare young men for the ministry.

Crisis of Faith

I came to a crisis in my faith. Everything I was hearing contradicted what I was taught and believed all my life. My spiritual crisis came to a moment of decision in an experience similar to the one Billy Graham had as a young preacher. I drove to Baconsfield Park on the other side of Macon. The Park consisted of seventy-five acres of beautifully landscaped grass walkways, with roses, tulips, and daffodils beautifully encircling the tall trees deeper into the park. From time to time I would go there, walk through the woods, and pray.

On this day I came there as a troubled young ministerial student. Deep into the trees I found a tree stump. Placing my Bible on it, I knelt and prayed, "Father, I'm hearing men much wiser than I will ever be saying the Bible is filled with contradictions and errors. I have been taught that Your Word is true and without error. I'm going to just take Your Word by faith. From this day forward I will read and live and preach the Bible, trusting You to prove it to me as what it claims to be." The only audible sound was from a few squirrels meandering in the leaves. Some birds sang overhead. I didn't hear any voices. Something was singing in my heart. "The B-I-B-L-E, yes, that's the Book for me. I stand alone on the Word of God, the B-I-B-L-E."

That day I arose from my knees with a new faith and confidence deep within. That has been many years ago now. God has proved to me over and over again that His Word is absolutely inerrant and trustworthy. I can sing today what I used to sing in Vacation Bible School: "I know the Bible was sent from God, the Old, as well as the New; Inspired and holy the whole way through, I know the Bible is true."[15]

I promised the Lord that, if I ever had an opportunity, I would do something to help deal with the liberalism that was destroying the faith of so many young students. In subsequent years I would attend Baptist associational meetings or state Baptist meetings. I would hear representatives from Mercer state to the approving messengers, "All our professors believe the Bible." I knew what they were saying was not true. I knew, because I heard just the opposite in my classes. There didn't seem to be any way to deal with the problem, however.

Backslidding

I actually backslid while at Mercer. No, you aren't about to read some juicy gossip about moral failures. I was so busy studying the Bible to take tests that I neglected to study it for my own spiritual nourishment and growth. Texas groceryman Howard Butt came to Macon for a citywide crusade. Mr. Butt was part of the group God used mightily in the 1950s to bring revival to thousands of Southern Baptist young people. I attended the meetings every night. One night he spoke on "My heart, Christ's Home." He talked about the devotional room. Long story short, God convicted me of my neglect of the daily quiet time. I started having an early morning Bible reading and prayer time. I came to see a preacher wins or loses the battle in his quiet time. Like Elijah we must "hide thyself" (1 Kings 17:3) before we can "shew thyself" (1 Kings 18:1). More than one preacher has fallen because he neglected his daily time alone with God. When a preacher falls in public, it very often is because he has already fallen in private.

The spiritual battles I experienced don't tell the whole story of my years at Mercer. I received a very good education there. I am grateful for the good, competent professors who taught me. There were many fine young men and women who, just like myself, believed the Bible and were committed to serve the Lord as pastors, ministers of music, missionaries, and laypeople. There were some special times with many who remained friends for a lifetime. I grew in my Christian life.

I remember a group of us decided we would start getting up very early in the morning to pray for an hour before breakfast. My first morning the alarm clock went off. I drug myself out of the bunk and headed to my designated place of prayer on the campus. I got on my knees and started praying. I prayed and I prayed. I prayed for everything that came to mind. When I finished my "hour," I looked at my watch. I had been praying for ten minutes! I started over. I peeped at my watch—five minutes. I learned that prayer is glorious but also hard work.

Pranks

And, yes, I was the prankster. One night a boy in our dorm decided to go to bed early to prepare for a test. When he went to sleep, we changed the clock so it went off at midnight. He got up and so did we. He showered, shaved, and headed for the cafeteria line. We went back to bed. He sheepishly came back around 12:30 a.m.

There was the boy who could sleep through Armageddon. We picked up Rip Van Winkle and his mattress. Then we dissembled the bed, taking it, his desk, chair, everything in the room out on the flat roof of the dorm porch. We then placed him and mattress back on the bed. When he woke up the next morning, he was on the roof!

One morning after Halloween, to the astonishment of all, we saw a wagon hanging by one corner on the top of the spire on the chapel. I don't know who did. I promise I was not involved. But, I must say, I admire the skill of those who got the wagon perched so high.

Eatonton

God also opened the doors for ministry during my college career. John Atherton, the minister of music I mentioned above, had come to Tabernacle in Carrollton from First Baptist Church, Eatonton, Georgia. The Eatonton Church needed an interim minister of music. At his recommendation I was asked to fill that role. I would drive over on the weekend. I stayed in the home of a very godly couple. Their son was a Southern Baptist missionary in Africa. The church was small. The pastor, Otis Brooks, was kind to me. He gave me my first Greek New Testament.

Shortly after I got there, he resigned. I've often wondered if my music was that bad! I was then asked to do some of the preaching. I would lead the music, then bring the message. I picked up some of the visitation responsibilities. I remember attending a Sunday school meeting. The mayor of the city was the Sunday school director. He conducted a routine meeting, then asked if anyone had anything to say. "Yes, sir. I have been visiting over in the housing projects and there are kids all over the place.

I believe if we ran a bus over there, we could get lots of them to come to our Sunday school."

The mayor's face turned red. "We have all we need or want in our Sunday school!" End of discussion.

I knew I wouldn't be there long.

Centralhatchee

And I wasn't. In Heard County, Georgia, just below my home county of Carroll, Centralhatchee Baptist Church needed a pastor. The local associational missionary (now called director of missions), Paul Jackson, was a member of the church. He knew about me. So he recommended me to be their pastor. As an eighteen-year-old boy, I was called to be their pastor! I would drive back and forth from Macon to Carrollton. The Centralhatchee Church requested of the Tabernacle Church that I be ordained to the gospel ministry.

Brother Tippett formed a presbytery for the purpose of examining me concerning my salvation experience, call to preach, and doctrinal soundness. I remember how nervous I was when I met with the preachers who formed the examination council. I answered the questions to the best of my ability. They seemed to be satisfied with my answers. Then they gave me practical words of wisdom. They talked of the preacher's finances, his personal moral life, and promptness in paying his bills. One pastor told me something I never forgot. "Jerry," he said, "just as sure as the Lord made a possum, He made a tree for him to climb. If God has called you to preach, He will give you a church. Don't ever leave a church unless He gives you another one." Pretty good advice for restless young preachers today.

An ordination service was held on a Sunday afternoon. John Tippett, Paul Jackson, and my grandfather, W. O. Johnson, participated in the service. I remember my grandfather breaking down as he prayed, "Lord, help him."

I have often marveled at the patience of the people. I went into the deacons' meetings scared to death. Paul's daughter, Shirley, fifteen, was the Sunday school director. She later spent her life as a Southern Baptist missionary in Nigeria. His other daughter, Marjorie, fourteen, was the church pianist. She later married a boyhood friend of mine, Fred Barr, who was my minister of music in Rome, Georgia.

My sermon barrel contained only a few messages. One Saturday night I started flipping through my Bible trying to find a sermon for the next morning. I went from Genesis to Revelation. Nothing. I got on my knees and cried out to God, "Lord, I've just been a pastor for a month. I've preached the whole Bible and don't know what to preach in the morning!"

I remember when August revival meeting came around. I ran out of sermons! And no one was getting saved in the services. I spent a whole afternoon in the woods behind the church. The Lord gave me some messages. And some people were saved the rest of the week! I learned you must depend on the Lord for your messages. And leave the results up to Him.

Many unusual experiences were mine during my brief stay at Centralhatchee. One Sunday afternoon I was invited to attend a deacon ordination service at a small church just below Centralhatchee. I was called upon to lead in prayer. They got on their knees. Not to be outdone, I got down on mine. In my most spiritual voice I said, "Let us pray." Much to my astonishment, everyone started praying! I had never heard that before. So shocked was I that I opened my eyes and looked around. I tried to pray as best I could, but this method of prayer clearly created some disconnects on my royal telephone.

One of my members was Preacher Rufus McWhorter. He was a great encouragement to me. His wife was the best cook in the church. On Saturday when I was visiting, I always managed to wind up near their house around lunchtime! His daughter, Mildred, went on to become a legendary home missionary in the Southern Baptist Convention. She served faithfully for many years in inner-city missions in Houston, Texas.

About twelve months was all I could last at Centralhatchee. I was out of sermons, facing some problems, and didn't know what to do. My only answer was to hightail it to another church. A church in Carroll County needed a pastor. They issued the call to me to be their pastor, and I accepted. The folks at Centralhatchee were mad. I was making $150 a month. When I resigned, they owed me $75 for two weeks. They never paid me. I've never resented it. I never thought I was worth that much money anyway. And I just love telling that story. When I became pastor at Centralhatchee, the Sunday school was around forty. When I left, it was around eighty. So we grew, saw people saved, and a young preacher was learning to depend on the Lord for his messages and for the results.

Bethesda

Bethesda was a small church averaging only about eighty in Sunday school. The older people used to call it "Ole Bethursday." I became an instant hit. I was barely twenty. The word around Carroll County was, "Let's go to Ole Bethursday and hear that boy preacher preach." Used to make me so mad. The nerve of them. Calling a pastor, a man of God, "that boy preacher." Young people flocked to the church. R. E. McIntosh, a descendent of the famous Indian chief William McIntosh, was the Sunday school director. He drove a bus to Hubbard's Pant Factory in Bremen, Georgia. On Sundays he picked up young people and children for church. That was the first bus ministry I ever saw. R. E. followed me as pastor when I resigned the church. Shortly thereafter he had a massive heart attack. He died at forty-three.

The people were wonderful to me. Our church was really active. I would eat with the people. I was single. Sometimes I would wind up sitting between two single girls at homes of moms who wanted their daughters to marry a preacher. I made it a policy not to date members of my church. Actually, I dated little in those years. I was busy studying at Mercer, preparing my sermons, commuting back and forth to Bethesda, visiting on Saturdays and preaching on Sundays.

The Filling of the Spirit

During my three and one-half years at Bethesda, I preached as best I could, but there didn't seem to be much power in my messages. They were certainly biblical. I was in earnest. But something was missing. I met the pastor of another rural church, Mount Pleasant Baptist. His name was Irvine Phillips. Though he had a college degree, he was of the old-time style. He preached like a Tennessee windsucker, as they were called in those days. Which means he preached like a machine gun and caught his breath in sucking sounds along the way. But there was an unusual power about his preaching. I often visited in his home. He would talk with me about the Spirit-filled life. I never really heard much about it before he shared the truth with me.

Brother Tippett's emphasis was the lordship of Christ. Brother Phillips pointed me to the filling of the Spirit as the source of preaching and witnessing power. He pointed out that Ephesians 5:18, "Be filled with the Spirit," was a command. I remember the day I knelt in the altar of my church and asked the Holy Spirit to fill me. I didn't speak in a tongue. There was no emotional outburst. There was a difference in my preaching from that day on. I began to understand and affirm the line from the old hymn: "All is vain unless the Spirit of the Holy One comes down."[16]

Convictions

I learned another lesson in a rather unusual way. All my life I went to the movie theaters in Carrollton. We had only two, The Playhouse Theater and The Carroll Theater. The latter was my picture show of choice. On Saturday my father would give me two dimes. Nine cents got me in; five cents paid for the bag of popcorn; five cents paid for the Coca-Cola; and the remaining penny bought a piece of bubble gum! Saturday was the day for the cowboy movie. I loved Gene Autrey, Roy Rogers, Hopalong Cassidy, Lash LaRue, and the Lone Ranger. Although I did quit Roy Rogers because he kissed a girl in one movie! If you've got to kiss anybody, kiss your horse, for goodness' sake. The plots were always the same. At the end of the movie, the hero was in desperate straits. The bad guys were closing in. At the last moment he would prevail. I would throw my popcorn into the air, whoop, and pour my Coke down the back of the girl in front of me. We had simple pleasures in those days!

When I became pastor at Bethesda, I continued going to the movies. On Saturday nights I would see young members of my congregation. One day my father said, "Jerry, don't you think, now that you are a pastor, you ought not go to the movies?"

I didn't say anything, out of respect for my dad, but it made me so mad. "Who does he think he is?" I fumed to myself. "I'm the pastor of a church."

Not long after that, I was kneeling in the altar of Bethesda for a time of prayer. No one was there but me and the Lord. As clear as a bell the Lord seemed to say to me, "You shouldn't go to the movies." That did it. No more movies for me.

Since that time I have been to only three movies that I can remember. I was surprised to learn many years later that my friend Adrian Rogers didn't go to movies either. I don't think I have missed much. I'm not trying to impose my convictions on anyone else. Just the opposite. I learned through my experience that you must come to your own convictions about worldly amusements. Others can't impose their convictions on you. But, when the Holy Spirit speaks deep within your soul, it pays to listen. Don't worry what others may say, whether they make fun of you or not, or what is accepted practice. Get your convictions from the Word of God and prayer and the leading of the Holy Spirit.

Growth

The church always insisted I preach the summer revivals. After my first revival on the closing Sunday morning, the chairman of deacons came to me after the service. He asked me not to leave for a while. The men of the church were having a meeting and wanted to see me. Scared me to death! I just knew they were going to fire me. I entered the men's meeting with fear and trembling. The chairman spoke with broken voice, telling me what my ministry had meant to him that year. Other men, with tears, said the same thing. Then, to my utter astonishment, they presented me with a large monetary love gift. This was their way of expressing their love and appreciation to their pastor.

We had almost as many in Training Union as we did in Sunday school. We periodically promoted high-attendance days. During the three and one-half years I was there, we grew to an attendance of 120 in Sunday school. I became the chaplain of the state championship basketball teams at Roopville High School where my young people attended. The captain of the boys' team was Emerson Lyle. Emerson was not saved.

During a summer revival the other young people were burdened for Emerson. He was attending the services and was under great conviction. On a night he decided to slip into the church through the basement entrance. He walked right into the middle of a youth prayer meeting! He heard a girl call his name in prayer. At the invitation that night he came forward. Eight young people followed him. Shortly thereafter God called him to preach. He became the finest personal soul winner I have ever known.

Graduation

I graduated from Mercer in 1959. The church gave me a tape recorder for a graduation gift. It was bulky and heavy. The tapes were big, round ones. The quality was poor. But I could record my sermons and listen to them. And I could get tapes from well-known preachers as well.

My parents came down to Mercer for the graduation. They met many of my friends. We had a very happy time. The morning after the ceremonies I got in my jalopy and headed back to Carrollton. I didn't have a spare tire. When I completed the 120-mile journey, I drove up behind my dad's furniture store. I got out of the car, walked to the passenger side, and both tires, slick as onions, gave up the ghost! God protected me on the journey.

I planned to attend New Orleans Baptist Theological Seminary. One of the deciding factors in my choice of seminary was that some of my liberal professors referred to it as "that prayer meeting school." That was for me! To New Orleans I would go.

Schoolteacher

I couldn't leave immediately, however. There was the matter of money. I didn't have enough money to move to New Orleans and attend the seminary. I took a position at Central High, a new school made up of a merger of two Carroll County schools, Roopville and Whitesburg. I was to teach algebra and history. The principal and his wife, Render and Gladys Caswell, were also the coaches of the championship boys' and girls' basketball teams. The week before school began, Mr. Caswell informed me a teacher dropped out and that I would also be teaching eighth-grade science. I knew nothing about the subject. When a student asked a question, I would say, "You don't know the answer to that? That's so simple I'm not going to tell you. Find the answer for yourself." That night I'd find the answer as well!

I was strict. You couldn't get by with anything in my class. I left school to conduct a funeral one day, and there was a substitute teacher. When I returned to school, I heard the students had given the substitute a hard time. I informed the guilty parties I would meet them in the principal's office the next morning. They marched in that morning, knowing that the great white throne judgment had arrived.

"I don't know exactly what to do. I want us to pray about it."

The students hit their knees. One prayed, "Lord, I think whatever Mr. Vines wants to do will be the right thing."

The next boy prayed, "Me too, Lord."

The next boy prayed, "Lord, forgive us Christians for acting like the devil in front of these sinners."

When it was over, I said, "Go to the classroom. Today you are getting what is called 'mercy.' If it happens again, it will be called 'judgment.'" I often tell people I taught school two years: my first and last! But the experience was really a good one. I acquired a great deal of respect for schoolteachers. I also learned quite a bit about how to deal with young people during that one year.

I was saving up for seminary. At that time I was a bi-vocational pastor. The pressures of two full-time jobs, preparation for sermons and lesson plans, gave me a deep respect for bi-vocational pastors. I received two salaries—from the church and the school. I was living at home, rent free. Time was drawing near for me to head to seminary. I was single. I had been praying for a wife. There were no prospects in sight. I would go on to New Orleans. No clue what was just ahead. And how God was going to answer my prayer. Time had come for me to fall off Jacob's ladder.

Chapter 5

I Fell Off Jacob's Ladder

The third Sunday in May was a big day at "Ole Bethursday." That was homecoming or decoration day as it was often called. On that day former members of the church, those who had family buried in the church cemetery, and the community in general would gather. The church premises would be spruced up. Flowers would be placed on the graves. There would be singing, preaching, dinner on the ground, and a good time had by all.

Homecoming Message

The church was aware that their boy preacher and schoolteacher would soon be leaving for seminary. I was getting ready to attend New Orleans Baptist Theological Seminary in the fall. My final homecoming sermon was anticipated by the sad but supportive congregation. Special music for the day was indeed going to be special. I prepared a special message. In some ways this was to be my farewell sermon, though I would still be their pastor through the summer.

I did not want to disappoint. I was led by the Lord to prepare a message on the passage in Genesis 28 about Jacob's vision of the ladder between earth and heaven and the angels of God ascending and descending on it. I studied and prayed and prepared. I got up a stem-winder. I could hardly wait to deliver the message. Women would shout; grown men would weep; babies would be thrown in the air; I would sign my own Bible. Pentecost 2 was on the way!

The third Sunday in May arrived. People converged on the church. Before the Sunday school time was over, the auditorium was almost filled. The mens' and the ladies' amen corners to each side of the pulpit were filled with my best sermon supporters. They actually didn't really say, "Amen," out loud too much. They were a rather quiet people. But their nods of approval and teary eyes always helped me preach.

The congregational singing was electric. "Brethren, We Have Met to Worship," "How Firm a Foundation," "Amazing Grace" and other great hymns of the faith rocked the rafters. The choir never sounded better. Even those who would often get off-key stayed on tune that day. What a preparation for my "sermon of the ages." People were still coming in all through the congregational singing and the choir specials. I always liked to sit in a pulpit chair so I could see who was entering the building. If lost people were there, I wanted to know it. I saw personal friends and other encouragers enter. The last choir special was finished. They didn't clap in those days. The amens and nods of approval let me know the people were ready for my pulpit masterpiece.

Jacob's Ladder

I stood to preach on "Climbing Jacob's Ladder." I warmed to the subject. Early on in my fledging preaching career, I learned to follow the well-known dictum for sermon delivery: "Start low; go slow; rise higher; strike fire. Sit down in a storm." I was rising and striking. I was joining the angels in ascending and descending on Jacob's ladder. Then it happened.

The door opened and four people entered. A man and a woman. Two girls in their twenties. They quickly found a seat. My eyes immediately went to the blonde, dressed fit to kill and gorgeous beyond compare. She was the most beautiful girl I had ever seen. I fell off Jacob's ladder!

I can't tell you exactly what happened after that. The people probably wondered what happened to the message. I totally lost my train of thought. I remember consciously thinking, *I'm going to marry that girl.*

No kidding. It was love at first sight. I don't recommend young people do it that way. That's the way it happened to me, though. I can't tell you how the sermon ended. Whether there was any response during the invitation, I have not a clue. All I can tell you is, after the service I headed to the front door of the church. I only had eyes for the beautiful blonde young lady who knocked me off the ladder. As she came out the door with her mother and father, Mr. and Mrs. Paul Denney, and her friend, I looked immediately to see if there was a wedding ring on her finger. There was not! When I took her hand, I asked, "And to whom do you belong?" I was quickly told she was Janet Denney, the daughter of Paul and Velma.

A Pastoral Visit

I did a little investigative work. I had to find out where she lived, her phone number, all the proper contact information. Though I did not tell him why, my father was able to help me get that pertinent information. Her uncle, Hugh Striplin, was one of my father's all-day singing friends. He obtained the phone number from Hugh, and I called her. She was not there. I called several times; still no Janet. I was told she had gone on a cruise to the Bahamas and would be back in a few days.

Upon her return from the cruise, her mom told her, "Jerry Vines has been calling you."

"Who is that?," Janet asked.

"He's the preacher who preached homecoming at Bethesda on the third Sunday in May.

"What does he want?"

"I am not sure," her mother said.

Janet was working as secretary to one of Georgia Power's vice presidents. She was making really good money. Much more than I was making as a country pastor. She had graduated from West Georgia College, in my hometown, Carrollton. I transferred there from Mercer for one spring quarter while she was a student there. I transferred because I had a lot of revivals that spring. I never saw her. I didn't attend many classes, just enough to pass my courses. My future wife was right under my nose, and

I never knew it! She had been selected the first runner-up in the Miss Atlanta Pageant. The judges must have been blind not to crown her Miss Atlanta.

I soon heard her father was sick. Being the faithful pastor that I was, I felt it incumbent upon me to make a visit! They lived in College Park, Georgia, fifty miles from Carrollton. What is distance to the faithful, sick-visiting pastor? I made the trip and made the visit. While I was there, I asked Janet for a date. She accepted. Things were getting serious!

First and Only Date

"Where would you like to go?" Janet inquired.

"Is there a good revival we can attend?"

Revival? thought Janet. She called one church to see if they were having a revival. They were not. Relieved, she let me know and told me there was a religious movie at the drive-In. *The Story of Ruth*. Perfect! There are times when you have to adjust your convictions somewhat! After all, it was a Bible movie, you know.

The night for the date arrived. The time was to be 7:15 Friday night, July 29, 1960. I had my car washed and polished.

"I hope he doesn't drive a Chevrolet," she said.

At exactly 7:15 I rolled up in my white Chevrolet.

"I hope he doesn't wear white socks, " she declared.

I arrived in my dark pants, white shirt, and skinny tie. And white socks. Talk about GQ stylish!

Janet was breathtakingly beautiful. She was dressed in a white pique sundress, embellished with cobalt blue flowers She was elegant in white heels. Tanned and sun-bleached blonde from the Bahamas cruise, she looked like a preacher's wife to me!

To the drive-In theater we went. I really don't know much about *The Story of Ruth*. I wasn't interested in Ruth. I was interested in Janet. I didn't see much of Sister Ruth. My eyes were only upon Janet. Have I told you she was stunningly beautiful? After the movie we sat in the car at her house a long, long time. I think I left her house around five the next morning. Talk about being in love. The love bug laid one heavy bite on me.

Janet says there was only one date. But it lasted for five months. We still have the little Georgia Baptist schedule book where I recorded the times I saw Janet. From the first date on, there were eighty-two times we were together in those five months.

I was constantly on the road between Carrollton and College Park. I would leave after prayer meeting, drive the fifty miles there and back, just for a goodnight kiss. On one of those nighttime trips, I was headed to see Janet, and I saw lights coming and going in the sky. My first thought was, *Jesus is coming back.* I began to pray, "Please Lord, don't come back until I can marry Janet." Turned out it was the searchlights revolving at the Atlanta Airport near Janet's house. Talk about praising the Lord!

I didn't let the people at Bethesda know I was dating Janet. By no means because I was ashamed of her. During the years as their pastor, if I ever did have a date, I would get anonymous letters telling me what a mistake I was making dating that particular girl. I've always wondered if it was single girls or their mothers in the church sending the the anonymous warnings.

I would preach revivals and find myself the center of attraction for mothers and their daughters. I know it wasn't because I was handsome. I think they just thought it would be wonderful for their daughters to marry a preacher. Finally, I started taking Janet Bennett with me to the first night of a revival. Janet was my cousin. I never lied about it. I would just say, "This is Janet Bennett." People assumed she was my girlfriend. That seemed to do the trick. My cousin and I had a lot of good laughs about that.

After we married, my wife Janet found my cousin Janet's picture in my wallet. She was crestfallen. Until I told her the whole story. For that reason I just did all my courting of Janet in and around Atlanta. Things got serious, and marriage was planned before the people of my church knew anything about it.

The Nonproposal

Janet says I never proposed marriage to her. I just said, "Would you like to go to seminary with me?" She would. Just one little detail. There must to be a wedding first. Her birthday was December 18. The wedding date was set for December 17.

From the time of the engagement until the wedding, I went with Janet and her family to a number of places. Janet was an active member of First Baptist Church, College Park, Georgia. Her dad and his family were all Primitive Baptists. When I went with her to the Denney family reunion, I was thoroughly grilled by the Denney men.

"Do you believe in salvation by grace?" queried one.

"Yes, sir."

This seemed to satisfy him a bit.

I was carried to the sacred harp singing at Hopewell Primitive Baptist Church in Heard County, Georgia. The sacred harp singing was not new to me. I had heard it in my growing up years. The singers sang the notes, then the words. There was something hauntingly appealing about the sounds of singers singing, "Do, re, me, fa, so, la, te, do." I remember quite well Mr. Denney standing with his brothers and leading a song.

One Saturday the family wanted me to go with them to Emmaeus Primitive Baptist Church in Carroll County. The elder preaching recognized me immediately. He waxed eloquent: "Some of these little Jack-leg preachers are running around talking about 'saving the lost.'" Then he shouted, "JEEESUS said, 'Of all that Thou gavest me, I have lost NONE!" I got the message.

The people at my church were delightfully surprised. Their boy preacher was taking a bride. Showers and special parties were planned. The biggest shower was held in a clubhouse just a mile from the home where my mom and dad had been married by Preacher Bonner.

The Wedding

We were married on December 17, 1960, at First Baptist Church, College Park, Georgia. The wedding was a beautiful affair. She had just a few bridesmaids, and her twin sister, Janice, as her maid of honor. My best man was Richard Smith, a young man from Bethesda I led to Christ. Both families and friends were well represented. The Bethesda Baptist Church people were there in large numbers, beaming. The wedding ceremony was performed by Jim Stallings, a fellow student at Mercer and my best preacher friend. I only remember this from the wedding: when Janet came down the aisle on the arm of her sad-looking father, she was dazzlingly beautiful in her white wedding gown. The prettiest girl I ever, and to this day, ever have seen. And God gave her to me to be my wife, my helpmate, the mother of our children, and the best pastor's wife I could ever have desired.

Ideal Pastor's Wife

I was soon to learn there was much, much more to Janet than physical beauty. Physical attraction is normally first on the list. Other traits she possessed are equally beautiful. Janet has a keen mind, sympathetic ear, and spiritual depth that make her the ideal pastor's wife. Her insights into Scripture, especially the book of Proverbs, are remarkable. I watched her grow in her Christian life through these years. God could not have given me a better helper in ministry. The people always loved her. In fifty years of pastoral ministry, her name never came up in a controversial way. I'm sure the people loved Janet and just tolerated me!

After the wedding we headed for our honeymoon. We stopped at a motel just across town at Marietta, Georgia. She got on a pay phone and called her mother! The next morning we headed on up to Gatlinburg, Tennessee, in the Smoky Mountains for our honeymoon. We almost didn't make it up there. There was heavy snow and travel was difficult. When we got there, we saw only two other couples the entire time. They were newlyweds as well. We pretty much had Gatlinburg to ourselves. There were only two restaurants open. What did we care?

The Last Convert

I came to my last Sunday as pastor of Bethesda Baptist Church. During the three and one-half years I was there, the Lord had blessed in the salvation of souls. There was one man in particular I tried to win, to no avail. Carl Smith was one of the most respected men in our community. His sons, Richard and Donald, were outstanding basketball players. They soon came to Christ and I baptized them. I just couldn't win their dad, Carl. His parents were universalists, a rarity in that Baptist-dominated rural area. I witnessed to Carl many times. I was often a guest for meals in his home. His wife, Reba, was one of the outstanding cooks in the community. As you can see, I had a knack for finding the good cooks!

I claimed Carl for Christ. The last Sunday morning, I just knew he would come forward. He didn't. I was brokenhearted. That afternoon we had some candidates to baptize. We met at the pond where I baptized behind the house of Glen Jordan, our church treasurer. The people lined the banks of the pond. I waded out into the water. From there I gave a brief gospel message and issued an invitation for people to receive Christ and present themselves for baptism. We sang an invitation song. Much to my great joy, Carl Smith stepped forward! He was the last person I baptized at "Ole Bethursday." This taught me another valuable lesson. Preach the Word, exalt Christ, invite people to receive Him as their Savior. Then leave the results up to the Lord.

Bound for Seminary

Plans were made for our trip to seminary in New Orleans. I purchased a trailer, thirty-two feet by eight feet. No air-conditioning. The morning we were to leave, the trailer was hitched to my car. We had spent the night with my parents. They were standing in the yard as we drove away. My dad was crying. Janet and I were excited. We were on the way to seminary so I could complete my education to be a preacher and pastor.

Neither of us imagined where this journey would take us. God was leading us step-by-step. I often think of the words of the old gospel song: "In shady green pastures, so rich and so sweet, God leads His dear children along. . . . Though sorrows befall us and evils oppose, God leads His dear children along; Through grace we can conquer, defeat all our foes, God leads His dear children along."[17] Our journey together as husband and wife started. The road ahead was unknown but promising. There were new sights just down the road.

Chapter 6

That Prayer Meeting School

O ur trailer was thirty-two feet by eight feet. Did I tell you our trailer didn't have an air-conditioner? We were pulling it behind my Chevrolet. I was seeing sights never seen before by this small-town boy's eyes. We got to Slidell, Louisiana, and turned west toward New Orleans. I started seeing billboards advertising things that were brand-new to me. Clubs and shows and liquor and gambling. What ungodly world was this to which I was taking my new bride? The heat was stifling. As we approached New Orleans, I smelled the odor of strong coffee.

New Orleans Baptist Theological Seminary

Before long we turned into the entrance of the New Orleans Baptist Theological Seminary. "That prayer meeting school," as my liberal Mercer professors had derisively called it. Their derision wasn't far from the truth. Often God takes what is intended as a criticism and turns it into a compliment. The Pharisees said of Jesus, "This man receiveth sinners, and eateth with them" (Luke 15:2). Christ's enemies meant it as an accusation; we take it as an accolade! The school was known since its founding in 1917 as the School of Providence and Prayer." That is what it was to me.

As I winded our trailer down the street, I saw the administration and classroom buildings. The chapel, with no steeple, loomed before us. We went by the faculty houses, the dorms for single students, and the apartments for married ones. In the back of the campus was the trailer village. I contacted the proper people, and they assisted me in getting the trailer parked, connected to utilities, and ready for occupancy. The first night was unbelievably hot. Did I tell you we had no air-conditioning? In Georgia, where I lived for twenty-three years, we got a little break during the summer days. The temperatures subsided somewhat at night. Not New Orleans! Did I tell you we had no air-conditioning? Such heat was not conducive for a newly married couple to adjust to each other.

There was no food in our little trailer. I went across the highway from the seminary to purchase something to eat that night. I parked in front of a hot dog stand, opened the door, and said to another man exiting his car, "Hello, how ya doin?" He looked at me like I was ready to mug him! I soon learned that people in New Orleans weren't used to southern friendliness.

We ate our hot dogs. Now we must do some grocery shopping. Some students told us about Schwegmann's across from the campus. Never had we seen such a huge store. The place looked like a city. In my growing up years in Carrollton, I never shopped where alcoholic beverages were sold. Carroll County was dry most of the years of my childhood and youth. When alcohol was voted in, I didn't shop where any was sold. That was my conviction. Well, there were rows and rows of beer, wine, and liquor in Schwegmann's. I got the shock of my life at the checkout counter. I saw a Catholic priest with a buggy loaded to the top with all kinds of intoxicating beverages. I soon learned there was no place to purchase groceries that didn't serve it. I also soon learned that, though I was not to be of the world, I was still in the world.

Neither of us had a job. We were pretty close to broke. Because of her experience as a secretary to the vice president of Georgia Power, we thought she might easily obtain work at one of the downtown corporations. We headed out job hunting. In one of the offices, I observed the risqué behavior of those working there. This incensed me. No way I was going to expose her to such. I'd work the midnight shift to avoid that.

Janet and I both obtained jobs at the seminary. I was allowed to work only a maximum of eighteen hours per week on the grounds and maintenance crew. My job consisted of cutting grass, building cement sidewalks, and cleaning student apartments for newly arriving students. I made the fabulous salary of one dollar per hour. If it didn't rain. A maximum of $18 per week. Janet immediately was assigned to work as the secretary to William S. Garmon, one of the ethics professors. His grader at that time was a student named Kirby Godsey.

One afternoon I arrived at our trailer after Janet did. When I stepped in the trailer, she was in tears. The professor had made a suggestive remark about her. I was outraged. I immediately headed toward his office. Along the way I saw a new friend, Jimmy Jackson. I told Jimmy what had happened and what I intended to do. "Let's wait just a minute. You can't do that. You'll get kicked out of school. Let's go to the business office and get her reassigned." I cooled down somewhat and took his counsel. We told Mr. McLemore, the school's business manager what had happened. He immediately gave her a job in the business office. I have often said that Jimmy saved my seminary career. I would have been kicked out before I started if I had had the confrontation I was planning in the professor's office.

Conservative Atmoshpere

The atmosphere at New Orleans was in stark contrast to Mercer. I found a spirit of evangelism on the campus. The students and faculty, for the most part, were solid Bible believers. There were some liberal professors and some liberal students. The president was Dr. H. Leo Eddleman. Dr. Eddleman had been a Southern Baptist missionary in Israel. He was a solid biblical conservative. He was moving to see to it that every professor was a solid conservative. There were some professors on the faculty who weren't. Dr. Eddleman watched them carefully. Dr. Robert Soileau, a theology professor, and Dr. Frank Stagg, New Testament and Greek professor, were more liberal in their beliefs. The word around campus was that Dr. Stagg was singing about Eddleman, "His eye is on the Soileau, and I know he's watchin' me."

I went to see Dr. Eddleman one day. I told him of my concerns regarding the liberalism in the Southern Baptist Convention. I will never forget what he said. "Jerry, the only way to get their attention is to touch the money."

The majority of the faculty was decidedly conservative. One of my Old Testament professors was Dr. J. Wash Watts. Dr. Watts was Southern Baptist's first missionary in Israel. He was a Hebrew scholar. I had been taught that the Pentateuch was a compilation of several documents. The theory was known as JEPD, a higher critical approach to the Old Testament. I shall never forget the week Dr. Watts spent the entire lecture time in his class meticulously demolishing the documentary hypothesis. On the concluding day this godly old professor, with tears in his eyes, raised his Bible above his head and said, "Young men, the documentary hypothesis makes your Bible nothing more than a scrapbook!" We left the classroom shouting.

Dr. Gray Allison was my evangelism professor. To attend his class was like a revival meeting. He taught us how to lead people to Christ. Often on Friday he would ask us whom we were going to try to win to Christ on the weekend. He would tell us whom he would seek to win. Then we would spend the entire class in a time of prayer for the salvation of those people. The next Tuesday we would share our reports and rejoice in those who had been won to Christ.

Dr. Allison could be disconcerting to students who were rather liberal. I remember well one day as Dr. Allison stood at his office door and talked with a liberal student about the matter of personal evangelism. In exasperation the student declared, "Well, I just can't get that out of the New Testament." To which Dr. Allison quickly replied, "Of course you can't. It's in there to stay!"

A special blessing to me was the R. G. Lee Library. This was a room where the library of the fabled pastor of Bellevue Baptist Church, Memphis, Tennessee was housed. I would often go there at night to see the books that influenced him. I saw immediately his love for DeWitt Talmadge's works. And I developed an interest in being a wordsmith, as was Dr. Lee. Imagine my excitement and thrill when Dr. Lee preached the dedication sermon of our new auditorium at West Rome Baptist Church in Rome, Georgia, a few years later. Ninety-four at the time, he preached an hour and a half! A younger generation of preachers would do well to study his sermons.

I loved my classes. I took Hebrew and Greek, Old and New Testament, ethics and homiletics, theology and evangelism, counseling, pastoral ministry, and sermon preparation. My grades were even better than they were at Mercer. I was enjoying my studies immensely. Thoughts of pursing a Th.D. entered my mind.

French Quarter Missions

Each student was required to spend time each week in some mission activity. I preached at the Baptist Mission. Most of those there were alcoholics from off the streets of New Orleans. They would be marched into the chapel service at the mission, and we would preach to them. I remember one night when a liberal student tried to preach. They coughed him out of the pulpit. I discovered even a room full of drunks didn't have any respect for a liberal preacher.

One of the most memorable mission activities was my assignment in the French Quarter, just off Bourbon Street. The seminary had minivans. We loaded up the van with a portable organ, guitars, and a few preachers. We would set up on the corner to sing and to preach. One night a fellow student was preaching, and a drunk came behind him and put his hand on his shoulder. I quietly attempted to remove his hand. The drunk glared at me and said, "Don't you touch that hand." I retreated. Talk about preaching! The student really went at it.

One night on our mission activity I was handing out gospel tracts while a fellow student was preaching. A drunk came up to me and said, "Tell that guy to shut up." I told him that he was preaching about Jesus who could save him. "If he doesn't shut up, I'm going to kill him." He didn't, but I kept my eye on him.

On another night I was preaching. We had a PA system, and you could hear us a block or so away. In the middle of my message, a police squad car rode up. Six policemen got out and circled me. Really got me to preaching! They let me finish my message. Then they told me that a bar on the next block had called to protest. Seems our services were hurting their business.

I have never forgotten those street services. I met some scary characters on those sinful streets. One night I met an alcoholic who said he once preached the convention sermon at the Southern Baptist Convention. I got his name and checked it out. He indeed did preach the convention sermon. There were some tragedies walking those hellish streets. I saw the depths to which sin could carry people. I was learning the country preacher's words were true: "Sin will take you farther than you want to go. Sin will teach you more than you want to know. Sin will keep you longer than you want to stay. Sin will cost you more than you want to pay." I also learned something else. There is no depth of depravity so deep but that the love of God cannot reach it. There is no sin so bad that Christ's blood can't cleanse it.

No Church Would Call Me

I wanted to preach, but few opportunities came my way. I wanted to be pastor of a church. No one seemed to want me. I preached in view of a call at a church in Denham Springs, Louisiana. I met with the pulpit committee. There was a lady on the committee. I didn't like that. I thought only men in the church should be seeking a pastor. She said to me, "We only let our pastor preach two revivals a year." I was young and rather brash. "Well, what if the Holy Spirit leads your pastor to preach three revivals one year?" I wasn't going to let anyone tell me how many revivals I could preach. Looking back, I can see the wisdom of having women on a pulpit committee. I also know that a pastor can abuse his privileges if he isn't careful. But I still believe the pastor must be free to be led by the Holy Spirit. Evidently no church wanted me to be their pastor.

On Sundays Janet and I went to church. We attended Franklin Street Baptist Church, near the seminary. In later years the church, white in membership, nearly died. A young African-American pastor took the church, and it grew tremendously. His name was Fred Luter. He built it into the largest church in the city. In 2013 Dr. Luter was elected the first African-American president of the Southern Baptist Convention.

We also attended Mid City Baptist Church where Paul Driscoll was pastor. The church was quite an evangelistic center. Each year they baptized more than one thousand people. Dr. Driscoll preached brief sermons. But could he ever give an invitation! I can hear him now: "If you're lost, you're walking a spiderweb over hell. It could snap at any moment, and you'll fall into hell forever."

From time to time we attended First Baptist of New Orleans where J. D. Grey was pastor. He served First Baptist as pastor for thirty-five years. He also served as president of the Southern Baptist Convention. Dr. Grey was one of the major "movers and shakers" in the Convention. He and R. G. Lee, pastor of Bellevue Baptist in Memphis, were close friends. The services were upbeat and evangelistic. One feature of the service that appealed to me was the prayer time. He had the people to sing, "All your anxiety, all your care, Bring to the mercy seat, leave it there. Never a burden He cannot bear, Never a friend like Jesus."[18] This chorus set the atmosphere for prayer time. In later years in Jacksonville, I introduced the singing of prayer songs as we went to our special prayer time in the service.

Friends for Life

I met some ministerial students who became lifetime friends. I mentioned Jimmy Jackson. We have been friends all through the years. Another friend I met there was Jim Henry. We have maintained a friendship from those days until now. Another special friend I made was Grady Crowell.

Grady was from Mississippi. He had the longest drawl I ever heard. He could make a sentence go into the next day. His favorite saying was, "If the Lord leads." One day, playing softball, I came up to bat. Grady, coaching at third base cried, "Tiiiimmee ouut!" He came to me and whispered in my year, "Brother Jerry, if the Lord leads, lay down a bunt!" Grady was a tremendous soul winner. He always had a supply of gospel tracts. He would sweetly hand them out at the grocery store or wherever he might be. He would awaken in the middle of the night to go to the bus station, board buses at 1:00 or 2:00 a.m., and hand out tracts to the passengers.

Grady didn't lack for boldness. One week the noted liberal pastor from North Carolina, Carlyle Marney, was the speaker for a special series of chapel services. We were beside ourselves that such a liberal would be allowed to speak on our conservative campus. One afternoon Grady was driving on campus and saw Dr. Marney walking down the sidewalk, smoking a cigarette. Grady rolled down the window and shouted, "Smoke that cigarette, you liberal!"

Some outstanding preachers spoke in chapel. The most memorable to me was Dr. Charles Howard. Dr. Howard was a Bible professor at Campbell College in North Carolina. He also served rural churches. Southern Baptists discovered him in the latter years of his life. His week at New Orleans impacted me greatly. He seldom preached without tears. He spoke of personal soul winning. By the end of the week, the entire campus, professors and students, were engulfed in an ocean of their own tears. I learned preaching must not only have head; it must also have heart.

A Controversial Decision

Pretty soon we discovered Janet was pregnant with our first child. She was deathly sick. This was a new experience for me. I didn't have a clue what to do. I was not as attentive as I should have been. I was going to class, working on the campus part-time, and trying to be an understanding husband. We were running short on money. I wasn't sure we could continue my seminary education at that point. Love will take you just so far!

I remember a story Dr. W. A. Criswell told. He said a young couple in his church told him they were going to get married. "And how do you plan to support yourselves?"

"Oh, we are so in love. We've heard two can live as cheaply as one."

To which Dr. Criswell replied, "Sure. If one of you doesn't eat and the other one goes naked."

Janet and I weren't exactly naked. We did have a little to eat. But we weren't getting by. And Janet was so sick I knew something had to be done.

Paul Jackson, the associational missionary who had been on the pulpit committee that called me to my first church, moved to Cedartown, Georgia, to do the same ministry there. One of the churches in his association needed a pastor. The church was Second Baptist of Cedartown. Paul arranged for us to visit Second Baptist. I preached for them. They wanted me to serve as their pastor. I prayed about it and accepted their call. We would be moving back to Georgia. I planned to return to seminary at a later time.

Many of my friends were appalled. They told me I was making a big mistake. Some even suggested I was out of the will of God. Others said if I left, I would never return. They told me about student after student who left, never to return. I knew what they were saying perhaps was true. But I also knew I was made of different stuff. I would become the pastor of Second Baptist Church in Cedartown, Georgia. Our baby would be born. I would get my finances in better shape. In time I would return. Little did I realize the winding journey my return would take.

Chapter 7

Midnight Train to Georgia

J anet and I loaded up and headed back to Georgia. We would sell our
trailer. We were going to live in a pastorium! There was excitement
in the air around Second Baptist Church of Cedartown, Georgia.
Their new pastor was in his twenties. His wife was beautiful, and they
were expecting their first baby. The young couples in the church were
excited. Located in the Goodyear Mill Village, the church was well
known for a good ministry through the years.

Second Baptist Cedartown

Their most fruitful ministry had been during the pastorate of Buddy
York. Part Cherokee Indian, Buddy was quite the preacher. He was the
brother of Rudy York, the baseball player who played thirteen seasons in
the Major Leagues. Rudy was an accomplished first baseman and home-
run hitter. One sportswriter said of him, "He is part Indian and part first
baseman."

Buddy York was a powerful and bold preacher. In those years radio
preaching was well received. God used him and other effective preachers to bring a mighty revival to the area. Multitudes were saved. Second
Baptist was the beneficiary of many of those great revivals.

The church was for sure a mill village church. I had gone to school in Carrollton with students who lived in the Mandeville Mill Village. They were looked down on by those who thought they were superior to mill village people. I found them to be some of the finest young people in our high school. The same thing was true in Cedartown. Each morning the people in the village would walk to their jobs at the Goodyear Fabric Mill. Second Baptist had a four-room house right behind the church where their pastor and family would live.

We were so excited to move in. There weren't any closets. So we hung what few clothes we had on nails driven in the doors. We had one small bathroom off the back porch. We didn't care. Janet and I were in love, I was pastor of a church in town, and a new arrival was on the way.

The church was a country church in town. The music was decidedly southern gospel. The choir could really belt it out. The ladies in the choir had on their hats and their little ones under their arms. Talk about an animated choir! There was a lot of talent in the choir. A talented trio composed of the Abram twins, June and Joan, and Sherrie Stephens often sang. Our piano player, Virginia Redding, could really play. The people in the congregation sang at the top of their voices. Starling Redding led the singing. His high tenor voice could be heard above everyone as he would screech, "I have beeeen redeeemed!" What glorious singing we had.

At times the people would get so happy they would shout. That was new to me. One of the sweetest women in our church, Mrs. Bridges, would get happy. Her hair was beautifully gray and wavy. From time to time she would tear up and shout. I always heard, if you jump and shout, be sure you walk the straight and narrow when you hit the ground. She certainly did. There was a beautiful radiance about her. She was one of the finest, godliest ladies in our church.

Before the service began, the deacons would meet to pray with me. I was ready for them. They all prayed at once. I knew about that. But there was one good brother who seemed to be the last one praying. I soon discovered why. He would wait to begin praying until the rest of us had about worn ourselves out; then he would set in. Not to be outdone, I started waiting as well. Then, it was a contest to see which one of us could hold out the longest! They were good, godly men. I thank God to this day for their prayers, love, and support of a young, inexperienced pastor.

The people were very receptive to my preaching. I was doing topical preaching in those days. I was always a student, but the only method I knew was to take a topic, find some Scripture verses about it, and put together a message. The people didn't care. They seemed to enjoy just about everything I preached.

I routinely preached with my coat on. But the building was not well cooled, and it could get pretty hot. When I overheated, I took off my coat. I noticed when I threw my coat to my pulpit chair, loosened up my tie, and unbuttoned my collar, the people really thought I was preaching in the Spirit. I thought that was too much of the flesh, so I stopped going through my partial disrobing ceremony.

Radio Broadcasts

I immediately secured a radio program. I would go to the radio station early every morning Monday through Friday for a fifteen-minute broadcast. I also started a thirty-minute service at 12:30 right after the Sunday morning service. The choir would stay, sing one number, and I would bring a brief message, usually a recap of my morning message.

I started receiving money each month from one of our college students. Joe Kines was playing football at Jacksonville State University, Alabama. His roommate was Bobby Welch, a future friend and Southern Baptist Convention president. Joe's grandmother loved the daily radio program. He sent money from his limited funds to help pay for the broadcasts. Joe is one of the most respected coaches in college football ranks. He coached at several places including Florida, Georgia, Florida State, Arkansas, and Alabama. One year he was selected National Defensive Coordinator. Joe's Christian character impacted many players through the years.

Revivals

The people responded to my leadership. The attendance was growing. People were being saved. God was blessing. At our revival meetings

the attendance would be so large the people couldn't get into the auditorium. We set up loud speakers and chairs on the grass on either side
of the church to accommodate the crowds. Heaven came down in those
meetings.

One year we engaged in a two-week tent revival. The tent was erected
behind the church in the lot between the church and the pastorium. I
preached to the church the first week. F. M. Davis, a prosperous businessman and lay preacher from Marietta, Georgia, preached to the lost
the second week. For whatever reason there were lost people who would
never darken the doors of the church who would come to the tent. Many
who came were saved.

Joy Bell

The time for the birth of our baby was drawing near. Janet sang in
the choir. One Sunday, after I signed off the air in our after-service radio
program, I turned to the choir. Janet said, "It's time to go." And to Rome,
Georgia, we headed. I dutifully took my place in the fathers' waiting
room. On November 6, 1961, Elizabeth Joy was born. We called her our
Joy Bell. We have continued to call her that. She has indeed been a Joy
Bell to us. The people were thrilled there was a baby at the pastor's house.
They brought gifts, offered to babysit, and did everything they could to
make this happy occasion even happier for us.

Problems

The times were joyful. There were also problems. The people worked
together at the mill. They would get into a lot of squabbles during the
week. But, come Sunday, they would gather in God's house, and heaven
would come down. I was young and inexperienced. I really didn't know
how to deal with problems between members. Fortunately, most all of
the people liked me, and they kept squabbles between themselves rather
than with me.

I read old minutes of the church. I saw some of their misbehavior
through the years reflected in the minutes. In those years the minutes

could get rather specific, to the point of naming names. One Sunday I announced to the people I had been reading the church's minutes. If some of them didn't "straighten up and fly right," I was going to read the minutes publicly. That seemed to quiet things down somewhat.

At Wednesday night prayer meetings the people gave their testimonies. Those were sweet and blessed times. Our church custodian was Brother Williams. He served a term in Sing Sing for killing a man who made a sexual advance toward him. No one wanted to cross Brother Williams. One Wednesday night he stood to give his testimony. "I had a dream the other night," he started.

Oh me, I thought, *where is this going?*

He continued, "The Lord appeared to me and said, 'Williams, see that young preacher of yours?' I said, 'Yes, Lord.' Well the Lord told me, 'If you give him any trouble, I'll kill you.'" He turned to the people and said, "And, if you give him any trouble, the Lord will kill you!"

"Amen," I shouted.

Having the pastorium right behind the church provided some advantages. We could easily walk to church. There were disadvantages also. One or two of the members might show up on Sunday morning before church. We were trying to get ready. There really wasn't time to entertain unexpected guests. On weekend nights drunks would be dropped off on our front porch. I would load them in my car and drive them to their home. Often fights would ensue between the drunk and his wife. When I tried to break it up, the drunk would turn on me.

Preaching and Studying

I was busy preaching revivals. This helped me make ends meet. The church was generous, but there was just enough to get by, including the modest honorariums the churches gave me in revivals. We didn't have a lot to spare, but the Lord met our needs.

I preached from time to time at Cedartown High School. I was young and the students were receptive. In those years there was the freedom to preach the Bible and give an invitation for people to come to Christ. One of the young students who listened to me was Danny Watters. Danny

attended revivals at our church. Later he was called to preach and became
a close friend.

Though I intended to return to seminary in New Orleans, I wanted to
do some study while back in Georgia. I enrolled for a quarter at Columbia
Theological Seminary in Decatur, Georgia. I commuted back and forth.
I took a Greek intensive course in Ephesians, a class on 2 Corinthians
taught by noted scholar Phillip Hughes, and a course in counseling.
This was helpful to me and whittled away some credits of my course
requirements.

I gave myself to study. A small study was provided for me at the
church. That was not a very good arrangement. Often my study would be
interrupted by members who just wanted to come by and chat. One day
I was way behind on my sermon preparation. There was a knock on the
door. "Come in," I reluctantly said.

In stepped a member. He sat down and said, "Now that I'm retired,
I didn't have anything to do. I figured you didn't either. So I thought I'd
come by and chat a spell."

I wasn't filled with spiritual thoughts about then.

Flight to Eureka

The problems really got to me. I didn't know how to deal with them.
My solution was to run. The problems didn't involve me personally. The
majority of the people seemed to like me. They loved Janet and Joy. But I
just didn't know what to do. I wasn't sure if being a pastor of a city church
was for me. Maybe I needed to stay in the country. A pulpit committee
from Eureka Baptist Church in Carroll County contacted me. The church
was small, had a brand-new pastorium, and wanted me to be their pastor.

The people of Second Baptist Cedartown were shocked. Some were
sad. Others were mad. There seemed to be a general consensus I was making a big mistake. One of my biggest supporters, Earl Studdard, came to
see me. "You're making a big mistake. You aren't supposed to leave here,"
he said. I didn't like it at the time; looking back, he was probably right.

There were problems at Eureka from day one. The church was about
half the size of Second Baptist. There seemed to be little interest in

growing. There were suspicions of moral problems among some leaders of the church. There were many difficulties and challenges. I learned a valuable lesson. You really can't run away from church problems. They show up at your newest post of duty; they just have different names. To be sure, every church and every pastor have distinct personalities. There are times when those personalities do not match. Under those circumstances a move for the pastor might be best. But I found out the problems at Second Baptist were in capital letters at Eureka.

However, there were some wonderful people in the church. Many of them were very kind, supported us, and were with us all the way. Mr. and Mrs. W. T. Moore just fell in love with Joy. They often volunteered to keep her. Joy loved them, referring to Mr. Moore as "T." The Huddlestons were good friends. A young couple, they often invited us to share meals with them. Across the road behind our house was the Bill Pritchett family. Their daughter, Patti, was just a little girl. She aspired to become a pianist. She became an outstanding one and has taught piano to hundreds of students through the years.

I fellowshipped with some special country preachers during that time. Carl Tapley, Horace Wilson, and Charles Williams took me under their wing. Carl Tapley is still in my top ten greatest preachers I ever heard. Those men loved me, mentored me, and spent time with me. I have never forgotten them.

Double Blessing

Another special event took place during our first two months at Eureka. Our twins, Jim and Jodi, were born June 24, 1963. Only nineteen months after Joy was born. Less than three years of marriage, three children. Looked as if all our children were going to be born in the same year! You should have seen us. We had two bedrooms. I took one of them to be my study. Janet and I, Joy, Jim and Jodi were all in the same bedroom. When one of the twins would cry, Joy would sit straight up and cry also! Jim and Jodi have been double blessings to us all these years.

Janet was amazing with the children. When she fed the twins, she sat between them. She would pop the baby food in one twin's mouth; the other would cry. She would pop food in that one's mouth! I was not much help. All I knew to do was study and preach.

Unwelcome Excitement

The year in Eureka was not without excitement. Several pastors joined me in concern for the illegal gambling going on in Carroll County. I was especially concerned about the pinball machines. A cousin of mine was addicted to gambling on them. We went to the courthouse and took out an injunction against the machines. The sheriff picked up all of them in the county. Talk about a furor.

The man who owned the machines was well known to me. He was also the lead man in the illegal activities going on in the county. I knew him well. His son was on the Carrollton football team with me. We had also played on a championship little boys' baseball team. I remember vividly returning from a game in Waycross, Georgia with their family. The back floorboard of the car was full of whiskey bottles. We put our legs on top of them. I knew quite well who I was upsetting.

About midnight that night my phone rang. It was he. He was not happy. "Jerry, you had them pick up my pinball machines today. I'm drinking; I'm mad; and I'm going to shoot somebody tonight." He hung up the phone. No sleep for me that night. Every time I heard a car pass by the house I sat up in bed. The night was uneventful. The next morning I was still unnerved. During my morning devotions I read these words from Psalm 57, "Be merciful unto me, O God, be merciful unto me: for my soul trusteth in thee: yea, in the shadow of thy wings will I make my refuge, until these calamities be overpast" (v. 1). What a relief. I learned to take your stand for what you know is right and trust God to take care of you.

Back to Seminary

Though I often wondered if I was in God's will when I went to Eureka, I have never questioned God was leading us on a winding journey back to seminary. I resigned the church. Plans were made to return to New Orleans. This time, not with just a wife. But with a wife and three children. There would be no trailer this time. We would live in an apartment. We took the journey again. We arrived on campus, moved into our apartment. The small apartment had air-conditioning! Janet was not going to work. She would take care of the children. I would work. We would trust God to meet our needs.

God provided for us in unusual ways. On one occasion bills were coming due, and there were not sufficient funds to pay them. That morning before class I read these words in my devotions, "Trust in the LORD, and do good; so shalt thou dwell in the land, and verily thou shalt be fed" (Ps. 37:3). I prayed, "Lord, I am trusting You. I believe I am doing good to attain a seminary education. You have said we would be fed."

That day after class I went to our post office box. There was a letter from Bobby Rivers, general manager of Roy Sewell Clothing in Bremen, Georgia. He said he felt impressed to send me some money! There was a check to cover all the due bills and enough left over to take the family out for Sunday dinner! I learned that you can trust God to meet your needs. The words of the familiar saying are true: "Where God guides, He provides. Where He leads, He feeds."

Dr. Harrison

Dr. George Harrison soon became a favorite professor. Dr. Harrison was my Hebrew teacher and also taught Old Testament intensives. I had him the first year he ever taught a seminary class. Talk about tough! His tests and pop quizzes were unbelievably hard. Many a preacher boy walked after those tests. Perhaps you have heard this told as a joke. The story really happened in one of my classes under Dr. Harrison. So difficult was he that we were kept in a constant state of nervous anxiety. On this particular day Dr. Harrison called on a student to lead the opening prayer. He incorrectly thought we were having a test. His voice trembled as he pleaded for the Lord to help us all do well on the test.

Another student, hearing the fervent prayer, thought he had forgotten about the test. He exclaimed out loud, "Oh no!"

I determined I was not going to let his difficult tests intimidate me. I studied for a particular final exam all day and night. I had the material down. I was going to grade a solid one hundred. I was whipping down through the test when I came to this question: "Who was Joktan?" "Joktan?" I racked my brain. I couldn't come up with the answer. Turns out the only time he is mentioned, the only thing said about him is that he had thirteen sons (Gen. 10:26–29). I made a ninety-nine on the test. In later years when he led Bible conferences for me, I reminded him of that.

Dr. Harrison opened up for me the beautiful pictures of Christ to be found in the Old Testament tabernacle. His reverence for the Word of God and His love for the Son of God were evident. We became good friends. On occasions when he was away, he would ask me to lecture to his classes.

Pinnock Takes Campus by Storm

There was a new sensation on the campus. Dr. Clark Pinnock was brought on to teach theology. Dr. Pinnock was a brilliant young scholar and a strong conservative. He took the campus by storm. Students flocked to his classes. Though I never took a class from him, I did visit his classes from time to time. I did attend the nighttime prayer meetings he held in the chapel prayer room. I can still hear him praying: "Lord, bless part of this seminary, and judge part of it."

After chapel we would gather in the dining hall for coffee. After having a questionable speaker, we would see Dr. Pinnock loping through the dining hall. He was tall, had coke-bottle glasses, and always had an umbrella. "What about the chapel speaker, Dr. Pinnock?" Never missing step, he would declare, "He's a liberal."

He spared none of the liberal professors on the faculty. He could be scathing in his remarks. Dr. Frank Stagg had already left to become a professor at Southern Seminary in Louisville, Kentucky. The pressure became so great Dr. Soileau resigned under protest in 1969, accusing the administration and trustees of what he termed "oppressive practices."[19]

Dr. Pinnock became a featured speaker on Baptist state evangelism conference programs. He was exposing the liberalism in the convention. Those who sat under liberal professors knew he was telling the truth. The influence of Dr. Pinnock in birthing the conservative resurgence is unmistakable. One of his doctoral students was a young man named Paige Patterson. When the conservative resurgence officially began in 1979, Dr. Pinnock had moved on to a non-Southern Baptist school.

Back to Cedartown

Things were doing well. I was enjoying my studies. Janet was doing a superb job with the children. Graduation was ahead. The journey took another unexpected turn. Second Baptist, Cedartown, was without a pastor again. They contacted me about returning to the church to complete what God had sent me there to do previously. I had never been able to get away from my love for the church. There was much work to do. One problem: how could I complete my seminary education? The pulpit committee assured me I could commute back and forth to finish. The move was made. I was pastor of Second Baptist, Cedartown, for the second time. We moved into the same, but enlarged pastorium. They had added another bedroom and bathroom. The house was bricked. They had done a beautiful job. Janet was really happy with it.

I took up my role as pastor. I continued being a seminary student. During the week I stayed in the men's dormitory. Then I commuted home for the weekend. Through the generosity of Bobby Rivers again, there were some weekends I could fly. Some weekends I made the journey by car. Carl Tapley, one of my rural pastor friends, took the journey with me. Most of the time I journeyed by train. On Friday nights I would board the Pelican train to Birmingham, Alabama. Around midnight I would rush from the Pelican to the Seaboard Railway to Cedartown. I slept in the passenger car as best I could.

I met several of the railroad people. They took a liking to me. When the train arrived in Cedartown on Saturday morning, they slowed it down as it got near my house. I would jump off the train and head home to greet Janet and the children. I would shower and shave, then begin visiting. On average I would make thirty to fifty visits on Saturday.

One of those Saturdays I visited all day with no visible fruit. I thought I would quit. The Lord seemed to say to me, "Make one more visit." I went to the home of Mr. Landrum, who owned the service station where

I purchased gas. He was there, suffering from a severe headache. I led Mr. Landrum to Christ. Before I returned the next weekend, he died of a brain hemorrhage. I conducted his funeral and told the people about his salvation. As a result nine members of his family came to Christ. I baptized all of them.

I would preach both services on Sunday. On Monday Janet prepared me a lunch, and I would board the train for the journey back to New Orleans. I spent those Mondays studying for my seminary classes. During the ten months I commuted to school, 110 people came to Christ and were baptized. The church continued to grow.

No Need to Wait until Houston

I remember one trip quite well. I was studying my schoolwork. Behind me was a young man. I could tell by his language that he was probably unsaved. My Bible was on my lap along with my seminary textbooks. In a few minutes I sensed someone looking over my shoulder. I looked up. "Are you a preacher?" he said. I answered that I was. "Well, I'm going to Houston to see a preacher. My fiancé is a Christian, and she says she won't marry me unless I become one. I'm going to talk with her preacher."

Well, no need for him to go all the way to Houston to talk with a preacher. I asked him to come and sit with me. I was able to take the Bible and lead the man to Christ. I often imagine the surprise and joy of his fiancé when he arrived in Houston, a new Christian.

Pretty soon I completed my seminary work. I considered doing advanced work toward a Th.D. degree. Dr. Harrison mentioned it one time. He wanted me to do work in Hebrew and be his grader. None of my other professors encouraged me. I was interested, but there was a tug from Georgia. I was pastor of a church. I could now devote myself to being a full-time pastor again.

Preaching Change

I made a change in my preaching during my second time at Second Baptist. For the early years of my ministry, I preached topical messages.

The frustration of searching for a suitable text made sermon preparation difficult. My time to study was limited. I attended a Bible conference at Tennessee Temple University that changed my approach to preaching. I heard so much criticism of the school from Southern Baptists that my curiosity got the best of me. I was preaching a revival in Chattanooga and noticed in the Sunday paper they were having a Bible conference.

The next morning I went to the 8:00 o'clock session. The building was packed. There was a huge choir. The Bible teacher was a man named Warren Wiersbe. Dr. Wiersbe was pastor of Calvary Baptist Church in Covington, Kentucky. He stood to speak. He was matter-of-fact and very low key. He was teaching about Mary sitting at the feet of Jesus. He began to say things that caused me to say, "Where did he get that?" I would look at my Bible, and there it was. Right on the page! He was doing what I came to understand was expository preaching. That's what I wanted to do. This was the way to actually teach the people God's Word.

I announced to my people at Second Baptist I was changing my method of preaching. I was going to take a book of the Bible and preach consecutively through it. The people took a while to adjust to that kind of preaching. My sermons weren't as bombastic and emotional as before. But pretty soon they realized they were learning God's Word. And they were happy with the new method.

The church had several fine Bible students. Though most had limited education, they showed remarkable insights into God's Word. One of those was Ed Shellhorse. Ed lived across the street from us. He worked at the Goodyear Mill. Never owned a car. He would work the second shift, return home that night, bathe, and eat the meal his wife prepared for him. And then he would study the Bible.

Ed Shellhorse was a great encouragement to me. After the services he would walk down the street from the church with me. He was always kind and complimentary. Often he would say, "Pastor, I was studying that text recently and . . ." He would show me things in my passage of Scripture I had never seen before. I should have asked him about my passage walking to the church and not walking from it!

We had our share of sorrows. As the twins began to grow, we became aware Jodi had some physical difficulties. She was unable to use her left hand. She limped on her left leg. We believe she was injured at birth. Through all the tears Jodi became a great blessing to us.

My father had been enlisted to be our full-time minister of music. He moved to Cedartown. We got a two-for-one deal. My sister, Brenda, would be the pianist. My dad could really get it out of a choir. The church grew, the people were happy, and the Lord was blessing.

Things were looking good. I was devoting my time to the church. We were growing. The family was settled in. I was giving the people the Word of God. People were being saved. Looked like we would be there for a long time. Little did I know the next leg of the journey.

Chapter 8

It's a Fit or It's Not

Pretty soon there would be a pulpit committee from First Baptist Church, Fort Oglethorpe, Georgia. The church was located just south of Chattanooga, Tennessee. Though things were going well at Second Baptist, Cedartown, there was a restlessness in my spirit. I was receptive when the committee from Fort Oglethorpe came. In a matter of a few weeks, I accepted their call to be their pastor. Janet, Joy, the twins, and I said, good-bye to the sweet people. They seemed to understand the time had come for me to move on.

First Baptist, Fort Oglethorpe

The Fort Oglethorpe Church was a contrast in every way to Second Baptist, Cedartown. The people in Cedartown were primarily mill workers; those in Fort Oglethorpe were professional people. The music at Second was decidedly southern gospel; FBC, Fort Oglethorpe music was more formal, almost high church. The Second Baptist people were demonstrative and vocal; Fort Oglethorpe was rather quiet and subdued. Preaching was difficult. I struggled to deliver my messages.

I continued my new pattern of preaching through books of the Bible. Immediately I faced resistance. Almost every message I brought seemed to hit someone in the congregation rather hard. One Sunday I preached

the passage in James 3 about the tongue. After the service one of the deacons came to me and said, "Preacher, how did you know?"

"How did I know what?" I answered.

"That Mrs. So and So was in the congregation? She's never been here
before. She is the biggest gossip in town; and you preached about the
tongue. How did you know?"

I didn't know. The Holy Spirit knew and had just the message she
needed to hear ready for her.

On another Sunday I preached the passage from James 5 about the
rich. In the message I said, "It is dog eat dog in the business world." After
the service a deacon who owned a large grocery store accosted me in my
study. He accused me of attacking all businessmen. I held my ground.
That afternoon at the deacons' meeting, he proposed to raise my salary!
To try to buy me? I don't know. Whatever. I took the raise.

Sin in the Camp

A young deacon and his wife would make faces while I preached.
They would look at each other, smirk, and laugh. Their behavior really
bugged me. I didn't know why they responded so negatively to my preaching. I did some serious heart searching. Was something wrong with what
I was saying? Was I preaching in the wrong spirit? As best I could tell,
my motives and methods were pure. Sometime after I left the church, I
found out she was sleeping with her boss. He was a homosexual. I was
learning through the preaching experience that the Holy Spirit can take
the Word of God and apply it to the listeners, whether I know what is
going on or not.

There was a prevailing worldliness in the church. Though there were
many sweet, dedicated members, others were steeped in the ways of the
world. At our youth camp matters pretty much blew up. The adult counselors wanted to let the young people come to the services dressed in
bathing suits. I felt that one's attire set the atmosphere for their reverence
in the services. The adults wanted to let the couples go off into the woods
to be alone together after the services. I said, "Absolutely not." The camp
was a battle between me, the counselors, and our young people. The Lord

and I won. Many young people were saved. Many others surrendered to the lordship of Christ.

A Liberal in the Pulpit?

Our church was on the edge of Chattanooga, where Tennessee Temple University was located. Dr. Lee Roberson was president of the school and pastor of the founding Highland Park Baptist Church. Dr. Roberson was a good man, great church builder, and strong evangelistic leader. The influence of the church and school spread all through that part of the world. Though I faced some objections from strong Southern Baptist members in my church, I continued to attend their Bible conferences.

Often on Wednesday nights our people would go to their cars after the services, and there would be tracts on their windshields placed there by Tennessee Temple students. The tracts warned the people that they were listening to a liberal preacher. I suppose it was because I was a Southern Baptist. Tennessee Temple students were strictly forbidden to attend our church. This was not of Dr. Robertson's doing but of other officials at the school. In later years, when I was elected president of the Southern Baptist Convention, Dr. Robertson sent me one of the most gracious letters I received.

Though it was forbidden, some of the students slipped into our services. Word was getting around among the students that there was a young pastor there who was preaching the Bible, book by book. One of those young students was Paul Dixon. Dr. Dixon later became the successful president of Cedarville University, a Baptist school in Ohio.

Another Blessing

God gave us a special blessing while at Fort Oglethorpe. Our youngest child, Jon, was born there on November 30, 1967. Jon was born a happy boy with a mischievous glint in his eye. He has been a blessing to us. Our family was now complete. Janet continued to do an amazing job as a mother, while I filled my role as a pastor.

All the indications made it clear to me I was not a good fit for the church. I knew I would be moving on. I wanted to move on. Each afternoon I would go to an out-of-the-way Sunday school room. Down on my knees I would ask the Lord to send a pulpit committee. Nothing. I continued to pray. No word from heaven. Two years dragged by. Then, out of the clear blue, two pulpit committees showed up at the same time. One of the committees was from Tabernacle Baptist Church, Cartersville, Georgia. They told me God told them I was to be their next pastor. The other pulpit committee was from West Rome Baptist Church, Rome, Georgia. They told me God told them I was to be their next pastor. Someone was mistaken!

West Rome

As I prayed, I felt drawn to West Rome. My friend, Fred Barr, was the minister of music. He gave the pulpit committee my name. A time was arranged for Janet and me to journey to Rome to meet with the pulpit committee. We met at the historic Forrest Hotel in downtown Rome. The committee shared their vision for the church. I shared my convictions concerning ministry. Things seemed to immediately click.

On the way back that night Janet and I were so thrilled. We talked and talked. Out of nowhere I saw a blue light flashing in my rearview mirror. A Georgia State patrolman pulled me over. He looked in the car.

"Have you had anything to drink tonight?"

"No sir," I said," startled.

"Haven't you had just one teensy-weensy drink?"

"Officer, I'm embarrassed to tell you this," I said, "but I'm a Baptist preacher. I've been in Rome talking with the pulpit committee from West Rome Baptist Church."

He told me he pulled me over because I was weaving all over the highway. He asked me to be more careful and let us go. My enthusiasm affected my driving.

We moved to Rome in July 1968. Fred Barr had led the church to purchase a new pastorium for us. At the huge cost (for those years) of $35,000, the church bought a beautiful two-story house in a very nice neighborhood. There were enough bedrooms upstairs for the boys and girls to have their own rooms. Janet and I had our bedroom. We were living high! Fred Barr was not only a tremendous minister of music. He was also an astute businessman. He told the church the house would be worth far more than that in the years to come. He was exactly right.

Uniting a Congregation

Upon arrival at West Rome, I discovered I was now pastor of a divided congregation. The division was over the previous pastor. Brother Melvin Smith had been pastor of the church for twenty-four years. The early years of his ministry were fruitful. He led the church in several building programs. The church held worship services in a temporary building until a larger one could be built. Brother Smith was a good and godly man. He didn't have a strong voice. When the church moved from its earlier worship location to the next one, the people had difficulty hearing him. Over a period of time the people became divided between those who supported the pastor and those who did not. The division also seemed to be along generational lines. The older people supported Brother Smith; the younger couples did not.

I sought the counsel of my pastor, Dr. John Tippett. How should I go about following a man who had served as the church's pastor for twenty-four years? How should I handle the division? Dr. Tippett had followed a man at Calvary Baptist Temple in Savannah, Georgia, who had been there over fifty years. He gave me good counsel. When people said something nice about Brother Smith, I should say something nicer. In time those who loved Brother Smith would also give me their love. When someone said something critical about him, I should just reply that we must not look to the past but look to the future. His counsel worked. Fortunately, both sides loved and supported me. Our personalities matched! I saw God bring the people together. Some who were bitter antagonists became best friends.

Evangelistic Music

Fred Barr was the minister of music. His wife, Marjorie, was the organist. Fred and I attended the same high school and church together. Marjorie was the pianist at my first church. Fred came quite frequently to Centralhatchee to see Marjorie when I was there. He went on to get a degree in music from Florida State University, then a seminary degree in music from New Orleans Seminary. Marjorie graduated from Mercer University, as did her sister, and also attended New Orleans Seminary. Fred had a tremendous voice and was a very gifted choir man. Fred knew how to get maximum energy out of a choir.

Soon after my arrival, I shared with Fred that, though the music was good, we needed a little more gospel-oriented, evangelistic style to build the kind of church needed to reach the lost in Rome. I asked him to trust me and give it a try. He agreed to do so. After a few weeks he came into my office and said with great emotion, "I see what you are talking about." From that day on there was no finer evangelistic music program to be found anywhere.

Fred and Marjorie were assets to the ministry God had given me at West Rome in every way. People would come from all over that part of Georgia to hear the choir sing those glorious gospel songs. Bill Gaither's "Alleluiah" was being sung in the churches. Fred did it with the choir. People flocked to the church to hear it. Gaither's music became a good bridge to transition many churches to a more down-to-earth, heartfelt style of music. I don't recall any tension or worship wars during the transition. Obviously the Lord was in it. God is the author of peace, not confusion, as 1 Corinthians 14:33 teaches.

Sunday School Growth

I was trained in Southern Baptist Sunday school building. One of the study course books I read while a teenager was Arthur Flake's *Building Standard Sunday School*. His fivefold formula for building a strong Bible study program in the local church was the gold standard of the day. His formula was used all across the SBC to help churches build strong Sunday schools.

I soon became aware the Sunday school needed a major overhaul. When I arrived at West Rome, the attendance was below two hundred. I studied the organization. I soon discovered many of the classes were stagnant and stale. They were little more than social clubs. They were interested in themselves and lacked vision to reach out to the lost. When I talked with the Sunday school leaders, I discovered they were content with the status quo and had no desire to change. I couldn't get the classes to budge. I decided to do an end run.

I announced that I was starting a pastor's auditorium class. No one currently enrolled in a class was eligible to attend. I would build the class from scratch. Only nonattenders could come to my class. My first Sunday there were six present. I was on the way! I visited people. I called them. Before I was done, the class grew to over one hundred in attendance. On Saturday nights I would call every person attending and get a commitment from them to attend the next morning. At the end of the Sunday school year, I would give my little talk and tell them all to go to a Sunday school class. Every year all but about forty would do so. Our adult classes were growing whether they wanted to or not! As a result, other areas of the Sunday school were growing as well.

Sunday School Literature

The people weren't happy with the Sunday school literature. I had been using Warren Wiersbe's *Expository Notes in the New Testament* in my own Bible study. They were mimeographed lessons prepared for his Calvary Baptist Church in Covington, Kentucky. I moved our curriculum to these notes for Sunday school. On Wednesday nights I taught the lesson to the teachers. They taught the lesson to their classes the next Sunday morning. Through this method we developed some of the finest Bible teachers I have ever known.

One in particular was Mrs. Elizabeth Roberson. Elizabeth had rheumatoid arthritis. She became a wonderful teacher of ladies in Sunday school and young people in her home Bible studies. Because of the excellent teaching of many others, our Sunday school continued to grow. Moving from Southern Baptist literature didn't win me many friends in the state Baptist headquarters, however.

Training Union

The Training Union was very weak. Fewer than thirty-five people showed up on Sunday nights. I began to poll the people about their nonattendance. The answer was swift and simple—they didn't like it! I decided to offer several courses on Sunday night. There would be courses on the family, evangelism, teacher training, and Bible study. I taught a course myself in the auditorium. Our Training Union began to grow. We became the largest one in the state of Georgia and one of the largest in the entire Southern Baptist Convention. The people loved it. Southern Baptist leaders did not. The word was spreading that the young, brash pastor at West Rome Baptist wasn't a "good" Southern Baptist. There was no question that I didn't fit the mold of what was considered a good one.

Better Get in Line

I was summoned to the office of Jack Harwell, editor of the *Christian Index*, Georgia Baptists' paper. I went. In his Atlanta office he informed me that people in Rome and around the state didn't appreciate my independent ways. I was not attending the denominational meetings I should attend. I was doing some unconventional things in my church. I needed to get in line if I wanted to be a "good" Southern Baptist pastor. When he finished lecturing me, I asked him if he was through. He was. I told Jack I answered only to the Lord Jesus Christ and no one else. Jack informed me he would see to it I never got a big church in the state of Georgia. I left his office. What he said didn't shake me in the least. I read somewhere in the Bible that the Lord said He "openeth, and no man shutteth; and shutteth, and no man openeth" (Rev. 3:7).

I was pretty much shut out of any involvement in the Georgia Baptist Convention. Dr. O. M. Cates was the state evangelism director. He did use me to speak at some associational conferences. We would leave at the crack of dawn and drive to meetings in South Georgia. I was never used on the state evangelism conference because they wouldn't allow Dr. Cates to use me. One year our choir was invited to sing. They introduced everyone connected with the church, including the WMU director! Everyone but their pastor. The distinct impression was left that the choir was that of the First Baptist Church, Rome, whose pastor spoke right after they sang. I didn't care. I frankly didn't think I was qualified to preach in the conference. And I was so busy having the time of my life being a pastor and preaching at country church revivals, it mattered not to me.

At about that same time someone gave me a few sermon tapes by a young pastor at First Baptist Church, Merritt Island, Florida. What a powerful expository preacher! What a resonant, melodic, authoritative voice. His name was Adrian Rogers. I was immediately drawn to him. His messages were organized much like I was arranging mine. His main points and subpoints were alliterated. That's what I had been doing since I heard Warren Wiersbe do the same thing in his Bible studies. Rogers was a bold conservative. He was shortly to go to the historic Bellevue Baptist Church in Memphis, Tennessee. "I would really like to meet him," I said to myself.

A Busy Pastor

I was a busy pastor. I taught Sunday school and preached the morning service; I taught Training Union and preached the evening service; I taught the teachers and preached the Wednesday night service; I preached five days a week on my *What's the Good Word?* radio program; I led special youth Bible studies. When I hear some of our pastors today groaning that it's so hard to prepare one message a week, I just smile. Early in my ministry I had followed the advice of my hero, Dr. Criswell. He said, "Give your mornings to God and your afternoons to the church." I had formed the habit of spending the mornings in study. This proved to be one of the greatest moves I ever made in my schedule.

When I invited Evangelist Jess Hendley for a meeting at West Rome, he encouraged me to move my study to the pastorium. I experienced quite a bit of difficulty trying to study at the church. They were well intended, but people disrupted my study time with constant interruptions. I told the people of the change. I asked them to give me the morning time for uninterrupted study. They were gracious and willing. This proved to be a wise decision as well.

We started a lot of new ministries to help us reach people for Christ. I mentioned my daily radio program. We also broadcast our Sunday evening service. We started a bus ministry to bring people to church. The Georgia School for the Deaf was in nearby Cave Spring, Georgia. We sent a bus to pick them up and bring them to our church. There was an interpreter in the services. The church continued to grow.

Evangelism

Our evangelistic visitation was the heart of what we were doing to reach the lost. We gathered on Tuesday nights, teamed up two by two and went from house to house. Soon we needed someone to lead this for us. Emerson Lyle, the basketball star I mentioned earlier, was pastor of a rural church in Floyd County. I brought him on as our director of evangelism. Emerson became the finest personal soul winner I have ever known. He won scores of people to Christ. He also trained many of our people to be personal soul winners. I always went out with the people. I realized you couldn't lead the people to do anything you weren't doing yourself. The lost were being saved, and the church continued to grow.

Emerson mentioned to me a young theologian and pastor at New Orleans Seminary. He and Diane belonged to his church while attending the seminary. He really wanted me to meet him. His name was Paige Patterson. *I would like to meet him,* I said to myself.

Young People

Youth ministry was one of my major emphases. I built our youth ministry around summer youth camp. We conducted camps for our elementary and high school young people. I was always there. I preached hard on separation and the lordship of Christ. I brought strong preachers to preach at our youth camps. Roop Caswell, a pastor who had been a nationally acclaimed high school basketball coach, preached several times. Evangelist Jess Hendley, one of the greatest Bible scholars and revival/evangelistic preachers of all time preached on Revelation and other Bible subjects. The kids ate it up. I discovered early you can't fool young people. They know if you are real or not. And they want you to shoot straight with them. They can spot a phony a mile away. Heaven came down in those youth camps. I never saw the power of God any greater than I saw in some of those camp services.

My philosophy was this: the way to get the church moving was to begin with the young people. They are the second hand on the clock; it moves faster than the other hands. But, when the second hand starts moving, the minute hand moves; when the minute hand moves, it gets the hour hand going. When the young people get on the move for the Lord, the core of the church moves; then the whole church will move. Or it's like kindling wood. The kindling wood catches fire first; then the larger pieces begin to burn; finally, the old backlog begins to simmer, spit, and burn. The young people get on fire first; then the church core starts burning; pretty soon the big log of the whole church begins to burn. Our young people would return from camp. I would put them up to sing and give their testimonies. They would set the church on fire!

My study of church history seemed to indicate many of the great revivals and moves of God started among the young. The preacher used in the Great Awakening of the 1700s was George Whitefield, who was twenty-one when it began. God used Evan Roberts, at the age of twenty-six, in the twentieth-century revival in Wales. No doubt God used young people to keep the fires burning at West Rome.

I was involved with young people in the city. One of my deacons, Paul Kennedy, had been the football coach at West Rome High, where most of our young people attended. His assistant was his nephew, Nick Hyder. When I came to West Rome, Nick by then was head coach. We became friends. He asked me to be chaplain for his team. I readily agreed. A wonderful Christian, Nick witnessed to boys, took African-American players to live in his home, and was a positive force for Christ in the community. This connection opened many doors for me to win young people to

Christ. Nick later went to Valdosta High School in South Georgia where he became legendary for his state championship teams.

Music Crisis

We faced a crisis in our youth ministry. The Southern Baptist Convention was publishing musicals for youth choirs. In rapid succession *Good News, Tell It Like It Is*, and some others came out. The music was a definite shift in style and form. Churches all across the convention were using them with their youth choirs. Churches in Rome, Georgia, were also using them. Fred and I experienced great pressure. Some of our young people were going to other churches to be a part of these musicals. Parents started coming to us, saying we must do them as well, or we would lose the young people. Fred and I were greatly concerned. We both had a background in rock music; Fred was especially knowledgeable. Both of us played in bands. We were uncomfortable with the move toward a musical genre we considered unhealthy.

After much prayer, amid much pressure, we decided not to go that route. We were going to continue to have a style of youth music we believed was biblical and Christ honoring. Admittedly, the musicals in those days were mild compared to what you hear today. We just felt it was a step in the wrong direction. Where music in church has gone today convinces me we were correct.

The Fires of Youth Revival

Something amazing happened. We did lose a few young people. However, when the drum quit beating at the churches doing the rock musicals, young people started coming our way. The youth choir got bigger and bigger. God honored our convictions. During that period of time, thirty-seven young men and young ladies surrendered either to the ministry or some form of full-time Christian service. Today they are scattered literally all over the world, serving the Lord Jesus Christ. Among that group was a young man named David Allen. Dr. Allen is now dean of the School of Theology at the Southwestern Baptist Theological Seminary in Fort Worth, Texas. Dr. Steve Drake serves at LifeWay. His brother, David, is a pastor. I have always believed we would not have seen God move in such power if we had compromised with worldly music. I could name many more.

We had some wonderful Bible conferences and revivals in those days. I mentioned Jess Hendley. There were always many people saved when he came to preach. He was a friend and mentor. Another mentor was John Phillips. I was introduced to his phenomenal Bible teaching ministry when a member of my church gave me his book, *Exploring Romans*. He came to the church for glorious Bible conferences. From time to time I would meet with these men. They poured their lives into me. I am grateful for what they taught me.

On my study wall I have five pictures: Billy Graham; W. A. Criswell; Jess Hendley; Warren Wiersbe; John Phillips. These men influenced me more than any others. I thanked them while they were here; all but Graham and Wiersbe have gone to heaven. I look forward to thanking them again over there.

First Baptist Jacksonville Revival

One revival was significant in my ministry. Soon after I began broadcasting the Sunday evening service, I started receiving in the mail a check to cover a month of evening services. The checks came from a man who was not a member of West Rome. I soon located Herman Cooley. I visited him and his wife, Alice. They joined West Rome. He became a great friend. He mentioned to me that his daughter, Angie, and son-in-law, R. O. Stone, were at First Baptist Church, Jacksonville, Florida. R. O. was the minister of music. Angie played the piano. He also talked about his three grandsons, Ricky, Randy, and Rodney. They sang together as the Stone Brothers. I asked him to get them to come up to sing for us. They did and were an instant hit with the congregation.

Later I was able to get Homer Lindsay Jr., pastor of FBC, Jacksonville, to come for a revival. He brought his youth choir and orchestra. His young people teamed up with ours during the day for survey work and door-to-door evangelism. At night we had revival services. Dr. Lindsay preached; the choir and orchestra sang and played. The building was packed. We had a glorious revival with many coming to the Lord.

This was the beginning of a special friendship between the Vines and Lindsay families. We took several vacations together. I preached several revivals at First Baptist, Jacksonville. Upon my return I would always tell Janet, "There's just something special about those folks." I felt a special affinity with them. They were my kind of people.

My family was doing well in those years. Joy, Jim, Jodi, and Jon were involved in all the activities of the church. Janet continued to be a superb mother. How she took care of them and managed to make all of the activities of the church I will never know. Her children rise up and call her blessed.

Doctoral Work

As if I didn't have enough to do, I wanted to pursue further education. I had graduated from New Orleans Baptist Seminary. I aspired to go further. My family and church made it unfeasible to pull up stakes and head back to New Orleans again. I heard about a new school in Jacksonville, Florida, that was offering a Th.D. through correspondence courses. The concept was developed by Dr. Robert Witty, president of Luther Rice Seminary.

So innovative was the program that most of the standard schools looked down upon it. I really didn't care. I just wanted further training. Southern Baptists looked with disfavor on that "independent" school. I didn't care about that either.

The program was intense and difficult. I worked on it late at night after the family had gone to bed. The program took me five years to finish. My faculty advisor, Dr. Lizelle Owens, had his Ph.D. from New Orleans. He told me I did a lot more work for my doctorate than he did for his. In May 1974 Janet and I traveled to Jacksonville, Florida, where, in the auditorium of the First Baptist Church, I was awarded the Th.D. My friend Dr. Patterson takes pleasure in saying I messed up the Th.D. program so badly they discontinued it and now offer only a D.Min! Of course, today online learning is available from many of the finest, most prestigious schools in the land.

I wrote my doctoral dissertation about my home church, Tabernacle Baptist in Carrollton, Georgia. I proposed to prove this thesis: Every church has a distinct personality. Every pastor also has a distinct ministry personality. If the pastor's personality and the church's personality fit, there will be a successful ministry. But, if their personalities do not match, there will be problems. The church may be a fine church. The pastor may be a fine pastor. But, if they don't fit each other, there will not be a successful ministry. I was able to demonstrate this thesis in the history of my home church. I saw the same pattern in my own ministry. The churches where I encountered difficulty didn't match my kind of ministry. The churches where I saw a fruitful ministry were churches where the congregation and I were of one mind and heart.

Preacher Boys

As I indicated, we were having a lot of young people surrendering to full-time service. And a large number of our young adult men announced their call to preach as well. Some of my best Sunday school teachers and church leaders were announcing their call to the ministry. One of them was Jim Goodroe, an executive with Southern Bell Telephone Company. I was losing good workers. I became uneasy.

Sherrill Dunn asked for an appointment with me. Sherrill was a graduate of the University of Tennessee. He was a medical technologist with Battey State Tuberculosis Hospital there in Rome. He and his wife, Phoebe, were some of my best workers. He was a deacon and Sunday school teacher. She was our church pianist. The day for the appointment arrived. When Sherrill sat down, I said, "Sherrill, if you're here to tell me you have been called into the ministry, I'm going to hit you in the mouth." Sherrill turned pale. "Pastor, that's exactly why I am here. God has called me to preach." I was immediately apologetic. Sherrill went to Southern Seminary. When he was finished, God had him ready for me.

The New Auditorium

We were out of space. The temporary auditorium was packed. We purchased houses near the church for Sunday school classrooms. There was a pressing need for a larger, more permanent auditorium. A building committee was appointed. Plans were drawn. Duke Westover, representing a design-build firm, led the construction of a building to seat twelve hundred people, including the balcony. The construction was completed in 1972. The opening service was glorious. The room was packed. The music was heavenly. I preached a sermon on Christ entitled "Consider Him." Dr. R. G. Lee, fabled pastor of Bellevue Baptist in Memphis, preached the dedication message that evening. In his nineties, Dr. Lee preached an hour and a half! No one seemed to mind. Great days were ahead.

The church was experiencing steady, continual growth. We grew from fewer than two hundred in Sunday school to over nine hundred. We were always among the churches with the largest number of baptisms in the state. Janet and I and the children were very happy. I fit the church and the church fit me. What better place to remain for a lifetime? This was not to be. There were strange stirrings going on in my soul. Was the glory cloud indicating another move?

Chapter 9

"I'm Giving You a Difficult Assignment"

There was a restlessness in my spirit. I recognized this uneasiness in previous pastorates. Things were doing well at the church. The church was growing, the people seemed happy, and the future looked bright. Janet and the children were very happy in Rome. I could see many years of fruitful work. West Rome was the kind of place where a preacher could plant his life and have an ongoing fruitful ministry. But I was not one to stay long. My earlier pastorates were fairly brief. I was at West Rome five and one-half years and counting. I couldn't really put my finger on the source of the restlessness. Did God have other plans for me?

A Pulpit Committee

Without my knowledge Dr. Homer Lindsay Sr. had sent a letter of recommendation to Dauphin Way Baptist Church in Mobile, Alabama. Dauphin Way was without a pastor. Dr. Lindsay served as pastor at First Baptist Church, Jacksonville, for over thirty years. His son, my friend Homer Jr., had served as co-pastor with him for several years. The church experienced phenomenal growth. I preached several revivals there, and Lindsay Sr. became a friend and mentor. He suggested the Mobile church's pulpit committee should come to hear me preach.

Evidently several of the members made more than one visit to Rome, Georgia. I was unaware of their presence until the Sunday that Luther Davis, chairman of the committee made himself known to me. He asked if they might meet with me that afternoon. I agreed and asked them to come to our house. After lunch the committee arrived. We sat in the living room. Janet and my oldest daughter, Joy, knew what that meant. I can still see Joy standing in the hallway shaking her head no.

Dauphin Way was one of the most prestigious churches in the Southern Baptist Convention. Their pastor, Harold Seaver, served as chairman of the SBC Executive Committee. Pastors Herschel Hobbs and Jaroy Weber were elected president of the SBC after they moved on from Dauphin Way.

I arranged to make a visit to Dauphin Way. Once I was there, the committee showed me around the city. They showed me the impressive church facilities: a beautiful auditorium, Children's World, bus ministry, parking lots. The next stop was the spacious pastorium. The church's morning service was televised on a local network station. The telecast reached a large area in South Alabama, Florida, and Mississippi. The influence of the Dauphin Way pulpit was considerable.

They also showed me the long-range plan for the church. They had already built a Christian life center with a basketball court, running track, pool tables, etc. Also, there was a drawing showing the new auditorium to be constructed on the corner, next to the current worship center. Would I be willing to have two morning services until this structure could be built? They shared with me their vision to reach the city for Christ. I was thrilled to hear the committee members express their desire to have a Bible-preaching pastor who would lead them in an evangelistic ministry.

I well remember returning to Rome, Georgia, late that night. Before I went home, I stopped by the church. I turned on the lights in the auditorium. I looked at the place where I had seen so many people come to Christ. In that room God's presence and power manifested itself so many times. How could I leave such a precious place?

I went into my study. I buried my face in the carpet. There was the definite impression that I was to leave West Rome and move to Mobile to be pastor of Dauphin Way Baptist Church. I did not hear an audible voice; it was louder than that! The Lord said to me, "I am giving you a difficult assignment. I want you to go to Mobile."

I talked with Janet about it. I told her I believed the Lord's plan was to go to Mobile. As always, Janet was willing to go wherever I sensed the Lord was leading. I shared with her that He had told me it would be a difficult assignment. Neither of us realized all this was to mean. The road is not always smooth pursuing the will of God for your life. Dauphin Way issued me a unanimous call, which I accepted.

The announcement that I was leaving was made to the church. The sweet people of West Rome were shocked and saddened. I received some sweet letters from people who thanked me for what I had meant in their Christian lives. Some wrote, thanking me for leading them to Christ. Many of them urged me not to go. Yet they seemed to reluctantly say, "The will of the Lord be done." The last Sunday came. The services were sad but sweet. The Sunday night service concluded. The last amen was said. I lingered for a while. When everyone else was gone I walked into the auditorium one more time. I looked around. I thanked the Lord for all the blessings. I then turned and walked out, not looking back.

Dauphin Way Bound

We were on our way to Mobile! I wrote a letter to the congregation setting forth my philosophy of ministry and vision for the church. I requested that the letter be read to the congregation before they voted on me. The pulpit committee, well meaning, didn't read it; they thought it was unnecessary. I didn't know this until some years later.

Bobby Rivers, the general manager of Sewell Clothing in Bremen, Georgia, heard I was going to Mobile. He told me, "We can't have a Georgia preacher going to Mobile and not look good." So he took my measurements and tailored for me six suits and six sports coats with matching trousers. He sent me to his outlet store and had me select shirts and ties to go with them. My suits were virtually every color in the rainbow! My sports coats looked like Halloween tablecloths! I was a walking Joseph A. Bank commercial! That was quite a shock to the Dauphin Way congregation. They were accustomed to their pastor preaching in a black suit. One pastor even preached in a Prince Albert coat. With tails!

My personal conviction through the years is that I should always look my best when preaching. When I went to see Presidents Reagan and Bush in later years, I always dressed in my very best. When I preach, I represent the King of king and Lord of lords. I want to look like it. Just my personal conviction. Not trying to impose it on others.

A Brief Honeymoon

The first days were like a whirlwind. There was the first Sunday with all its excitement. There was new furniture to purchase. The children were enrolled in school. Sunday school departments hosted us for special social gatherings. There were interviews with the local newspaper and television stations. And there was the deacons' and wives' banquet.

I was asked to speak to the deacons and their wives at the banquet. Tell them what I expected of them. I stood to speak before people who were all ears. I remember going through the Bible's standards for a deacon. I thought, "There's no need to say this. It's a given." But I said it. "No person should be allowed to serve as a deacon who is a social drinker." I felt what I had said was totally unnecessary. All of them knew you couldn't serve as a deacon and have anything to do with alcoholic beverages!

After the meeting one of the deacons approached me. He was on the finance committee. He taught the largest Sunday school class in the church. He had the leading law firm in the city, his offices taking up an entire floor of the bank building downtown. His father had been one of Dauphin Way's pastors. "Well, if you can't drink and be a deacon, I guess I'll have to resign." I laughed and slapped him on the back. He didn't laugh. He didn't smile. He was serious. I accepted his resignation on the spot. He also resigned from the finance committee and the Sunday school class. The shock waves went through the church. My honeymoon never occurred.

Shortly thereafter he took me up to the Bienville Club on the top floor of the bank building. Quite impressive. I wasn't accustomed to dining in such opulent surroundings. He said to me, "If you don't let men who drink serve as deacons, you're going to destroy the church."

I replied, "I don't have many convictions. Not nearly as many as I should. But, those I do have, the world will crumble before I will compromise them." He left the church. Five years later we had a special celebration at the church. We honored previous pastors who served at Dauphin Way. He was in the service. He came up to me at the conclusion and said, "You're doing a great job at the church."

Staff Changes

The pulpit committee recommended to me I change the staff when I got to Dauphin Way. This seemed unfair to me. I didn't want to create difficulty for the current staff members. Beside that, I could work with anyone. Their counsel was correct. I was too inexperienced working with a large staff to see the wisdom of a pastor having his own staff. I did bring Emerson Lyle with me from Rome to be my minister of evangelism. In addition I needed someone to do hospital ministry. I saw quickly I couldn't visit the fifty plus members who would be in the hospital daily and do the preparation necessary to preach through books of the Bible. Sherrill Dunn was finishing up at Southern Baptist Theological Seminary. In his secular employment at Battey State Tuberculosis Hospital, he spent his time going in and out of hospital rooms. Perfect! He came to be my assistant, doing hospital visitation. I would keep the rest of the staff.

Big mistake. The minister of music was a good man. He was popular with the people. I wanted to make a few adjustments to the style of music used in the services. Nothing drastic, just a little more exciting and upbeat. He came to me and said a church in Florida had offered him $4,300 more per year to be their minister of music. If I would let him go to the finance committee and get them to raise him to that, he would stay. I told him no. To do that would place his ministry on a mercenary basis. And I would have to let the other members of the staff do the same. "Pray about it. If God leads you to Florida, go. If not, I will talk with the committee about a raise for you."

He went immediately to a good friend on the finance committee. The man came to my study and tried to put pressure on me. I told him the same thing. A for-sale sign was placed in the minister of music's front yard. Everyone got the message. We were without a minister of music.

R. O. Stone was the minister of music at First Baptist in Jacksonville. He and I were good friends. I stole him from Homer! Talk about excitement in the song service. R. O. was gifted with the unique ability to lead the music with joy and happiness. His big smile and winning way created real participation by the people. Angie was a fabulous pianist. His boys, The Stone Brothers, came along with the deal. The overwhelming majority of the people were elated. Some were not. I got some letters telling me the dignity of the service was being destroyed. I ignored them.

R. O. and I planned a new format for the Wednesday night service. We would have the 120-voice youth choir he developed to sing. I announced I would begin a survey of the whole Bible. R. O. had a video clip of a rocket blastoff at Cape Kennedy. As the youth choir marched in, 5-4-3-2-1, blastoff! The youth choir sang, "It took a miracle to put the stars in place; it took a miracle to hang the world in space. But when He saved my soul, Cleansed and made me whole, It took a miracle of love and grace."[20] The fifteen hundred-seat auditorium was packed to the ceiling. What a launch for our Wednesday night service!

The next day I came to church, and R. O. was on the bottom. That morning he received a phone call.

"Are you the man responsible for the video clip last night?"

"Yes mam, I surely am!," he said, waiting for effusive praise.

She proceeded to chew him out unmercifully. I thought it was funny. R. O., not so much so.

Friends, Projects, Difficulties

I met some lifetime friends while in Mobile. Fred Wolfe was pastor of Cottage Hill Baptist Church. Fred was a strong conservative. His young associate, Len Turner, drove us to places to eat. We had great fellowship together. Those friendships have continued to this day.

The church grew and grew. The Sunday school was doing well. We led the state of Alabama in baptisms year after year. The services were packed. No question we needed to build that new auditorium soon.

First the preschool building desperately needed a renovation. "Why do we need to do that?," some asked. "It's the finest preschool facility in the state of Alabama.

"It was in 1937," I replied, "but the rooms are so run down and the odor is so bad over there, I can't reach young couples with children. We've got to renovate." And we did. But the new auditorium must be built. I started making plans to that end. There was resistance. I was somewhat surprised but thought it was just the people wanting to be inquisitive and thorough in the planning.

"I'm giving you a difficult assignment." I remembered the words the Lord had spoken to my heart. Unexpected, out-of-the-ordinary difficulties appeared. There were some eruptions in the services. One Sunday I arrived for the early service and saw several police cars on the premises. A large African-American man with a black robe and silver cross was sitting in my pulpit chair. He announced he was the prophet and had come to deliver the message. The police got him and carried him away. One Easter Sunday morning, I declared, "When Peter said, 'My Lord and my God' he was declaring that Jesus is God!"

A man in the balcony jumped up and shouted, "Jesus is not God!"

I shot back, "In the name of the Lord Jesus Christ, sit down and shut up!" He went down like a shotgun blast had hit him.

In the middle of a service one morning, a young woman stood and began to speak in a tongue. I stopped, waited until she finished, then continued my message. When she came out of the building that morning, I told her at the door, "In the name of the Lord Jesus Christ, don't you ever do that in this building again."

Have you ever seen snake eyes jumping up and down? Hers did that and she said, "I am the Christ."

Southern Baptist missionaries from Africa were in the service. They told me it was exactly the same language they had heard from African witch doctors.

That wasn't the last encounter with the tongues issue. A Baptist church in Mobile was one of the first in the Southern Baptist Convention to get involved in the tongues movement. They became aggressive in their attempts to spread tongues to other Baptist churches in Mobile. A family from the charismatic Baptist church joined Dauphin Way. I later learned they were planted specifically to infiltrate our church with charismatic doctrine. I said nothing. I just started preaching through 1 Corinthians. I carefully exegeted chapters 12–14. Within a month the family quietly left the church. Those sermons became the substance of my book *God Speaks Today*, published by Zondervan. I later republished it with the title *The Corinthian Confusion*.

A Whosoever-Will Church

There were other difficulties. I made it plain to the pulpit committee I was a "whosoever will" preacher and would only be pastor at a church where people of all races were welcome. Our church in West Rome received its first African-American member without a ripple. I never heard one word of complaint from the congregation as African-Americans were saved, baptized, and became members of West Rome. The Dauphin Way committee felt the same way.

Then the first African-American person came forward during a Sunday morning invitation. As we always did, the young black man was carried out for counseling. This was standard procedure for all who came forward. After the service the deacon who counseled the young man said to me, "Pastor, he gives evidence of a genuine salvation experience. What should we do?"

"I will present him for membership tonight," I said.

My boys rode home with me that morning. "Dad, is the black man going to join the church tonight?"

"Yes, boys," I said.

"What if the people don't vote to let him?"

"I'm going to resign the church."

That got their attention. "Where will we go, Dad?"

"I don't know, but I'm a 'whosoever will' preacher. God will provide a place for us."

The word got around. The evening service was always filled to capacity. That particular night it was jammed to the rafters. There was tension in the air. The young African-American man was presented. I said to the congregation, "Folks, I know this is unusual for you. There are times when you have to trust your pastor. This young man has been saved and is being presented for membership. I want to be as fair as I know how to be. We are going to take a yes and a no vote. If you welcome this young man in the name of the Lord Jesus into the fellowship of our church, please stand." Boom! The overwhelming majority of people stood to their feet. "If you do not welcome him in the name of the Lord Jesus into the fellowship of our church, please stand." I believe there were six people who stood. The people left that night rejoicing at a tremendous breakthrough. I am not positive, but I believe we were the first Southern Baptist Church in South Alabama to receive an African-American person into membership.

The next morning the "carnal corral," as I called them, heard what happened in the evening service. Of course, they weren't present in the service. One deacon called me. He was irate. I responded to him, "You weren't there, so you don't really know what happened. We usually charge, but I'm going to give you a service tape free, so you can hear for yourself." I was accused of being paid by the NAACP to integrate the church. The uproar was something else. Mattered not to me. I was a "whosoever will" preacher at a "whosoever will" church!

Through all of the difficulties, I strongly sensed the Lord was with me and had a plan and purpose for my being there. The overwhelming majority of the people were loving and supportive. I probably changed some things too quickly. Someone said, "Vines has changed everything in the church except the signs on the bathroom doors." Ouch! Some of the difficulties I ascribe to my youth and inexperience. Probably my brashness and stubbornness didn't help either. I was growing and learning. In spite of it all, God was blessing. I was seeing lost people come to Jesus and Christians growing in their faith.

Scott Hunter and his wife, Debbie, joined Dauphin Way. They started coming on Sunday nights to hear my series on the book of Revelation. Scott was an outstanding quarterback at the University of Alabama. He also played eight seasons in the NFL. Scott was a magnificent physical specimen. He kept himself in perfect physical condition. I did not. He was growing in the Lord. One night he said to me, "Pastor, doesn't the Bible say the body is the temple of the Holy Spirit."

"That's right, Scott," I said hesitantly. *Where is this going?*

"Well, Preacher, isn't it important for us as Christians to take good care of God's temple?"

Ouch! In addition, my doctor told me I was tired all the time because I was out of shape and needed exercise. I started jogging, a habit I have maintained to this day.

I was able to begin my first book ventures at Dauphin Way. The high visibility of the Dauphin Way pulpit caused publishers to ask me for man-uscripts. I had wanted to do some writing, but a busy pastor's schedule hindered me. At Dauphin Way I touched my writing toe into the waters of publishing. My first book was *Family Fellowship*, in 1975. Published by Crescendo, it was a compilation of my messages in the Epistles of John. This was later republished by Loizeau in 1989 under the title *Exploring the Epistles of John*. As I mentioned, I published *God Speaks Today* with Zondervan. This was later republished in 2006 with the title *The Corinthian Confusion*. Victor Books published *I Shall Return—Jesus* in 1977. This became my best-selling book. Broadman Press published *Fire in the Pulpit* in 1977. *Great Events in the Life of Christ* came in 1979. My book *Interviews with Jesus* was published in 1981. The material for the book was actually gathered at Dauphin Way. This was republished as *People Who Met Jesus* in 2009.

"I'm giving you a difficult assignment." There were more difficulties ahead. Inside the church and farther away.

Chapter 10

Our Ascended Lord

There were difficulties beyond my local church as well. Southern Baptist leaders were not happy with me. Soon after I arrived at Dauphin Way, the state executive in Alabama said to a group of new pastors, "The two most dangerous men in the SBC are Adrian Rogers and Jerry Vines." I was mighty proud to be in such big-time company! The state convention office wanted to know what I was doing at Dauphin Way. A deacon and his wife obliged. Each Monday morning they called and gave a report of what I had said and done on Sunday.

Most people knew I was less than enamored with the direction of Southern Baptist schools. Having heard firsthand the liberalism taught by my professors in college, and a few at seminary, giving money to pay their salaries was problematic to me. One of the professors at the local Mobile College, an Alabama Baptist school, regularly mocked and made fun of me in his classes. And I was his pastor!

Preparing for the Evangelism Conference

Yet the state Baptist leaders couldn't ignore me. I was pastor of one of the largest, if not the largest, Baptist congregations in the state. So I was invited to preach at the Alabama Baptist Evangelism Conference. The conference was to be held at Dauphin Way. I knew I would be under the microscope. I would be examined carefully. That really didn't make any difference to me. I had a great burden to preach a message that would exalt Christ and bless the large congregation of pastors who would be in attendance.

I had preached a message or two on the ascension of Christ in Acts 1. The subject interested me greatly. At that time I had not heard or read a sermon on the subject. I began to study the passage and other passages that touched on the subject of our Lord's ascension. As I studied, the subject gripped my heart. I read everything I could about the Lord's glorious return to heaven. I became overwhelmed with my theme. Many times at night, after the family was in bed, I would be in my study reading and researching. Sometimes I became so moved and thrilled that I sometimes put my hand in my mouth to keep from shouting and alarming the family. I studied day and night. I spent a good six months on the message. When I got it all together, I chose as my title "Our Ascended Lord." My main divisions were: (1) The HISTORY of It; (2) The THEOLOGY of It; (3) The DOXOLOGY of It.

Ascension Day

January 27, 1976, rolled around. Big guns were there to preach. John Bisagno, pastor of First Baptist Church, Houston, Texas, was preaching. The man I wanted so much to meet, Adrian Rogers, was also scheduled to preach. I didn't feel intimidated. God had given me a message! I was to preach in the afternoon session. The service started off rather slowly, and the session was somewhat boring. Right after lunch isn't the best time to speak to pastors with full stomachs. The time came for me to preach.

Bisagno and Rogers were sitting in the choir loft behind me. I struggled as I started the message. Then something happened. God came down upon me in mighty Holy Spirit anointing. I was carried up to another level. I felt as if I were a bystander to the whole scene. I was there and yet I was somewhere else. The place exploded. Preachers "amened" and shouted. We were all carried into the heavenlies. When I finished, I was exhausted and physically spent. I went to bed that night and didn't awaken until ten the next morning.

Word about the message spread like wildfire. Requests for tapes of the message poured in. From that time until now, there has not been a week in my life someone has not written, called, referenced, or mentioned to me the impact of that message. I take no credit for it. I knew then, and know even more now, that the Lord gave me the message and anointed me to preach it. He continues to use it even now for His glory alone.

Unexpected Elections

That year I was elected president of the Alabama Baptist Pastors' Conference. Much to the chagrin of convention leaders. Without my prior knowledge a seminary friend jumped up and nominated me for president. I received more votes than the convention's choice.

Adrian Rogers, president of the Southern Baptist Pastors' Conference, asked me to preach the ascension message at the Norfolk, Virginia, conference. I preached it June 14, 1976. The response was similar to the first time I preached it. After lunch Janet and I and Danny and Becky Watters sat up in the higher level of the meeting hall. The time for election of officers came. The word got around that Bailey Smith, pastor of the large, evangelistic First Southern Baptist Church, Del City, Oklahoma, was to be nominated for president. I was looking forward to voting for him. He was nominated. Election was assured.

Then out of nowhere a pastor from Alabama came to the podium to make another nomination. *Good grief,* I thought, *What is he doing?* His voice followed that familiar Alabama preacher's cadence. I leaned over to Janet and whispered, "He's fixing to really embarrass somebody." As he continued, an alarming thought struck me: *He's nominating me!* He hadn't asked my permission to do so. I jumped up and ran down toward the platform to decline the nomination. When I got to the platform, photographers started taking my picture. I was the newly elected president of the Southern Baptist Pastors' Conference! This thrust me into the spotlight of Southern Baptist life. I did not seek it. I was uncomfortable with it. Shy by nature, I really didn't like it. I could not avoid it. God was evidently in it.

I was president of the Alabama Baptist Pastors' Conference and the Southern Baptist Pastors' Conference at the same time. I was also nominated that year for president of the Alabama Baptist Convention. I lost by twelve votes. On the afternoon just before the election, I saw buses beginning to arrive. The state convention organized pastors and churches to bus people in to vote for the other candidate. That's the only organized busing for political purposes I ever personally saw.

During those years I was also seeking a deeper understanding of the issues surrounding biblical inerrancy. At the suggestion of Dr. Patterson, I attended the Chicago Council on Biblical Inerrancy. This was held in 1978 at the Hyatt Regency O'Hare in Chicago. The conference was convened by James Montgomery Boice, Carl F. H. Henry, Norman Geisler, Harold Lindsell, and others. The outcome was the Chicago Statement on Biblical Inerrancy, signed by nearly three hundred evangelical scholars. I learned at those sessions that inerrancy is a far deeper issue than most realize. The scholarly presentations convinced me even more that the Bible is God's Word, without error.

The Pressler Strategy

I was preaching at an evangelism conference in Jacksonville, Florida. The meeting was held at my friend, Homer Lindsay Jr.'s church. A judge from Texas, Paul Pressler, asked if he could come to see me and Homer. We met for lunch at the Hilton Hotel. Judge Pressler knew Homer and I were concerned about the liberalism in the convention. He explained to us how we could turn things around. I remember quite well the conversation Homer and I had as we crossed the blue Main Street Bridge over the St. John's River, returning to the church. We both agreed that it would be wonderful if Judge Pressler's strategy could be successful. We also both agreed it couldn't happen. How wrong we were!

Nomination for SBC Presidency

The next year I led the pastors' conference in Kansas City, Missouri. I thought the conference was a good one. A number of Southern Baptist preachers were on the program. I also used non-Southern Baptists Stephen Olford and Warren Wiersbe. I was criticized in Baptist Press for my "independent" program.

The night before the SBC meeting itself began, Adrian Rogers and I were talking. I called him "Ole Golden Throat" because of his resonant, rich voice. He called me "Dr. Kudzu." He said, "Dr. Kudzu, I think I'll nominate you for president of the convention." That was fine with me. Sure, why not? There was no master plan, no organized effort to get out the vote. Nothing. Just a conversation between newfound friends. The next morning he did nominate me. Several others were nominated, among them Dr. Jimmy Allen, pastor of First Baptist Church, San Antonio, Texas. The results of the first ballot were announced. There was to be a runoff between me and Dr. Allen. I was sitting by my predecessor, Dr. Jaroy Weber, who previously served as SBC president. He leaned over to me and whispered, "You are the next president of the Southern Baptist Convention." The thought stunned me. I was frightened stiff.

I later learned I led by a good margin on the first ballot. I also was told by Jack Brymer, editor of the *Florida Baptist Witness,* that panic struck the pressroom. W. C. Fields gathered the state editors together and told them to spread these two "facts" throughout the convention hall: (1) I cut out Southern Baptist literature when I came to Dauphin Way. Fact: We used all SBC literature throughout our church. (2) I led the church to discontinue giving to the Cooperative Program. Fact: No funds were deleted or cut. Dauphin Way actually gave more to the CP than First Baptist, San Antonio, the previous year. On the strength of these two rumors, according to knowledgeable analysts, I lost to Jimmy Allen in the runoff.

I look back on this and realize this was surely in the plan of God. I was young, inexperienced in Southern Baptist life, and totally unprepared to serve as president of the denomination. My time would come later.

Frightening Difficulties

There were still some bizarre, frightening things going on at church. Our daughter, Joy, returned to Rome to go to college. On a Sunday night during the offertory hymn, one of the men of the church stepped into the auditorium from a side door. He motioned to me to come. I turned to Emerson Lyle and told him to take the service until I returned. I didn't return.

The man was a FBI agent. He told me there was a call for me from the sheriff's office in Floyd County, Georgia, where Rome is located. He told me the caller said there was a tragic accident involving a member of my family. Joy was the only member of the family in Rome. He took me to the preschool building. The phone was off the hook, on a table. I picked up the phone and said, "Hello."

On the other end was a voice that sounded broken, "Preacher Vines. It's awful." The voice collapsed into tears. At that moment the phone went dead. I was later to learn phone service in all of Mobile went down at that time.

In my mind Joy was dead. I fell to my knees in anguish and prayer. One of my deacons took me to a nearby hotel and restaurant where we often dined. In a while we were able to get a call through to the Floyd County Sheriff's Office. There were no accidents anywhere in the county that day. I next called West Rome Baptist Church. Larry Hipps, the bus minister, answered. I asked him if Joy was at church that night. Yes, and he thought she was with a group of students at a nearby pizza parlor. I asked him to keep me on the line, get to another line, and call to see if she was there. He did and she was. She was safe and sound. I was greatly relieved but greatly shaken.

Several details have caused me to believe the whole affair was demonic. First, the phone in the preschool building was not listed. The phone was used only to make calls, not receive them. Second, everyone in Mobile called me Dr. Vines. In Rome I was called either "Brother Jerry" or "Preacher Vines." Third, the strange loss of service by the phone company was clearly unnatural. I was told by many that the whole Mobile Bay area was known for demonic activity. I took this to be another demonic attack.

Houston, We've Got a President

The summer of 1979 came. We were headed to the Southern Baptist Convention in Houston, Texas. Many urged me to run again for the presidency. I was willing to run, but I wasn't sure about it. I preached that year at the pastors' conference. But, my message was not the one that energized the people. Dr. Criswell preached the closing message that night. As always, his remarks were the telling ones. Before his message, out of the clear blue, he said, "We will have a great time here if for no other reason than to elect Adrian Rogers as our president." The gathering of almost ten thousand pastors erupted. That did it for me. That was my signal I was not the man.

I went to the room in the evening and told Janet I was convinced I shouldn't be nominated. "Well, you'd better find Paige Patterson then." The hour was late, around 10:30. I found Paige in the lobby and told him I was not the man; Adrian should be nominated. However, there was one small problem. Adrian refused several times to allow his name to be placed in nomination. His wife, Joyce, was most adamant he should not run.

In just a few minutes Adrian and Joyce came into the hotel lobby. I told Adrian. He invited Paige and me to come up to their room. The men sat in chairs and on the floor. Joyce sat on the bed. We talked and prayed; we prayed and talked. Joyce would hold up fingers, indicating where she thought things were. About 2:30 in the morning she put up ten fingers! Adrian agreed to run. We wept and rejoiced. Then to bed, for there was work to do in the morning.

Adrian Rogers was our candidate. Someone must nominate him. Everyone we asked refused. Looking back on that, I marvel at the lack of courage of some good men. Finally, Homer Lindsay Sr. was approached. He knew and loved Adrian since he and Homer Jr. were students together at Stetson University. Adrian preached many great revivals at First Baptist, Jacksonville.

We went to a skybox Judge Pressler had rented. We were up there several times. We liked the free snacks and deserts! We helped Dr. Lindsay prepare a nominating speech. Those on the platform below began to point fingers at us. We thought they were waving at us. We waved back! The scene was set.

That afternoon we moved down to the main hall for the election. The tension was palpable. Nomination speeches were made. Several moderate candidates were nominated, hoping maybe to get the election into a runoff. In addition to Adrian, Robert Naylor, Bill Self, Abner McCall, Douglas Watterson, and Ed Price were nominated. After what seemed an eternity, the results came in. Each candidate's vote and percentage total was announced. "Adrian Rogers: 6,129 votes, or 51.36 percent" For a moment there was stunned silence. "51.36 percent?" Adrian Rogers was elected on the first ballot without a runoff! Then the convention erupted. There were shouts and cheers and hallelujahs and "praise the Lords"!

Homer Lindsay Jr. was sitting by me. He jumped up, ran down a few rows where one of our seminary presidents was seated. Homer picked him up and danced him up and down the aisle. The dear man looked like Godzilla had him!

And thus the Conservative Resurgence was officially underway. Dr. Rogers's election was the first in a string of seven presidents known as the Conservative Resurgence Presidents. Houston was not my year. My time would come.

The Difficulty That Became a Blessing

The words hit me like a laser beam. "You will have to be completely silent for the next two weeks. You have a nodule on your vocal cord. Surgery is the only way to remove it." So said the doctor.

For several months at Dauphin Way I experienced hoarseness. Especially on Monday after preaching three services the previous day. But a nodule? Surgery? Pretty frightening to me. The thought I might not be able to preach was traumatic. To bundle the whole experience, let me tell you what happened.

Dr. Stephen Olford, who experienced similar difficulties, recommended I seek the assistance of Dr. Friedrich Brodnitz, the eminent throat specialist in New York City. Janet and I made our way to the Big Apple. He did not recommend surgery. Unless I corrected the vocal habits that had produced the nodule, it would reappear, even after surgery, he indicated. Taking his counsel, I went to a speech pathologist. Correcting some vocal abuses, the nodule disappeared in a month's time! Since then I have only had minor throat difficulties—nothing serious. Then entire ordeal became a great blessing to me. I recount the entire experience in a book on preaching I will mention later.

Build the New Auditorium

Meanwhile in spite of difficulties and odd happenings, things were going well at the church. We were growing, leading the state in baptisms, and cramping our facilities. We really needed to build the new auditorium. I decided it was time to have a vote to move forward with planning and construction. The Wednesday night we voted was the largest crowd I ever witnessed for that service. After the service we voted on whether to move forward toward the construction of a new auditorium. The people voted not to do it. I was shocked.

That's what the pulpit committee had brought me to Mobile to do. I later learned the vision for a new auditorium was the vision of the previous pastor and the pulpit committee. The church never signed on to it. This was the reason for the resistance I experienced along the way. The auditorium project became "Vines' project," not the church's.

At that point I felt I could lead the church no further. I did not want to force the church to do something they did not want to do. I did then, and do now, believe in a congregational form of church government. There seemed to be a sense of release. The difficult assignment the Lord gave me was now completed. I was free to go.

I never brought the problems of the church home with me. Janet and the children obviously knew about some difficulties that were open and public. But I never talked about church problems at home. And I never, ever mentioned any people by name. I have seen more preachers' children than I want to count who were told about church difficulties when they were young who were scarred for life. I have personally counseled many pastor's children who turned from the church and some from the Lord because of the way their father was treated. Children and young people are too young and immature to hear about those kinds of things. I made a concerted effort to keep things happy, fun, and upbeat at home regardless of church difficulties.

Wiping Dust Off

The church back in Rome was without a pastor. I was contacted. Would I be interested in returning to the pastorate at West Rome? Janet and I built a home there on seven acres of land on the side of a mountain. This was going to be our retirement home. Would it become our next home? Janet and I prayed. We felt the Lord wanted us to return. I announced my resignation at Dauphin Way. The people were stunned. One sweet lady on the pulpit committee came by the house on the day we left. She said, "This isn't the way it is meant to be."

The day I drove the family out of Mobile, we crossed Mobile Bay. I stopped at a viewing spot and looked back at the city. Then I wiped the dust off my shoes. Looking back on this, I was following something the Lord told his disciples to do (Matt. 10:14). He didn't instruct his disciples to tell it! I was young, immature, and rather impulsive. Looking back with more mature eyes, I could have handled many issues differently. I never before faced some of the difficulties I encountered. More patience on my part could have greatly helped the situation.

The vast majority of the people didn't reject me or my message. I was given a difficult assignment. I learned many important lessons during the five and one-half years I was at Dauphin Way. I think I preached some of my best messages there. I learned to preach when it was not easy and when I caught flack for preaching the truth. I will be forever grateful for the godly people of Dauphin Way and the spiritual victories God gave us.

West Rome Baptist—Second Time

Once back at West Rome, I faced something of the same challenges during my first pastorate there. The people were divided over their last pastor. My job was to get the people back together. I believe that is one of the reasons the Lord sent me back. The years of my second tenure were years of healing and peace. God gave us souls and growth.

One of the highlights was my friend Adrian Rogers preaching a revival for me. The week he was there I thought it would be good to schedule a press conference. He was president of the Southern Baptist Convention at the time. To have him speak there I thought was newsworthy. Much to my disappointment only one person showed up for the news conference. Jack Harwell, editor of *The Christian Index*. Frankly, I was embarrassed. Jack thought I set him up. I did not. He was just the only one who came.

My concern about the liberalism in Southern Baptist life was still uppermost in my thinking. There was no thought in my mind that I would ever be nominated again for president of the convention. That mattered not to me. I would take my stand for the Word of God. I would lead my church to be Bible believing and evangelistic. I would do whatever I could to turn the convention back to its conservative roots.

Boredom overcame me during my second tour at West Rome. Not because I didn't love the people. I did. Not because there weren't people to be reached. There were. The analogy I have used is this. If a coach has been leading the New England Patriots, it would be rather uninteresting to return to coach a high school team. I mean, I was used to a lot of activity, a large-city atmosphere, and a major center of ministry. But I was faithful. I was able to get the people back together and spiritually healthy again.

Criswell Calling

In November 1981 an unusual experience happened to me. Dr. Patterson invited me to come to Criswell College in Dallas to speak in chapel and read to the faculty a paper he asked me to prepare. Ike Reighard, a young pastor friend in Georgia, flew out there with me. As we made our approach, the pilot aborted the landing because another jet was on the runway. Young Ike was duly scared.

Ike was there when Dr. Criswell, unannounced, came to the faculty meeting, and asked to speak. Then he proceeded to ask me to come to First Baptist, Dallas, and be their pastor. I would preach to the world from that pulpit. Ike thought he was observing history in the making. After Dr. Criswell left, Paige took me to an adjacent room. He was white as a sheet. He told me he knew nothing beforehand about what Dr. Criswell had just done.

Ike was wide-eyed with excitement. He thought he was witnessing the changing of the guard; Elijah handing off to Elisha. On the way back to the airport, Ike said, "Are you going to take it, Doc?"

I smiled at him and said, "Do I look crazy to you? Not on your life!"

I knew enough about the situation there to know it would be a most challenging assignment. I felt no leading from the Lord to tackle another difficult assignment. I did write Dr. Criswell, my hero, and ask for him to spell out the particulars of his invitation. I still have the letter. A masterpiece. Classic Criswellian language. You really don't know what he was proposing! I wasn't the first or the last to get such a perplexing invitation.

God was preparing me for the next, and greatest, era of my ministry.

Chapter 11

I Hadn't Got Where
I Was Going Yet

I was not known to stay long in my churches. My first four churches I stayed an average of sixteen months. The word on me was, "Vines is a pretty fair preacher. He just doesn't stay anywhere very long."

I tell people, "I hadn't got where I was going yet!" The longest and most productive period of my ministry was just ahead.

Family Vacations

Homer Lindsay Jr. and I became good friends. I will refer to him as Homer from now on. I mean no disrespect for him as a friend, pastor, and God's man. He often told the people that he was "just ole Homer." Before the people I always referred to him as Dr. Lindsay; privately I called him Homer. He did the same with me. Before the people he always referred to me as Dr. Vines; privately I was Jerry.

As I indicated previously, the Lindsay and Vines families became good friends. We started taking vacations together. I well remember one such vacation to Disney World in Orlando in the month of July. Janet and I never experienced such heat. I was planning on fainting; Janet beat me to it! We both wound up being cared for in the clinic. So Homer and Shirley tended to their children and ours.

We took other vacations together in the mountains. That was far better. One particularly pleasant vacation spot was Bent Tree in North Georgia. One of the First Baptist families, the John Nills, owned a cabin there. They were so gracious to let us use it. On one of those occasions, we decided to make a trip to Dahlonega, Georgia to eat at the well-known Smith House. The food was brought to the table in bowls. Talk about some big-time eating! Homer devoured a big bowl of stewed apples with biscuits.

After the meal he and I mapped out a short-cut back to the cabin. Before it was over, we were on a dirt road on top of a hill with barely enough room to turn the car around. Homer got out to direct me. I decided I would get the car cool for him, so I rolled up the windows. Homer let out a bloodcurdling scream. I thought a rattlesnake bit him. Turns out I rolled the window up on his fingers!

Co-Pastors?

One year after we returned to West Rome, Homer and Shirley met me and Janet at Calloway Gardens. We walked, talked, and enjoyed delicious meals together. During a time when he and I were together alone, he asked me if I would come to First Baptist, Jacksonville, and serve with him as co-pastor. I laughed it off. He said no more about it. I thought he was just kidding around.

A year went by. On another vacation he reminded me he mentioned being co-pastor with him the previous year and that I just laughed about it. He told me he was dead serious. He prayed about it a year before he first mentioned it to me. He continued praying for the second year. Would I do this for him—pray about it for a year? I saw he was serious. I agreed to do so.

As I prayed, at first, I didn't think much about it. However, the more I prayed, the more I sensed God was in the matter. We met and talked together several times during the year. Just what did he mean by co-pastor? Did he have in mind an associate pastor? No, Homer, replied, he meant a coequal in every way. I would be pastor of the church just as much as he. The church would understand they were calling me to be their pastor. Upon his retirement or death, there would be no question that I was pastor of the church.

The obvious question to me was, is this biblically sustainable? I gave myself to a careful study of the New Testament teaching concerning the office of the pastor in a local church. I soon found three words are interchangeably used to refer to the same office: *pastor, bishop* (overseer), and *elder.* A comparison of passages indicated that each is a biblical term for the spiritual leader of a congregation (Act 20:17, 28; 1 Pet. 5:1–2). I also found these three titles refer to the several functions of the spiritual leader: elder = the function of consultation (counseling); overseer (bishop) = the function of administration (leading); pastor (shepherd) = the function of edification (teaching and preaching). I did not find a different group of men who would be teaching elders and ruling elders. The word referred to one and the same office. I believe churches today that go to an elder system mistakenly make a distinction between a teaching elder and a ruling elder. I find no biblical justification for such a distinction.

I also found that the terms were used in the plural. There seems to be biblical justification for a multiplicity of men who would minister in the church in a variety of roles. There is one who might be called the lead pastor. Probably Peter was the lead pastor of the Jerusalem congregation. Some think it was James. Whichever, clearly there always seems to be one in particular who would take the lead.

Homer was unquestionably the man God used to move the church to a new level of growth and evangelism. There was a need for someone to teach the people. The responsibilities of a large congregation were more than one man could fulfill. Was I to be that man to step alongside Homer and serve as co-pastor with him? All the signals indicated this to be the case.

In my Bible there is still the list of pros and cons I wrote down as I considered the will of God in the matter. Looking back on the list after thirty plus years, all the pros, none of the cons, came to pass! God's will for me and my family was to move to Jacksonville!

Let me insert here that subsequent events indicate the arrangement was of God. I do not think, however, such a partnership will work in most churches. This was not a new and revolutionary model for First Baptist, Jacksonville. Lindsay Sr. and Lindsay Jr. served in that model for four years. I'm not sure it is a model of ministry that will work in most places. Through the years I received numerous inquiries from pastors considering such a ministry combination. There are so many factors to be considered. Is the church large enough to justify it? Will the church accept it? Are the two men secure in themselves and not prone to jealousy? Are their wives compatible? There are many other aspects to consider. The arrangement worked for me and Homer. There is some doubt in my mind whether it will work in most other places.

Jacksonville Bound

I was not unknown to the people of First Baptist, Jacksonville. I preached in revivals and other conferences there. I seemed to be well received by the congregation. Homer presented me to the deacons. They were unanimous in the affirmation of the move. John Blount, chairman of deacons, presented me to the congregation as their pastor, to serve along side Dr. Lindsay. There was excitement among the people in Jacksonville.

There was not excitement among the people at West Rome. My second tenure was but three years. They agreed for Emerson Lyle and Sherrill Dunn to return with me from Dauphin Way. The people were not happy. The chairman of the finance committee asked me if I would like something in particular as a going-away gift. The car I was driving, a beautiful white Buick, was one of the Peach Bowl official cars. I purchased it, and owed just over $5,000 on it. Perhaps the church would pay that off for me. He took this to the finance committee. They liked the idea. They took it to the deacons. They didn't like the idea.

What no one knew at the time was that finance chairman Clyde Chester was going to give the money for the car but let the church have the joy of giving it to me. When the deacons turned it down, he did it on his own. He got the blessing and not the church. Looking back, I understand the feelings of the men. They were hurt and felt I was leaving too soon after I returned to Rome. I met with the deacons and talked it through. They were kind and understanding. They were my best friends. I loved them and they loved me. There was just no option for me. The clear will of God for me was to go to Jacksonville.

Our family moved in July. To hot, humid Jacksonville! We acquired an adequate home for $119,000. This would be our home the entire time we lived in Jacksonville. Arrangements for the children were made. Joy, our oldest, worked at the University of Jacksonville. Our oldest son, Jim, was playing football at Carson-Newman College in Tennessee. His twin, Jodi, was working at Pine Castle Center. Our youngest, Jon, would attend and play football at Terry Parker High School, where a fine Christian, Jim Scroggins, was coach. The team chaplain was Bob Tebow. Things were set, and we were ready for a new ministry.

In a matter of days after the move, I made my way to youth camp at Lake Yale, Florida Baptists' camp facility. Homer asked me to write a curriculum on evangelism to be used in the Sunday school. A good deal of the work was already done before I left Georgia. There was a little bit more to do. Homer graciously gave me his room where I could complete the work. He would humble himself and go over to the junior high section of the camp. In those years Lake Yale was not air-conditioned. Sweat poured off my body as I typed out the closing lessons on "Acts Alive." We used this curriculum many times to teach our people how to lead souls to Christ. Several hundred thousand of those lessons were sold to other churches. I received no royalties whatsoever for them. This was the way I wanted it to be.

Oh yes, about that "gracious" giving of his room. Homer moved to the junior high camp. Where his room had air-conditioning! Through the years I never let him forget it. He loved to tell it and have a good laugh. That was the beginning of many laughs we enjoyed through the years.

Unified Leadership

Homer and I agreed on how we would function as co-pastors. We would always be united before the deacons and the people. Matters would be discussed in private before we went to the deacons and the people. When we were making decisions, we didn't always agree. During those times we committed the issue at hand to the Lord in prayer until we came to agreement. We did not move forward without agreement. If, after prayer, we still didn't reach agreement, we would do nothing, or one would yield to the other. There were some times when I would realize Homer had more knowledge and experience than I in the matter before us. I would yield to him. On other occasions Homer would feel I was more likely to have the best approach. He would yield to me. Then, we went before the people in unity.

Sometimes I was wrong. Homer would say, "I told you so." At other times Homer was wrong. I would say, "I told you so." This worked beautifully for us through the eighteen years we served as co-pastors. Actually, we agreed virtually all of the time. We shared the same goal: we wanted to win as many people to Christ as we possibly could. We both wanted to help Christians grow in the Lord. God blessed our partnership in an amazing way.

Pastors and Staff

Those were exciting days in the life of our church. The Sunday school was growing by leaps and bounds. Guinell Freeman was recognized as the most able educational director in the Southern Baptist Convention. Under her leadership the church became one of the largest Sunday schools in America. Her friend, Fran Hawk, served alongside her in a variety of educational roles, most notably as children's director. Francis Hendrix was the full-time church training director, something unheard of in churches at the time. She developed the largest church training ministry in the nation.

Dr. Lindsay Sr. brought Guinell and Fran to the church from Southwestern Baptist Theological Seminary. Neither of them ever married. They married the church. During the early years when Dr. Lindsay Sr. was trying to get the old downtown First Baptist Church moving, they each made fifty visits per week. And turned in written reports on each visit. I wonder how many pastors or staff members would or could do that today!

There were other staff members, of course. Most of our staff stayed with us several years. If their attitude was good and they were willing to work, we helped them be successful. Since Dr. Lindsay Sr. came to the church, it was understood the pastor exercised sole authority in bringing the staff member to the church or in releasing him/her should it become necessary. There were times, not many, when staff members left under less than desirable conditions. I will not go into the details of any of the necessary departures. I would only give it from my perspective, and no good purpose would be served. Whether the deacons or church understood or agreed with a staff decision, they always supported Homer and me.

This provided for a great amount of harmony and unity in the church. The staff was to be an extension of the ministry of the office of the pastor. Homer and I were pastors of every area of the church's ministry. The staff members were to do what we would have done in their particular area of ministry. Homer and I were the worship pastors, the educational ministry pastors, the youth pastors, etc.

Men Leading

In those years there was a men's department in the Sunday school. The men all gathered in the first auditorium, The Hobson, seating about eight hundred people. The Jim Reid Ensemble played as the men gathered. Talk about fun and excitement. This also gave Homer and me direct access to the men. We could tell them directly what we wanted to do and where we wanted to go. This was a tremendous innovation by Homer that helped the church to be a strong, men-led church. Some of the godliest, finest, most capable laymen I have ever known led in those years. A book wouldn't be large enough to list all of them. They are all in God's list of "mighty men."

Of course, many godly, dedicated ladies served in many capacities. Thank God for the ladies. A church can't do without them. The men, however, should take the lead in the congregation. One of our biggest problems today, as I see it, is the "feminization" of the church. I don't blame the women for this; I blame the men. They have abdicated their responsibility to be spiritual leaders. Our churches are weaker for it.

Church Growth

Another auditorium seating three thousand was completed prior to my time at Jacksonville. Homer asked me one time before I got there if I thought it would ever be filled. "Of course," I replied, "if the Lord wants you to build it." Since 1943 the church established a cash policy. The money was raised. The large auditorium was constructed debt free. People were coming in droves.

I also encouraged him to televise the morning services. Telling him of the tremendous drawing power of our television ministry at Dauphin Way, he followed suit and drew thousands to downtown Jacksonville. Pretty soon it was necessary to have two morning services.

The visitation was strong. Our adult Sunday school classes were organized by zip codes. Prospects were assigned to the adult classes according to zip codes. The young people's Sunday school classes were organized by schools. Prospects for their classes were assigned by schools. There was a ladies' Tuesday morning visitation and a men's Tuesday night visitation. At its peak we averaged twelve hundred out visiting every week. There was never a week we didn't hear of people won to Christ in the homes. We always knew we could expect new converts to walk down the aisles in every service.

Homer and I both preached through books of the Bible. We came to the conviction this was the best way to teach God's Word to the people. I preached the 8:00 a.m. service and the Sunday night service. Homer preached the 10:45 a.m. service and the Wednesday night service. This worked beautifully.

When I came to Jacksonville, the first book I preached through was Acts. This was the Bible pattern for how to build a church, develop an evangelism program, strengthen believers, and send out missionaries. The people came. On Sunday nights I preached through the book of Genesis. The singles would run from Church Training to get a seat in the evening service. People sitting in the aisles of the balcony was a common sight.

The music was heavenly. Homer and I both believed you needed a gospel, evangelistic music program. All kinds of choirs were developed: a chancel (adult) choir, singles choir, youth choirs, and children's choirs.

And orchestras on top of that. The music was exciting and soul stirring. On Wednesday night the children were robed and marched into the service. Each Wednesday night one of the children's choirs would sing. Talk about exciting!

The people were taught the great hymns of the faith. Never dull or boring, they were sung with upbeat arrangements. Heart music to prepare the people to hear the Word and the pastors to preach the Word was presented every service.

Pretty soon after my arrival, we constructed a preschool building. The money was given and in hand when we started it. This provided space for the young couples' babies. We started building garages. The first one was the preschool garage to provide parking for those with infants. We constructed crosswalks so they could go directly from their cars to Sunday school for their babies and themselves.

Homer and I believed in a strong ministry for young people. In addition to camps and youth choir, Homer developed a strong discipleship program. There would be two or three months of Saturday visitation. They gathered prospects for our church and won many people to Christ. The young people would board school buses and fan out throughout Jacksonville. When they were finished with their survey work, we took them to a bowling alley, swimming pool, or some other recreational facility. Thousands of young people learned how to share their faith in this program. Scores committed to the lordship of Christ and Bible separation. Those who answered the call of God to full-time Christian service are today ministering all over the world.

Another outreach that helped us win people to Christ was a Thursday business luncheon. Each Thursday people could come to our dining room to get a delicious, inexpensive meal. I presented a brief Bible study. I kind of slipped up on the people when I spoke. Presented in a matter-of-fact way, I hit them before they knew I fired! Attendance grew to around seven hundred people each week. We saw many people come to Christ through this luncheon. To this day I meet people who tell me they date their conversion to one of those Business luncheons.

The people were easy to serve as pastor. They were sweet, kind, supportive, and willing to follow our leadership. Since the days of Dr. Lindsay

Sr. the church had been willing to let the pastor be the spiritual leader of the congregation. God greatly blessed the church because of this. Often I said, "If we asked the people to march into the Saint Johns River, they would have fallen into line!" There were times when we asked the people to follow us in projects that failed. They were never accusatory. They just picked us up, brushed us off, and said, "What do you want to try next?" This didn't create a cavalier spirit on the part of Homer and myself. Rather, it caused us to be prayerful and careful about what we asked the people to do.

Strong pastoral leadership has its advantages and its disadvantages. If the pastor of the church is godly, capable, Christlike and seeks the will of God for the church, this works well. If not, such willingness on the part of the people to follow the pastor can create great misery for the church.

Great FBC, Jacksonville Christians

Some of the greatest Christians I have ever known were in the fellowship of First Baptist Church, Jacksonville. The men who served as deacons were marvelous. In twenty-four years I was never in a deacons' meeting where anyone was unkind, sharp, or acted in any way that was disrespectful to me. Our deacons' meetings, normally only two per year, were like revival meetings. Time would fail me to mention all of the great deacons who served through the years. Nor could several volumes hold the stories of some of these remarkable Christians. Some members of our church were really most unusual. Colorful to say the least. Let me give some brief snapshots of just a few.

Jimmy Tharin was a high school classmate of Homer's. A bill collector, he had little interest in the things of God. On a weekly visitation Homer and R. O. Stone led Jimmy to Christ. He became wide open, all out, sold out for the Lord. His "amen" in church shook the building. Some of the members were upset and asked Homer to tell Jimmy to turn down the volume. Homer replied, "I'm not going to do it. I'm trying to wake some of you up!"

At the end of one revival I preached before I became the pastor, Jimmy, Judge A. C. Soud, and I were standing beside my car. "Jimmy, let me hear one more 'amen' before I go." Jimmy let out an "amen" so loud a policeman driving by stopped his patrol car and got out to see what was going on! Jimmy became a great soul winner. He memorized hundreds of verses of Scripture. He tragically drowned when he fell out of a boat and got caught in some rope.

Then there were the two Franks. Frank the bricklayer and Frank the egg man. Frank the bricklayer couldn't read. He visited in homes, told the people he couldn't read, and asked them to read the verses in his Bible that had been marked. One year he led forty-three people to Christ having the lost people read the verses to him! Frank the egg man was another unusual character. He always said his business wasn't what it was "cracked" up to be! He taught himself to play the piano. Sometimes Homer called on him to play in the middle of a service. Frank played magnificently and the people applauded!

There were scores more than I can mention here. "For the time would fail me to tell" (Heb. 11:32) of the heroes in the FBC "Hall of the Faithful." One of the great joys of the ministry to me has been to get to know the great saints of God. Those thousands who faithfully serve the Lord without attention or a lot of praise. Those multitudes who listened to me preach, faithfully prayed for me, and loved me in spite of my many failures and shortcomings.

As if I didn't have enough to do, Dr. Paige Patterson urged me to write two books—one on sermon preparation and the other on sermon delivery. Both books were written in one summer. Moody Press published them with the titles *A Practical Guide to Sermon Preparation* (1985) and *A Guide to Effective Sermon Delivery* (1986). These books were later revised by Dr. Jim Shaddix, professor of preaching at my alma mater, New Orleans Baptist Theological Seminary. The two books were merged into the one volume *Power In the Pulpit* (1999). This has been continuously sold since 1985/86. Many preachers indicate to me this book on preaching is beneficial to them.

Our Greatest Revival

We always scheduled revivals. Spring and fall revivals were not uncommon. The greatest revival in the history of First Baptist, Jacksonville, was led by one of my mentors, Dr. Jess Hendley. Upon my recommendation Homer and I invited Dr. Hendley to preach a revival meeting beginning one Sunday morning, going throughout the week, and closing the next Sunday. The best way for me to describe it is to paraphrase the words of the hymn: "Heaven came down, our souls to greet, and glory crowned the mercy seat." When the meeting ended, there were 375 professions of faith; 350 of them were baptized! These were not just "walk an aisle, sign a card" professions. The counseling ministry in the church was one of our main ministries. Those who counseled those who came forward were carefully trained. Each person was taken to a counseling room and counseled by a trained soul winner. This does not guarantee they were all saved, of course. Only God knows that. We did make every effort to lead people to a genuine experience with Christ.

One experience in the Hendley revival will illustrate what a tremendous movement of God it was. Keith Palmer was a son of Ernie Palmer, the owner of the local Toyota dealership. Janet and Shirley visited at his home previously to talk with his wife, Renee. So unconcerned was Keith he didn't even bother to stop mowing his grass to greet them. Keith came to the revival and fell under deep conviction. Dr. Hendley was called by some "Hellfire and Brimstone Hendley." One time Dr. Hendley said to me: "Jerry, people just say they believe there is a hell. I really believe there is one, and I don't want anyone to go there." One afternoon Keith was driving from his Toyota store to the revival. He said he was so under conviction he received Christ as his Savior in his car. He was afraid he might have a wreck before he got to church, be killed, and go to hell! Keith became one of our deacons and a member of our finance committee.

Those were busy, blessed days. The work was occupying me day and night. Sermons must be prepared. Visits must be made. Staff meetings must be held. There was more to be done than one pastor could do. Actually, more than two pastors could do. Even more than our dedicated, hardworking staff could do.

I had another full-time job going on alongside my duties as pastor, husband, and father. This other full-time job would bring me challenges, criticisms, and conquests I never would have imagined.

Before I turn the page to the next chapter in my life and times, I'll just say that I finally "got where I was going," and it was a fit!

Chapter 12

Conservative Resurgence

Homer and I shared similar concerns regarding the Southern Baptist Convention's drift toward liberalism. I first become aware of it at Mercer University. Homer encountered it at Stetson University, where he and Adrian Rogers graduated. We weren't really sure much could be done about it.

Baptist Faith and Message Fellowship

Early on I met other people who also were concerned about the convention and wanted to do something about it. I met Bill Powell in the early seventies. Bill was a former Home Mission Board servant. He had formed the Baptist Faith and Message Fellowship. He published a journal and held conferences around the country. His intention was to make Southern Baptists aware of the liberalism making inroads in the convention. I preached in some of Bill's conference. Adrian Rogers and I preached at a Baptist Faith and Message Fellowship meeting in Nashville in 1974. Adrian was the new pastor at Bellevue Baptist in Memphis. I had just gone to Dauphin Way in Mobile. I remember asking Adrian if he had been homesick when he first got to Memphis. He replied that he had been. I was homesick as well.

I never joined the Baptist Faith and Message Fellowship. I was sympathetic with what Bill Powell wanted to do. At times there was a tone that concerned me. I did preach in some conferences on several occasions. I met many other men around the country who were concerned about liberalism in our convention.

No Return from Apostasy

I recounted previously about Homer and I meeting with Judge Paul Pressler. And our agreement that, though we would desire to see it, we didn't think his plan would work. I listened to a lecture by a church history professor in earlier years who said there never was an instance in the history of the Christian church where a conservative denomination that turned downward toward liberalism and apostasy ever recovered. His thesis was that there never would be. He felt once a denomination departed from the Bible, there would be no return. I agreed with him. This accounts somewhat for my feeling that Judge Pressler's plan would not work.

Judge Pressler and I became great friends. Both of us had children with special needs. I appreciated his willingness to endure severe persecution for his efforts to turn the convention around. In 1978 I shared breakfast with Paul at the Atlanta Southern Baptist Convention annual meeting. At that time he was a member of a Presbyterian church and was effectively teaching 250+ high school students in a Bible class. At breakfast I said to Paul, "Paul, are you going to minister to 250 high school students or thirteen million Southern Baptists?" Judge Pressler told me later that God used my question to convince him to do what he could to turn the convention back to a conservative theological position.

Dr. Paige Patterson was the theologian of the conservative movement. At the time he was president of Criswell College. Emerson Lyle met him while a student at New Orleans Seminary. He mentioned him to me. I met Dr. Patterson and was impressed with his scholarship, strong convictions, and willingness to endure whatever persecutions came his way. He and Paul Pressler endured unbelievable attacks during the Conservative Resurgence. At one annual convention meeting I saw Paige standing against a wall by himself. I walked over and spoke with him. He began to weep and thanked me for speaking to him. Through the years he and his wife, Dorothy, became close friends. The practical jokes we have pulled on each other are legendary. More later. Back to the story line.

Books

Through the years I was doing a lot of reading on the issue of the inerrancy of the Bible. I read the books of Dr. Criswell. I also read *The Message of Genesis* by Ralph Elliott, professor at Midwestern Baptist Theological Seminary. His book was prime evidence of the drift toward liberalism by many of our professors. I also read Harold Lindsell's *The Battle for the Bible*. Dr. Lindsell was a noted Bible scholar and editor emeritus of *Christianity Today*. In contrast to Dr. Criswell's books, Dr. Lindsell's book named names. He documented what many of us had been saying.

In 1985 Janet and I went to New York to celebrate our twenty-fifth wedding anniversary. We stayed in the brand-new Marriott Marque on Broadway. One afternoon I was browsing around the hotel. I ran across a booksellers convention. As I scanned the exhibits, I saw a book entitled *Called to Preach; Condemned to Survive*. The book was written by Dr. Clayton Sullivan, professor of philosophy and religion at the University of Southern Mississippi. As I leafed through the book, I was captivated by what I read. Dr. Sullivan left Mississippi as a Bible-believing young preacher boy to attend Southern Seminary. While there he lost his conservative faith. His book documented everything we were saying was taking place in many of our colleges and seminaries! I told Dr. Patterson about the book. Soon it was being read all over the convention. Something must be done. My desire and prayer that something might be done to rescue the convention increased.

Strained Relations

Homer was also desirous something might be done. Homer never lacked for courage and boldness. When I arrived in Jacksonville, I soon discovered that relations between the First Baptist Church of Jacksonville and the Florida Baptist Convention were not good. Located across the Saint Johns River from one another, there was little desire on the part of either to board the boat of peace and cross the river. Homer was pretty vocal in his criticisms of the state convention. The convention officials reciprocated. None of the employees were permitted to be a member of First Baptist Church though there were some exceptions to the directive. Looking back on those years, I can only rejoice in how things have changed. My friend, Dr. John Sullivan, executive director-treasurer of the state convention became a member of the church. For several years I had the joy of being John and Nancy's pastor. We enjoyed sweet fellowship together. Other state convention servants, too numerous to mention, became valued and involved members of FBC, Jacksonville.

Homer led the church to have its own missionaries. A group of men in the church formed the Christian Light Ministries, Inc. to circulate sermon tapes and to send out missionaries. The church supported a number of those missionaries. Many of them, like Judy Russell in the Philippines, have served the Lord for many years. This indicated a clear intention to support only those who were biblically sound. The church seemed to be on a track away from the SBC.

But by 1982, there was hope. The election of Adrian Rogers in 1979, Bailey Smith in 1980, and the election of Jimmy Draper in 1982 were encouraging to both of us. We must continue to win presidential elections. These conservative presidents, as Paul and Paige had so well articulated, would select the committee on committees that would ultimately result in conservative boards of trustees for our SBC entities.

Conservative Meetings

Homer felt we should begin to have a series of conservative meetings in Florida to rally conservative pastors and laypeople. They needed to be aware of the issues and encouraged to attend the annual SBC meeting. We sent out invitations to pastors all over the state of Florida. We were pleasantly surprised by the large turnout at the luncheon meeting. There were 353 present. I guess the fact they received a free meal helped! The atmosphere at the meeting was like a revival. Homer minced no words. He attacked the liberalism with characteristic Lindsay fire and bluntness. Others spoke. Homer urged the pastors to get their maximum number of messengers to the convention.

We were not aware at that time of a network working throughout the states of the convention to get messengers to the annual meeting. Dr. Patterson told me in subsequent years we were intentionally not told about it. Certain pastors, because of their high visibility, were not included in the networking. These pastors might well be candidates for president. He and Paige enlisted men in each state to organize and get messengers to the convention. I was aware, of course, that there was a massive effort to get people to the conventions. But I was unaware a network had been formed.

This was certainly better for me. Religious politicking was always distasteful to me. I am not naive enough to not know, however, that any-time there is an election, politics plays a part. There is either good or bad politics. Looking back, I believe most of the politics for the conservative cause was well intended. Were mistakes made? Of course.

Homer and I were pleased with the turnout for and results of the meeting. Baptist editors were not. We were immediately attacked. This was nothing new. The attacks were numerous and vicious since the election of Adrian Rogers in 1979 and even before. Homer and I didn't care. Our convictions were strong, and we were willing to pay the price for those convictions. Neither of us aspired to Convention leadership of any kind. Both of us wanted to win souls to Christ and build a New Testament church.

But on the way to wherever, something unusual happened. The more the Baptist media attacked us, the more popular we became. Pastors began to rally to us. We were articulating what thousands of conservative pastors were feeling in their hearts. In some ways we became folk heroes. A folk hero is someone who may or may not exist. Homer and I certainly existed! A folk hero is also someone who helps the common people and fights against the powers that be. We certainly fit the latter definition.

God gave me a great love for grassroots, rural, small-church pastors. I never forgot how some of these dear men took me into their fellowship, loved, and prayed for me when I was a boy preacher. To this day my best friends are rural preachers. God was doing something I never dreamed could happen. Momentum was building. Conservative men were being elected. Trustee boards were changing. We were part of something God was doing that was far bigger than we could understand. God had chosen to let us have a small part in it. The "impossible" was occurring. A denomination was being turned from liberalism back to conservatism.

Cruise of the Cardinals

At the suggestion of Adrian, Maurice Templeton invited me to be one of the preachers on a cruise to the Bahamas. This was the beginning of twenty plus years of such cruises. Maurice was a great Christian layman and friend of preachers. This also began a personal friendship with Maurice that is meaningful to me. I greatly enjoyed these cruises. Often some of us would get together and discuss convention concerns. Possible presidential candidates would be mentioned. Along the way moderates began to refer to these cruises as "Cruise of the Cardinals" where a supposedly elite group would determine the next conservative presidential candidate. This was not true. The candidates were sometimes not determined until the night before the election. You'll read about this in just a few minutes.

I have put it this way: all over the SBC there were pastors with a melody going on in their hearts. Paul Pressler and Paige Patterson came along and put the words to the music. Homer and I were just two of thousands who helped play the song.

We didn't always conduct ourselves as well as we should have. One meeting at First Baptist Church, Dayton Beach, is a case in point. Things got pretty worked up during the meeting. Pastor Bobby Welch, a good friend, said the liberals hid behind "smoke screens." The "amens" resounded all over the building. Homer spoke a few choice words for the liberals as well. My time came. I told of one of my preacher boys who had gone to Southern where they "raped his faith." I should never have said it. I received a letter from Southern Seminary president, Dr. Roy Honeycutt, reproving me. I replied with a letter of apology. I did not back down from my concern about what happened to my preacher boy. But I did apologize for the improper language. I apologized to Dr. Honeycutt; I confessed to the Lord and asked for His forgiveness.

During all this time Homer and I were continuing to lead the church in evangelism and growth. The Sunday school was growing. People in large numbers were being led to Christ. The church training program was vibrant. At Homer's suggestion I started an annual pastors' conference (more about this later). I was working methodically, expositionally through books of the Bible. I was trying to be a good husband to my loving and supportive wife, Janet. I was seeking to be a good father to my children. How I kept all those balls in the air I will never know. The Lord helped me.

Charles Stanley

The annual meeting of 1984, to be held in Kansas City, Missouri, was approaching. Who would be the conservative candidate for president? There was no clear consensus. Some wanted Charles Stanley. He would be an excellent choice. Homer and I agreed that, if nominated, Charles would be elected. We also knew he was extremely controversial with much of the convention leadership and the Baptist media. The circumstances that surrounded his becoming pastor of First Baptist Church, Atlanta, Georgia, had antagonized many.

Among them was Dr. Russell Dilday, president of Southwestern Baptist Theological Seminary. Dr. Dilday was pastor of Second-Ponce de Leon Baptist Church when Dr. Stanley became pastor at First Baptist. Although I am not sure of the accuracy of the accounts, there seems to have been an exodus of several hundred people from First Baptist to Second-Ponce de Leon when Dr. Stanley assumed the First Baptist pastorate. Again, I do not know for certain, but there might have been a reception for those members who left. I presume Drs. Stanley and Dilday could clarify this for us.

Also, the network telecast of First Baptist's morning worship was pulled and given to Second-Ponce de Leon. This forced Dr. Stanley to seek another outlet. There was a small, fledging television channel seeking to grow. They agreed to pick up the First Baptist telecast. The name of the small channel was the Turner Broadcasting Network. We all know the rest of the story.

Under Dr. Stanley's leadership the church experienced phenomenal growth. Along the way a large number of members from Second-Ponce de Leon joined First Baptist. This didn't make Charles the most popular pastor in Atlanta either.

Homer and I agreed Stanley would be elected. We also agreed that his election would be like a red flag in the face of the moderates. His election might precipitate a split in the convention. Someone else should probably be nominated as the conservative candidate.

Janet and I went to the annual meeting in Kansas City. Homer and Shirley did not attend that year. Once in Kansas City I became engulfed in what was going on. Who would be the candidate? No one seemed to know. Contrary to what some moderates believed, things weren't all that well organized. The effort was made to get conservative messengers there, believing they would vote conservatively. There was no cut-and-dried plan about who would be the candidate.

God Changed His Mind

The night before the election we still didn't have a candidate. A group of us were in a hotel suite, talking and praying. The talk began to move in the direction of Charles Stanley. There was a consensus on the part of those present that he was the man. Charles would have none of it. "God has told me not to run," he said.

When Charles said that, I spoke up: "Brethren, God has told Charles not to run. It is wrong for us to try to convince him to do something God has told him not to do." There was agreement in the room. The talk then turned to my friend, Ed Young, pastor of Second Baptist Church, Houston, Texas. Again there was consensus. Looked like Ed was the candidate.

I'm not sure what time we prayed and dismissed the meeting. The hour was between two and three am as I recall. I went to my room. Janet awakened and said, "Well, what did you all decide?"

"Ed Young is going to be nominated," I said.

"He will make a good president," said Janet, and we went to sleep.

The next morning I slept in a bit. I was weary and needed some rest. I got up rather late. After breakfast I made my way to the convention center. I saw Paige Patterson coming toward me hurriedly and perspiring profusely.

"Where in the world have you been?" he blurted.

"Well, I slept in a little because I was so late getting to bed last night."

"We want you to nominate Charles Stanley for president," he declared.

I stopped dead in my tracks. I looked at him in stunned disbelief. "Charles Stanley?" I responded, "I thought God told him not to run."

"Well," Paige answered, "God changed His mind and wants Charles to run."

He recounted to me that early in the morning Ed Young made clear he didn't have liberty from the Lord to run. Charles was wrestling with the Lord. Statements from Bertha Smith and others caused him to reconsider. That morning, with many tears, he let Paige know he would be willing to run.

The Nomination Speech

"There's not much time. Let's go to see Charles," I said. When I entered the room, I never saw such a sight in my life. No one was willing to nominate him. Prominent pastors, who will go unnamed, crawfished. No one in the room could be persuaded. Now I was being asked to do it.

Paige asked me to step out of the room with him for a moment. He began to weep. "Jerry, I know I have asked you to do a lot of things. Could I ask you to nominate Charles?"

We returned to the room. I said to Charles, "Charles, when there is an election someone wins and someone loses. If I nominate you, are you willing to lose?"

Charles didn't hesitate an instant: "It doesn't matter to me. If God wants me to lose, I had rather lose than win." That bound my heart to Charles Stanley forever. He was my kind of man. Success didn't matter to him. All he cared about was doing what God wanted him to do. I agreed to do it.

"Time is running out. The time for nominations will be soon," someone said. I went with Paige, Adrian, and some others to compose a nominating speech. My hands were shaking from nervousness. I wrote down some things I wanted to say. How much did First Baptist, Atlanta, give last year through the Cooperative Program? We didn't know. We all knew the amount would be relatively small. Dr. Stanley had led the church to have many of its own missionaries. His television ministry *In Touch* was growing worldwide and received a large portion of the church's funds. None of us knew the amount through the CP. We were pretty sure, whatever the amount, it would not be enough for the moderates. "Let's ask Charles."

Charles didn't know either! Adrian Rogers, referencing the church's own missionaries and the worldwide TV ministry, said, "Say, 'First Baptist Atlanta just may be the greatest missionary giving and sending church in the history of the Southern Baptist Convention.'"

I nominated Charles Stanley for the presidency. I didn't read it but spoke from memory and from my heart. I used the sentence Adrian recommended. I didn't mention the Cooperative Program giving of the church because I didn't know the amount. There was no attempt on my part to be devious. I was later accused of mendacity.

Dr. Stanley was elected on the first ballot with a vote total of 7,692 (52.18 percent of the votes cast). This happened in spite of the efforts of the Baptist media, SBC entity leaders, and moderates in general to stop it. Of course, he was elected because of the sovereign plan of God. Though unpopular with moderate pastors, there was something those pastors hadn't considered. Their laypeople watched Dr. Stanley weekly on *In Touch*. When their pastors attacked Stanley, they didn't understand why they would attack a man who was preaching the Bible. They loved to hear him preach. No doubt that day many laypeople from moderate churches voted for him.

The Red Flag

Upon my return to Jacksonville, I saw Homer. He knew already Charles Stanley had been elected president. He did not know I had nominated him. When I told him, he had the most puzzled look on his face you have ever seen. His eyes became question marks. I told him everything that transpired. He saw the wisdom of it and was elated.

What Homer and I feared though certainly came to pass. Stanley's election was a double red flag in the face of the moderates. The uproar could be heard from Nashville to Fort Worth to the entire moderate world. Homer and I were wrong again though. As future events would demonstrate, the election of Charles Stanley was indeed what needed to happen. The election brought things to a head. There was no doubt the election the next year in Dallas, Texas, would go a long way in resolving the battle.

The Road to Dallas

Before the Dallas meeting I wrote an article entitled "Some Call It Heresy." This was in response to Dr. Bruce Corley and Dr. Russell Dilday calling dispensational premillennialism heresy. In my article I pointed out that a large number of pastors and theologians in SBC life, past and present, held to dispensational premillennialism. While I never made such a view a test of fellowship, I felt to call it heresy was over the line. Dr. Dilday heard about the article. He flew to Jacksonville for a meeting with me and Homer. *Florida Baptist Witness* editor, Jack Brymer, was at the meeting. Dr. Dilday wanted me to withdraw the article. Too late. The *Indiana Baptist* already had it and would soon publish it. I was able to get one clarification in the article Dr. Dilday requested. In the meeting Homer said, "Russell, we're going to win in Dallas." Dr. Dilday became animated and said, "We're going to burst your brains out in Dallas." Such was the intensity of feeling in anticipation of the meeting in Dallas.

Dallas Convention

The year leading up to the Dallas annual meeting was one of furious organizing. Both conservatives and moderates feverishly enlisted people to attend the convention. When the week for the annual meeting arrived, people descended on Dallas in record numbers. Before it was over, a record-setting 45,519 messengers were registered. They came from everywhere. Pastors of rural churches all over the convention arrived with their full contingent of messengers. The hotels were crowded. Dallas streets around the convention hall were congested. I actually became concerned that people might be injured as masses of people pressed upon the doors the first morning, trying to get in. Messengers brought lunches and drink boxes. They were prepared to keep their seats all day long.

I preached that year at the Southern Baptist Conference of Evangelists. The meeting was held at First Baptist Church, Dallas. My subject that afternoon was "The Tears of Paul." The building was packed. The atmosphere was electric. We shed some tears along with Paul that day. We rushed from First Baptist to the convention hall. The time for the election of president was soon.

Charles Stanley was reelected for a second term. He received 24,453 votes, to win by 55.3 percent over moderate candidate, Dr. Winfred Moore, pastor of First Baptist Church, Amarillo, Texas. In the history of Southern Baptist elections for president, this was the most votes any president ever received. I think there will never be a vote larger than that one. And probably there will not ever be a larger crowd attending an annual convention meeting.

The convention sessions themselves were studies in chaos. People were jammed in the hall, and the room was rather hot. Tempers flared. One night a conservative pastor friend of mine got into a nose to nose with a moderate pastor. "We need someone neutral to pray," someone suggested. They called upon me. Hardly neutral, I prayed as best and as quickly as I could. A bad scene was averted.

The platform was free for "whosoever will" to congregate on it. All kinds of motions were introduced. A liberal pastor from Virginia introduced a motion to replace Dr. Stanley's committee on committees nominations with the state convention presidents and WMU directors. Homer was on the platform. He lumbered over to the liberal pastor and said, "You're going to split this convention."

The liberal pastor hotly replied, "I know who you are, Homer Lindsay. You don't intimidate me. Find you some country-bumpkin pastor and intimidate him."

Homer grabbed him by the shirt collar and drew his arm back, ready to land a blow. Evangelist Jay Strack, who preached several revivals for us, saw what was happening. "Homer, Homer, you're on national television." Homer stepped away.

Decently and in Order

The chaos and lack of order made it apparent to all some strong parliamentary direction was needed. Dr. Stanley acquired the services of Dr. Barry McCarty, one of America's leading parliamentarians, to serve in the1986 Atlanta Convention. This was obviously of the Lord. Dr. McCarty has served as SBC parliamentarian from that time to the present day. His wisdom and skill have helped the convention presidents navigate their way through some difficult waters. Dr. McCarty helped the annual meetings to be conducted decently and in order.

At the 1986 convention in Atlanta, there was no doubt who the conservative candidate would be. Adrian Rogers had agreed to be nominated. Adrian was elected by a 54.22 percent margin over Winfred Moore, who had run against Stanley the previous year. Adrian was reelected at St. Louis in 1987, winning by 59.97 percent over Richard Jackson, pastor of North Phoenix Baptist Church, Phoenix, Arizona. The percentages were getting higher and higher. Clearly the convention was moving in a more conservative direction.

The Peace Committee

Beside the election of Adrian Rogers in 1986, there was another significant event. Many earnestly desired some kind of peaceful resolution to the controversy. Surely something must be done, or the convention was going to split. There must be a last-ditch effort to keep this from happening. The moderates, who were consistently losing the presidential election, saw the handwriting on the wall. A recommendation was forthcoming that an effort to reconcile differences between conservatives and moderates be made.

I had never been much of a committee man. I served one time on the SBC Committee on Committees. This was in the early years of my ministry at Dauphin Way. Dr. Jaroy Weber, my predecessor, had appointed me when he was president of the SBC. I remember how bored I was. I just didn't enjoy meetings. I didn't even like staff meetings at my church. I surely didn't like meetings on a denominational level. No meetings for me! Little did I know what kind of meetings were straight ahead.

Chapter 13

Purity before Peace

P aige Patterson made another request of me. Would I agree to serve
on a peace committee. A what? Paige explained that Dr. Franklin
Paschal, a former SBC president, suggested such a committee to
carefully examine the issues causing conflict and seek solutions to them. I
was not optimistic. He told me that an equal number of conservatives and
moderates were to be on the committee. And some who were perceived
to be somewhere in the middle would also be appointed. There would be
pastors and laypeople. With some reservations I agreed to serve.

Committee Members

A committee of eighteen was submitted and approved by the convention in session. The committee was later expanded to twenty-two members. Among the conservatives who had been engaged in the controversy
were Adrian Rogers, Charles Stanley, Ed Young, and myself. Notable
moderates included William Hull, Cecil Sherman, Winfred Moore,
and Daniel Vestal. Mrs. Morris Chapman (Jodi) and Mrs. A. Harrison
Gregory (Christine) were selected. Herschel Hobbs, the noted pastor-
theologian, was a member. Several laymen, including Harmon Born and
Charles Pickering, were on it. Jim Henry and John Sullivan, both conservatives who had not been visible in the conflict, were also selected.

Charles Fuller, who took no side in the controversy, was selected to be the chairman.

We were given this assignment: "That this Committee seek to determine the sources of the controversies in our Convention, and make findings and recommendations regarding these controversies, so that Southern Baptists might effect reconciliation and effectively discharge their responsibilities to God by cooperating together to accomplish evangelism, missions, Christian education and other causes authorized by our Constitution, all to the glory of God.[21] Whew! Pretty tough assignment, wouldn't you say?

My longest meeting ever was to begin! I realized I was going to be in an arena with much theological discussion. As I prepared for the meetings, I gave myself to reading much of what professors in question had written. I didn't read everything but did read quite a bit of their writings, including scholarly articles. I was getting ready to enter into theological discussions with scholars. I was going to be as prepared as I possibly could be.

Meetings

The committee began its meetings. Fourteen meetings were held in all. We met in several places—Nashville, Glorietta, etc. More and more we seemed to gravitate to the Airport Marriott Hotel in Atlanta, Georgia. This was a location somewhat central to the members of the committee. This was to be my second home for a period of time.

I will not seek to give a recounting of all that transpired in the meetings. Others will chronicle these meetings and deliberations. Now that the proceedings have been unsealed, historians will write about the committee's deliberations for years to come. Doctoral dissertations will be written by young Ph.D. students. Nor will I attempt to place what I recount in this chapter in chronological order. I will just share from my viewpoint some little-known aspects of our times together.

I will try to give some background not commonly known. I am aware my recounting will be from my perspective. Others on the committee might well interpret them differently.

Cecil Sherman

I met some of the moderates for the first time. There was Cecil Sherman. I actually met him at one of our early megachurch pastor meetings. I well remember the day a few years ago when we were discussing the problems of the convention. Cecil said to Adrian, "Adrian, you probably wouldn't let me teach in one of our seminaries."

In his deep, resonant voice Adrian replied, "Cecil, I wouldn't let you teach Sunbeams at Bellevue Baptist Church."

I really liked Cecil. There was an honesty about him I respected. He never tried to hide what he believed.

In one of our after-the-meeting discussions, Cecil, pastor of Broadway Baptist Church in Fort Worth, said, "We baptized fifty people last year. Some of my people were concerned that I was getting too evangelistic. Yuk yuk yuk!"

Cecil Sherman was the member of the committee who proposed we release our first finding: that there were substantial theological differences between conservatives and moderates. He was exactly correct. And honest enough to say it. The Peace Committee reported that "the primary source of the controversy is theological differences, but found there are political causes as well." Score one for the conservatives. And Cedil Sherman was the person who clearly articulated the primary problem.

William Hull

William Hull was pastor of First Baptist Church, Shreveport, Louisiana. He previously served as provost of Southern Seminary. His article "Shall We Call the Bible Infallible?" was one of the articles that fired the controversy. I found Dr. Hull to be the most brilliant moderate on the committee. And he was a perfect gentleman. Always polite and respectful, Bill Hull was easy to like. In January 1987 Dr. Hull sent me his book on John 3:16 entitled *Love in Four Dimensions*. He signed it, "To Jerry Vines—colleague on the SBC Peace Committee, 1985–87." I wrote him a few months ago and told him his book remains the finest treatment of John 3:16 I have ever read.

One night in an outside-the-meeting talk, Adrian asked Bill if he believed Jesus actually turned the water into wine. Dr. Hull replied, "We all believe in the miracle of the wedding." Catch the nuance? His answer illustrated the statement: neoorthodox theologians use our vocabulary but not our dictionary.

Herschel Hobbs

I knew Dr. Herschel Hobbs since my days as pastor at Dauphin Way. Dr. Hobbs was pastor there before he went to First Baptist, Oklahoma City. He was considered to be Southern Baptists' pastor/theologian. He was also a denominational statesman. Early on in our meetings, Dr. Hobbs reminded us that he was the chairman of the committee that revised the Baptist Faith and Message statement in 1963. His discussion of the meaning of the phrase that the Bible is "truth without any mixture of error" was a landmark for the Peace Committee. He took us to 2 Timothy 3:16, which includes the statement, "All Scripture is given by inspiration of God." He pointed out that the Greek word translated "all" meant the whole and every part of the whole. He said the intention of the 1963 revision committee was that the whole Bible, including every part of it, is inspired of God.

Dr. Hobbs's presentation stays with me all these years since those committee meetings. Another opinion was developed in my mind at that time. If men like Dr. Hobbs had come to some of the concerned conservatives and indicated they knew there were problems in our schools and would commit themselves to work them out, the controversy might have been avoided.

Christine and Jodi

Christine Gregory was a delightful member of the committee. Christine was from Danville, Virginia. She was active in WMU work in her church and on a national level, having served as national WMU president from 1975 to 1981. I called her our "mother superior." Sometimes after the night sessions of the committee, I would take "Mother Superior" and Jodi Chapman, a friend for many years, to the restaurant for desert. I often brought her flowers or other gifts and publicly gave them to her at beginning of the meetings. I well remember the night she shared with me her pastor preached a sermon about Peter and the boys sharing a six-pack of beer on the Sea of Galilee. Such preaching broke her heart. I believe Mrs. Gregory was the kind of Christian woman who would have been a blessing to any conservative pastor.

Crucial Votes

Because of our fellowship in the conservative movement, four of us were drawn together. Adrian, Charles, Ed, and I would often meet in one of our rooms to discuss upcoming issues, make plans for the meeting, and pray together. Ed Young was the great grey owl of night owls. You just prayed the meeting wasn't in your room. Ed could keep you up most of the night!

There were times when we seemed to be hopelessly outnumbered on certain crucial votes. We would pray. In the meeting we would be astonished that we carried the day. Sometimes by huge margins. God moved, and the majority of the members of the committee would line up with us. Looking back, it is apparent to me the large majority of the Peace Committee members were conservative theologically. For whatever reason some aligned themselves with the moderates. Others chose not to take sides in the controversy.

The great desire for the convention was that there might be peace. Adrian made it most clear, however, that it was not to be a peace at any price. Pointing to James 3:17, Adrian would remind us that "the wisdom that is from above is first pure, then peaceable." Though Charles Fuller was the chairman of the committee, Adrian was clearly the leader. During those months of meetings, I saw just how wise he was. And how much a Christian gentleman. I saw him under times of intense pressure. He never wavered in his convictions concerning the Word of God. I never saw him conduct himself in a manner less than Christian.

I actually felt sorry for the laypeople on the committee. They took the view, "Can't we all just get along?" They strived to be peacemakers. I'm not sure they really understood the depths of the theological differences between those who were on the committee. Most of them were good, godly, and sincere laypeople. I would have been proud to have most of them as members of my church fellowship. With one or two exceptions!

Committee Drama

There were some dramatic moments during our deliberations. During one of our meetings, I received a call from Steve Drake, one of my preacher boys from my church in Rome, Georgia. Steve was a student at Southern Seminary. Steve was finishing one degree and wanted to pursue his doctorate. As Steve recounted to me on the phone, he went in to the provost and expressed his desire to enter the doctoral program. Upon finding out Steve was one of my preacher boys, the provost told him he wouldn't fit in the program and indicated it would be futile for him to seek admission.

I was steamed. I returned to the meeting and told the committee about the call. Dr. Fuller called for a recess and said he was going to call Dr. Roy Honeycutt, president of Southern. When we returned, Dr. Fuller said he placed the call. Dr. Honeycutt said there surely was a mistake. They would love to have Steve enroll in the doctoral program! Steve did enroll, earned his doctorate, and later became a professor at Southern. I would really like to know what transpired between Dr. Honeycutt and the provost over that debacle!

Never will I forget when the seminary presidents appeared before the committee. In particular, when Dr. Russell Dilday, president of Southwestern, came. The atmosphere was tense. Matters concerning political campaigning came up. Adrian asked Dr. Dilday if he had been involved in political campaigning. He emphatically stated that he had not. Then Adrian asked him if he had sought to get out the vote to try to defeat Charles Stanley for reelection in Dallas. Dr. Dilday forcefully affirmed that he indeed worked to get the vote to defeat Stanley. Then, looking at Charles, he declared, "That man was not worthy to be president of the Southern Baptist Convention." Things went downhill from there.

I was sitting next to Stanley. "Don't say anything, Charles," I whispered to him. Charles didn't move a muscle. He was as solemn as a sphinx. Dr. Dilday went on and on.

When he left the room, Dr. Jim Slatton buried his head in his arms and said, "If I hadn't heard it for myself, I wouldn't have believed it."

Southeastern Subcommittee

The committee was arranged into subcommittees. We were to go to the various entities to discuss issues. I was placed on the Southeastern and Southwestern subcommittees. I remember well my trip to Wake Forest to visit Southeastern Seminary. Before the visit I received some letters from current students who told me of the liberalism they had heard in the classrooms. And the profanity. They requested a meeting with our subcommittee. Jim Henry was chairman of our subcommittee. I passed their request on to him. Dr. Henry arranged for a meeting with the students the night before our official visit. We met in a large room in the motel where we were staying. What the students told us was deeply concerning. They told us of the liberal teaching they were hearing. And the profanity used by some of the professors. If things were as bad as they were saying, the problems at Southeastern were greater than we thought.

The next day I walked on the campus of Southeastern for the first time. I felt a spirit of oppression. I really don't know any other way to describe what I sensed. We met with Dr. Randall Lolley, president of the seminary. Dr. Lolley had stirred further controversy by praying a dedicatory prayer at a brewery. We were hosted with a lavish meal. We were shown pictures of school dignitaries. Then we were ushered into the conference room. There Dr. Lolley thanked us for coming. He assured us all the professors were Bible believers and any fears we might have were unfounded.

End of subject. Kumbaya. Time to pray and dismiss.

I put my briefcase on the table. "Dr. Lolley," I said, "I have been reading some of the things some of your professors have written. I think at least nine of them might need to be tried for heresy." Boom! Nitroglycerin hit the room. I pointed out Dr. John Durham said David didn't write as many as one of the Old Testament psalms. I discussed some of the neoorthodoxy of several professors. Dr. Lolley expressed outrage over the meeting the night before with the students. Needless to say, kumbaya was a bit off-key. We made our report to the rest of the Peace Committee at our next meeting. Dr. Sherman was indeed correct. Our findings proved there were major theological differences between us.

The Glorieta Statement

In October 1986 our meeting was held at Glorieta Baptist Conference Center, New Mexico. All leaders of our SBC entities, including seminary presidents, would meet with us. As a result of that meeting, the six seminary presidents issued what became known as the "Glorieta Statement." Among other things included in that statement, they said, "The sixty-six books of the Bible are not errant in any area of reality."

Cecil Sherman went ballistic. He was merciless toward the presidents. He let them know in no uncertain terms he felt betrayed. He defended them in Peace Committee meetings; now they deserted him. In rather salty language he expressed his displeasure. He resigned from the committee.

There was some initial euphoria around the convention. Many hailed the Glorieta Statement as the breakthrough that would resolve the conflict. I was not so sure. I learned well during my Mercer days that neoorthodox theologians could say one thing and mean another. I feared the statement was just an attempt by the seminary presidents to calm things down, convince people everything was fine, and go on their merry way. As it turned out, neither side was happy with the statement.

Dr. Sherman was correct and justified in his feeling of betrayal. Some of the presidents incurred the wrath of their faculties upon their return to their respective schools. Several attempted a clever spin to the statement. What they meant by "not errant" was that the Bible is inerrant in matters of spiritual reality, not necessarily in scientific, historical, etc. matters of reality. The controversy was still on.

The Report to the Convention

The time for the Peace Committee's report to the convention drew near. A subcommittee was appointed to draw up a final report. All the committee members were to have input. When the first draft was prepared, I could hardly believe my eyes. What they penned bore little resemblance to the results we found and the decisions we made. I expressed my displeasure forcefully. One committee member kept pressing for the report to be as they composed it. I refused to go along with it. He was most unhappy with me. Before it was done, the report was pretty much in agreement with what the conservatives on the committee had intended and the full committee had voted. We would have a final meeting in Saint Louis the night before we were to give our report.

The night of our final meeting was a night I will always remember. There were efforts on the part of some to change the report yet again. The conservatives on the committee were adamant. We refused to budge. Adrian told the committee we would go directly to the convention floor and tell the messengers just what transpired in the meetings if the report was changed.

The hour was getting late. Things were at an impasse. The whole report was hanging in the balance. In the early morning hour Ed Young leaned over to me and whispered, "They don't know us, do they. Vines? We can wait 'em out, can't we?" I nodded a sleepy head of agreement. Ed then made this motion to add to our report to the convention these words:

> We recommend that, in view of the intense public
> discussions of the last few years, the trustees determine
> the theological positions of the seminary administrators
> and faculty members to guide them in renewing their
> determination to stand by their commitment to the
> Baptist Faith and Message Statement of 1963, to the
> Glorietta Statement of their intention to work toward
> reconciliation of the conflict in the Convention, and
> to their own institutional declarations of faith as the
> guidelines by which they will teach their students in

preparation for Gospel ministry in the churches, mission fields and service to the denomination.[22]

A sleepy Bill Hull seconded the motion to add this to our recommendations. The vote was unanimous in the affirmative. We had only wanted a few of our professors' theological positions ascertained. Now this called for the entire administrations and faculties of our seminaries to be polled to determine their theological positions!

The conservatives on the Peace Committee realized every desired outcome in the committee deliberations. Looking back on it, all I can say is that the Lord was with us and gave us victory on every hand.

The next day the report was presented to the messengers. By a vote of more than 95 percent, they approved the Peace Committee report. The report confirmed what conservatives incessantly said for years: theological problems existed. Also, the report showed that many of the charges the moderates leveled against the conservatives were untrue.

In these passing years I often look back on my time on the Peace Committee. In many ways the work of this committee guaranteed ultimate victory for the conservative cause. Was it worth it? Since that time our seminaries all now have presidents, administrators, and faculties who affirm the absolute inerrancy and authority of the Bible. Many faculty members thank me for my service on the Peace Committee. Scores of students thank me for making it possible for them to attend a seminary that is theologically conservative. They encourage me to believe the numerous days, multitudes of meetings, and long nights were worth it.

I will await the judgment seat of Christ to hear whether I receive a "well done, thou good and faithful servant."

Convention Sermon

Meanwhile, there was preaching to do. At the previous year's convention I was selected to preach the convention sermon at the 1987 meeting in Saint Louis. I always took these kinds of preaching assignments seriously. I began my preparation early. At the time the issue of the inspiration of the Bible was front and center in the SBC controversy. Both conservatives and moderates were writing and preaching on the subject. The seminary presidents announced their intention to hold three national conferences on biblical inerrancy. The first one was held at Ridgecrest, May 4–7, 1987.

In my preparation I was soon led to do an exposition of 2 Timothy 3:14–4:13. This is a key passage one must consider in regard to the Bible's inspiration. Here the Bible speaks for itself about its inspiration. I arranged the message around three divisions: (1) The INTENTION of the Bible (3:14–15); (2) The INSPIRATON of the Bible (3:16–17); (3) The IMPLICATIONS of the Bible (4:1–13). I did some word study. I included some down-to-earth stories. I used a little humor. And I pulled no punches. Then I titled the message "A Baptist and His Bible."

Time came for the delivery of the message. I was physically exhausted. The marathon meeting of the Peace Committee and the tension of our report to the messengers laid me low. I begged the Lord for strength and clarity. He met my need as only He can do.

That morning before I was to deliver the message in the afternoon, Shirley Lindsay came down with a severe reaction to food she had eaten. Her body was covered with red whelps. Hives. Janet was with her. Others stayed with her so Janet and Homer could hear the message.

The atmosphere in the meeting hall was unbelievable. I preached as best I could. I tried to be kind to those who did not believe in inerrancy. I was not kind to destructive criticism, calling it "that old thief." I said that old thief, destructive criticism, "clips faith's wings with reason's scissors." The messengers shouted "amen," applauded, and leaped from their seats. Lest you think I am taking credit for the message, I am not. I fully believe the Lord gave me the message, helped me deliver it, and I give Him all the glory. I attempted to let the Bible speak for itself. Some have called the message the water-shed sermon in the Conservative Resurgence. Whether or not that is true, only eternity will reveal.

I shall now proceed to brag. Dr. Carl L. Kell and L. Raymond Camp, professors of communication and moderates themselves, later wrote a book entitled *In the Name of the Father: The Rhetoric of the New Southern Baptist Convention*. In that book they take the position that the conservatives won because they had the more effective preachers. Though they didn't intend it positively, I'm sure, they were complimentary of *A*

Baptist and His Bible. They even included it in full in an appendix. They say it was "the finest national statement on biblical inerrancy we found during our research for this study." They also said, "In the words of southern folklore, 'If you don't want to believe the man, don't listen to him.'"[23] Not really bragging. The Lord did it, not me.

Dr. Adrian Rogers was presiding as president that day. He sat behind me as I delivered the message. Adrian said about the message: "[It] is a wonderful example of scholarship, conviction and truth presented from a heart on fire, and a heart in love with Jesus and His Word. . . . It was very obvious that Dr. Vines was causing sympathetic vibrations in the hearts and lives of people to whom the Word of God is precious."[24]

OK. I have asked the Lord to forgive me for my narcissism. I now ask your forgiveness.

The message remains to this day unchallenged. To my knowledge no Southern Baptist scholar has questioned the accuracy of my exegesis of this crucial passage about the Bible's inspiration.

When the message was over, the first person to approach me was Charles Stanley. He engulfed me in a bear hug. I thought he would break my back! Then he whispered in my ear a prediction that would change my life forever.

Chapter 14

"God Just Told Me . . ."

There is a difference of viewpoint among good men when it comes to how God speaks to us. Some believe God speaks directly today as He did in times past. They are not hesitant to say, "God told me." Others are more cautious, believing that God has spoken His finest and final Word in the Scriptures (Heb. 1:1–2).

This does not mean the former group doesn't believe in the finality of revelation as found in the pages of the Bible. Most all would agree, I am sure, that whatever we may think God is saying to us must be weighed against the revelation of Holy Scripture. Few take the unscriptural view that there is continuing revelation today on the same level as the Bible.

I have tended to say, "I sense the Lord is telling me . . ." or, "It seems to me the Lord has told me. . . ." Looking back on my life, there are times when I clearly discerned the voice of God in leading me. There were other times when I thought it was the Lord; turns out, I was listening to my own inner voice of desire!

Stanley Prediction

The first person I saw when I finished delivering "A Baptist and His Bible" was my friend Charles Stanley. As I previously indicated, he enveloped me in a crunching bear hug and whispered some words in my ear.

The words were startling. He whispered, "God just told me you will be the next president of the Southern Baptist Convention." Immediately my mind raced back to my loss in a runoff in 1977. Few, if any, were defeated for the presidency and were later elected. Being president of the Southern Baptist Convention was not on my bucket list. I was happy being pastor of First Baptist Church of Jacksonville, preaching around the country, and supporting efforts to turn the SBC back to its conservative roots. I heard what Charles said. I filed it somewhere in my memory bank. But I wondered, *Did God really tell him that?* Later the same day Charles told Jim Hefley, author of the comprehensive *The Truth in Crisis* volumes, "The message automatically nominated the president." Did it? Would it?

Homer was enthusiastic about the message. He felt it should be put in booklet form and mailed to every pastor in the convention. This was done, financed by First Baptist, Jacksonville.

Our church put funds into the conservative effort. The conservative effort operated on a shoestring. Moderates often said enormous financial resources funded our efforts. Not true. Homer and I were often in meetings when thousands of dollars were pledged to fund conservative periodicals like *The Southern Baptist Advocate*. Unfortunately, most of the pledges were never met. Homer and I always sent the funds we promised.

Mixed Opinions

Homer felt strongly I should be the conservative candidate at San Antonio, Texas, in 1988. Others were not so sure. Homer attended a meeting of conservative leaders in Atlanta. I did not attend. There was quite a bit of opposition to me being the candidate. I agreed with their reasoning. First, I lost in 1977. Southern Baptists tended not to elect those who previously lost an election. Second, the meeting was being held in Texas. I was not as well known in the West as I was in the East. Third, the moderate candidate was going to be Richard Jackson. Though he ran and lost previously (1980, 1987), the moderates were fully committed and engaged to get him elected this time. Fourth, Richard Jackson was a most formidable candidate. His church, North Phoenix, was always at or near the top in baptisms and Cooperative Program giving: 1,206 baptisms the previous year; $1,062,000 CP gift. No one could question his conservative credentials. He was also a strong preacher. Richard and I were casual friends. I liked him. He preached for us in Jacksonville on several occasions.

Men wiser than I did not believe I could win over Richard. I concurred with their political reasoning. Homer did not. He didn't care what the arguments against my candidacy were. So he just told them they could do as they pleased. Vines was going to be the candidate! Homer never was intimidated by disagreement. Or by the majority. Sometimes he made it appear that God not only spoke directly to him but used a boom box! I only agreed to pray about it.

I Am the Candidate

At our annual pastors' conference (more about this conference later) in January 1988, Homer, without even telling me, announced I was going to be the conservative candidate in San Antonio. The grassroots preachers who were in the audience were ecstatic. They knew I was one of them. I started my ministry in rural churches. Since the beginning days of my ministry, God gave me a heart for the pastor at the crossroads. I was one of them, understood them, and loved them. Some of God's greatest men have served all their ministries in little, out-of-the way places. They never receive much recognition or praise. But they are heroes to me. They are the men who made the SBC great. Unfortunately, some of our SBC leaders have failed to understand or appreciate them.

There wasn't anything the conservative leadership could do. Not that they wanted to do anything. They were just concerned that the string of conservative presidents being elected would continue. I shared the same concern. But the words Stanley had whispered in my ear kept coming back to me: "God just told me you will be the next president of the Southern Baptist Convention." Did Charles indeed have "a word from the Lord"? I think many of the leaders, all of whom were my friends, gave a reluctant "the will of the Lord be done" as did those who saw there was no dissuading Paul from his trip to Jerusalem (Acts 21:14).

The grassroots preachers started making their plans. Many of them had limited incomes, little help from their churches, and few resources to get them to San Antonio. In spite of the logistic difficulties, hundreds of them planned to bring their maximum number of messengers to vote for me. In the Southern Baptist system of representation, a church, regardless of its size, can bring one messenger for a yearly gift of $250 to the convention. And they can have a maximum of ten messengers if the annual gift is $2,500. This means a church with one hundred in attendance can have as many messengers as a church with ten thousand in attendance. Some have questioned this system, but it has never been successfully challenged.

The moderates went all out to rally messengers to come to San Antonio to vote for Richard Jackson. Richard was all over the convention, speaking and urging people to come to San Antonio. I was also going many places and speaking as well. I enjoyed going to preach the Word. I didn't enjoy campaigning. The politics of the entire matter was unpleasant to me.

I did meet some wonderful people. On one trip to San Antonio to speak to pastors in that area, I was given some money to purchase a pair of cowboy boots. I was taken to the Lucchese Boots outlet. They gave me enough to purchase quite a beautiful, expensive pair. Their word to me was, "If we can't have a Texan as our next president, then at least you can look like one!" I still wear those boots on some occasions today.

The moderates had a layman who was willing to put big bucks into the election of Richard Jackson. John Baugh, Baptist layman from Houston, was active in the movement to resist the Conservative Resurgence. I knew of Mr. Baugh. His company, Sysco, purchased the frozen foods company of Hugh Davis, one of my deacons at West Rome Baptist, Rome, Georgia. For whatever reason, Mr. Baugh was antagonistic to the conservative effort. I have no verification of this, but some said he put a million dollars into that year's SBC presidential election.

The time for the annual meeting arrived. Finding hotel rooms was a problem for many. Conservative pastors and their members from rural areas planned to sleep in their cars. One pastor and wife brought a pup tent! When I found out about it, somehow a room was arranged for them. The mood seemed to be that Vines was "one of them," and they were coming to San Antonio to vote for him.

The night before the election, I spoke at the Pastors' Conference. My message was entitled "How to Go through the Fire," speaking from the narrative of the three Hebrew children in Daniel 3. I said, "They wouldn't bow . . . they wouldn't bend . . . they wouldn't burn!" The message was well received. But, the fireworks came in the final message that night. Dr. Criswell was bolder and more forceful than I ever heard him. He tore into the liberals. He said, "Liberals today call themselves moderates. However, a skunk by any other name still stinks." The conservatives roared. The moderates were incensed.

Contrary to what some charged, he wasn't calling liberals skunks. He was using an illustration to point out that a name change doesn't change anything. In that message he also held up a weekly paper from FBC, Jacksonville. The previous week we baptized 152 people in a single Sunday. He emphatically stated our conservative churches were not the problem in the SBC. This was also his way of giving his endorsement to my nomination for president.

The Election

I slept peacefully the night before the election. The day of the election Janet and I made our way to a seat high up in the meeting hall. Danny and Becky Watters were with us. Sitting near us was Dr. Kirby Godsey, president of Mercer University, my alma mater. Next to him was the pastor of my home church, Ron Stone. Though never using my name, he attacked me and campaigned against me, with my parents sitting in the congregation listening to him malign me. His attacks continued after my election. So much so that my parents joined another church.

The time for the nominations for president arrived. The tension in the room was gut-wrenching for me and Janet. George Harris, a friend of mine and pastor of Castle Hills Baptist Church in San Antonio, nominated Richard. Ralph Smith, pastor of Hyde Park Baptist in Austin, Texas, nominated me. James Craig was nominated. Anis Shorrosh, an evangelist, started making a nomination. As he spoke, it dawned on me. I whispered to Janet, "He's nominating himself!" And I was his pastor at Dauphin Way!

I was never offended at any who were nominated or who nominated anyone against me. I always felt anyone who felt led of the Lord could run for any office or nominate anybody. One of my closest friends today, Ed Young, nominated Jimmy Allen against me. Though I did not know Ed well at the time, I was not offended.

The ballot was taken. The convention program proceeded as the ballots were being counted. Talk about roller-coaster emotions. The messengers waited for the results. Sitting on the platform was my friend, O. S. Hawkins. I would look down, and he would be smiling and giving a thumbs-up. The next time I looked down at him, he would be shaking and burying his head in his hands in despair. With friends like these, who needs enemies?!

After what seemed like a millennium, the results were back: 31,291 voted. Shorrosh received 82 votes. James Craig received 276. Richard Jackson received 15,112 or 48.3 percent. I received 15,804 or 50.3 percent. I leaned over to Janet and whispered, "I won. I'm the president of the Southern Baptist Convention." She and I stood up and left the hall to go to our room. Janet later said that day was "the most nerve-racking day in her life."

I won the closest presidential election in the Conservative Resurgence. I won by the narrow margin of 692 votes. My friend O. S. called me thereafter "Landslide Vines." With friends like O. S. . . . ! I have always believed the Lord did a miracle in my election. He did it through the sacrificial efforts of so many faithful, unknown, often neglected pastors. They never sought the praise of men but just faithfully served the Lord in lowly places. I have never forgotten those dear people who made such sacrifices to come to San Antonio to vote for me.

Press Conference

I was hardly prepared for the whirlwind in which I found myself. There was to be a press conference, conducted by Baptist Press. Richard Jackson showed up for my press conference. I don't recall this happening before. Baptist Press editor Alvin Shackleford, moderated the press conference. Alvin, ironically, was also from Carrollton, Georgia. He and I attended the same high school. He was a few years ahead of me. He was brought up in Carrollton's First Baptist Church; I, in Tabernacle Baptist, Carrollton.

One of the main questions was about the low percentage of Cooperative Program gifts by First Baptist, Jacksonville. I was ready for the question. I pointed out that matters of conscience had made it difficult for the church to give to support liberalism. I also pointed out that the CP amount was $70,000 when I arrived in Jacksonville. The previous year the gift was $255,000, an increase of 257 percent. I said, as problems with liberalism in the Convention were being addressed we were "putting our money where our mouth is."

That night after the election, Adrian held a celebration and prayer time for me. The presidential suite was packed with leaders of the Conservative Resurgence and many friends. Several spoke, expressing their appreciation to God for the victory and committing their prayers and support to me and Janet. Adrian's son, Steve, quite the musician, presented a hilarious skit and song "I Heard It from the Great Vines," a parody of "I Heard It through the Grapevine." The chorus said: "Oh we heard it through the 'Great Vines.' Who says no error in God's Word you'll find. Scripture is given in inerrancy, and what God says is good enough for me. I heard it from the Great Vines." My mother and father were there. My father, never one to be reticent or shy, asked to say a few words. With tears he told of their love and support for me. After he finished, Adrian said that represented the best of what Southern Baptist people were about. Then they laid hands on me and Janet and prayed for us. I will never forget the love, encouragement, and support we experienced that night.

My election marked the culmination of ten straight years of electing conservative presidents. The plan Judge Pressler had laid out for Homer and me some years ago had come to fruition. There would be other conservative presidents to follow. Many of them. But historians have regarded my election as the one to guarantee the success of the Conservative Resurgence.

I attended the New Orleans Seminary luncheon the next day. The president of the seminary did not introduce me. Dr. Chuck Kelly, professor of evangelism, did. I don't know if the slight was intentional or not.

I was accustomed to being ignored, slighted, and attacked. I chose not to take offense when such things occurred. I remembered well when I was treated like a pariah at conventions. Few would speak. I just turned those kinds of things over to the Lord. I refused to let others' conduct control me.

Year One

I soon announced the theme for my presidency would be personal soul winning. I would call our denomination to renew its commitment to one of the activities that had made it great. And, should I be reelected, my second year emphasis would be building great soul-winning churches. I recommitted myself to being a faithful witness for the Lord. I purchased a little red notebook and recorded the date, name, and some brief explanation of people I won to the Lord that year. I was not doing this to be a showoff. I was trying to set an example for our Southern Baptist leaders and people.

Broadman Press always asked the sitting president to publish a book. In 1989 they published *Wanted: Soulwinners*, the theme of my first year as president. In 1990 they published *Wanted: Church Growers*, my theme for the second year. During my term as president, there was little time to put many books together. I did publish *Exploring Daniel* in 1990. I did this book in collaboration with my friend John Phillips, in Loizeaux's Exploring Series. *Exploring Mark* was to come in 1992, two years after my presidency. I also did *Basic Sermons on the Ten Commandments* in 1992. This was later republished in 2006 as *God's Perfect 10*. Most of my books consisted of sermons that were prepared for a reading audience. John Phillips and I parted ways so he could keep the Exploring Series as his. I published *Believers Guide to Hebrews* in 1993, as a new series.

There was no way for me to know the unexpected issues that would foist themselves upon me. The first week after the convention, I received an unexpected burden. When I arrived at church one afternoon, there was a police report on my desk. A professor at one of our seminaries had been arrested for making homosexual advances in the bathroom of a local department store. Turns out the person approached was an undercover detective for the Jacksonville sheriff's office. There was no choice in the matter. I must call the president of the seminary where the man taught. This particular president was not friendly toward me. I called him and told him the situation. He told me he was aware of the problem and had taken steps to remove the man from the faculty. He thanked me for the call.

I could never have imagined the demands that would be placed upon me as president. Invitations of all kinds poured into my church office. My secretary, Shirley Cannon, was inundated with calls from people who wanted to speak with me. There were meetings to attend. Did I say there were meetings to attend? Pretty soon it became obvious there was no way I could accept all of the invitations or attend all of the meetings. I did not miss a single Sunday at Jacksonville due to being president. I maintained the pattern I always followed: missing two Sundays for vacation and one Sunday before the annual SBC meeting.

There were certain meetings, however, the president really needed to attend. The two yearly meetings of the Executive Committee in Nashville were a must. I had to attend meetings of my order of business committee. I did attend meetings of the Foreign Mission Board in Richmond, Virginia, and the Home Mission Board in Atlanta. This gave me firsthand information about what was going on to reach people for Christ abroad and at home.

I attended the inauguration of Dr. Lewis Drummond as new president of Southeastern Seminary. I remember well marching into the chapel with professors and students lining each side of the walkway wearing yellow ribbons of protest. I also remember sitting next to Dr. Wayne Ward on the platform. Dr. Ward, a professor at Southern Seminary, was there. He and I ministered on some programs together. During the proceedings he leaned over and whispered, "Jerry, I don't know why people think you are so mean. You have always been kind and gracious to me."

I replied, "Dr. Ward, I don't know either. I have always tried to treat people with respect."

Southwestern Seminary

I was invited by Dr. Dilday to speak at Southwestern Seminary. I remember the day well. The chapel was packed and students lined the walls. I spoke on "Have You Heard the Good News?" from 1 Corinthians 15:1–8. After chapel Dr. Dilday arranged a press conference. When the press conference began, it was obvious it was a setup.

First question: "Dr. Vines, we understand you have a son who is a student at Liberty University, Jerry Falwell's independent, non-Southern Baptist school."

"Yes," I responded, "my son, Jon, is a student there and is the punter on the football team. As you know, I went to a very liberal Baptist School, Mercer University, where my faith was under attack for four years. I thank God every day my son attends a school where every professor believes the Bible is the inerrant Word of God."

The press conference didn't last long after that.

The White House

One of the highlights of that first year was the invitation to be the guests of President and Mrs. Ronald Reagan for a state dinner at the White House. Talk about excited. Reagan was my political hero. Janet bought a new dress. I rented a tux. The dinner was in honor of the head of Timbuktu in the Western African nation of Mali (yes, there really is a Timbuktu!).

What a night! We were serenaded by 120 Marine violinists. The president's daughter, Maureen, loudly made her presence known. General Colin Powell was there. Other dignitaries were in attendance. Janet and I were awestruck.

I was honored to sit at the table of eight with the president himself. He entertained us with Russian jokes he had collected. Next to me was Cyd Charisse, the actress and dancer. On the other side was a lady who was head of the New York Alzheimer's Association.

During the meal the lady said to me, "I understand you are a Baptist preacher?"

"Yes," I answered.

"Well, can you tell me what 'born again' means. I've always wondered about it."

Talk about God opening a door for witness. I shared from John 3 how she could be born again. I don't know if she ever was or not.

I asked President Reagan about his remarkable ability in giving speeches. He said his training as an actor, memorizing scripts, had greatly assisted him. The hour was magical. I don't recall anything we had to eat. I was too wrapped up in the atmosphere of prestige, celebrity, and power to eat much.

We went to another room. There New Orleans jazz artist Pete Fountain played "Muskrat Ramble," among other things. Then he closed with "Amazing Grace." After his performance, I asked him, "Mr. Fountain, do you know the 'Amazing Grace' about which you play?" He jumped like he was shot. Didn't mean to scare him. Just wanted to get in a good word for the Lord.

Committee Appointments

One of the most important, if not the most important, assignment of the president is to select the committee on committees. This committee nominates the committee on nominations. This process results in the selection of trustees for our various entities. Very often presidents give this assignment to others. Dr. Criswell stated he didn't understand the importance of this process and passed it off to convention leaders to do for him. Other presidents gave the assignment to a member of the church staff.

I didn't pass my responsibility on to anyone else. I made all the appointments myself. I did enlist the help of friends and conservative leaders in the various convention states. There was little chance I would know people in all of the states who would be qualified to serve on committees. So I put out the word. I announced simple requirements for a committee appointment. First, they must hold to the inerrancy of Scripture. I made this crystal clear all along. I never budged from this stipulation. Second, they should be people of irenic spirit. I wanted no hotheads on the committee on committees. History will reveal how successful I was in my appointments. I took the word of others on some of my appointments. I have been told by conservative leaders my appointments were the most solidly conservative of any president. I don't know if that is correct or not, either.

Divisive Issues

As the meeting in Las Vega approached, I made a request of our entity heads. To encourage our people in my desire for us to return to personal soul winning, I asked each entity head to share a personal witnessing testimony in their report. I never dreamed this would be a cause for displeasure. I was told that one of our leaders, discussing my request with his subordinates, slammed his fist on a table and said, "I'll not do it!" Maybe I was asking too much. Maybe I was putting them on the spot. At the time I didn't view it that way. I just felt that those of us who were leaders should set the example for the pastors and people of our convention.

From a divisive-issue standpoint the big one was the desire to establish a religious liberty commission in the convention. For years Southern Baptists had been a part of the Baptist Joint Committee on Public Affairs. This group had taken decidedly liberal positions on matters of national policy. James Dunn, head of the BJCPA, was not very popular.

I remember one night at a convention, Adrian Rogers confronted Dunn about his criticisms of President Ronald Reagan. "James, I don't appreciate what you have been saying about President Reagan." James replied he didn't have to stand there and take that and walked off. Adrian never was timid when it came to confrontation of a person with an opposing view. Always gentlemanly, he never lacked for boldness and direct engagement.

This issue was creating a great deal of heat. The moderates were using it as an issue to rally their people to Las Vegas. Was the time right to make this change? I was not sure it was. Other conservatives took the same view. Although the Executive Committee prepared a recommendation for the annual meeting, I asked them to delay it one year in the interest of harmony and peace. I felt it would take away from the emphasis on missions and evangelism so needed in Las Vegas. I made this request in a letter to Dr. Charles Sullivan, chairman of the EC.

I experienced a rare instance of praise from those on the other side of the aisle. My suggestion was widely applauded. North Carolina Baptist paper editor R. G. Pickett said, "Vines may have defused the most controversial item on the agenda (for the Las Vegas meeting)." The Executive Committee accepted my request.

In some ways my first year as convention president was enjoyable. Other ways it was not. I really enjoyed getting to know many people all over the convention. Seeing the work of our convention close-up gave me a new appreciation for what was being done to get the gospel to people the world over. I did not enjoy going to all the meetings. Sometimes I could be seen working on sermons during dull sessions of a board meeting. I just never was much of a meeting man. I much preferred to study the Word, preach, and visit in the homes of lost people.

The Campaign Begins

The annual meeting in Las Vegas was approaching. The moderates were going to mount another campaign to wrest the presidency from the hands of conservatives. The closeness of the election in New Orleans greatly discouraged them. But it also encouraged them. An incumbent couldn't be defeated. Or could he? The closest election in the Conservative Resurgence caused many to believe I was vulnerable. How many conservatives would go to Las Vegas, the gambling capital of the world?

The moderates began mobilizing. Richard Jackson was not going to run again. Was there another possible candidate? Someone who was an avowed inerrantist? Someone who opposed the efforts of the conservative leaders? Just ahead was a meeting that just might be the moderates last opportunity to stop what they considered to be a conservative juggernaut. What would happen in Vegas? What happens in Vegas stays in Vegas, you know.

Chapter 15

What Happens in Vegas Doesn't Stay . . .

A Southern Baptist Convention in Las Vegas, Nevada? Perish the thought! How in the world did it ever happen that an annual meeting would be held there? The decision for meeting places is made several years in advance. Contracts are signed and plans are made. This is very difficult, if not impossible, to change.

I was the first president to preside at an annual meeting in Las Vegas. I may well be the last. No meeting place was ever so controversial. How could we hold a convention in "Sin City"? We are going to hold our annual meeting at the mecca of gambling, legalized liquor and everything Southern Baptists oppose?

Going to Sin City

Others thought Southern Baptists should go to Sin City to be a witness for Christ. Count me among them. Sounds rather New Testament to me. Church planters in recent years have gone there and established strong churches. They are winning many people to Christ in Las Vegas. I never viewed it as a compromise. Christians are in the world but not of the world. They are sent into the world to announce the good news of Jesus Christ.

Southern Baptists would go there. But would they go in large numbers? Moderates didn't think conservatives would. The moderates were desperate. They would go there. Though I was an incumbent, they viewed me as vulnerable. First, because of the narrow margin by which I won in San Antonio. Second, because they had a strong candidate. Dr. Daniel Vestal, pastor of Dunwoody Baptist Church in Georgia was their man. Dr. Vestal was a Ph.D. graduate from Southwestern Seminary. He was an avowed inerrantist. He and I had served together on the Peace Committee. I really liked Daniel. He didn't like the conservative movement.

The moderates launched an all-out campaign to get Dr. Vestal elected. He was all over the convention, speaking and meeting with moderate groups. They seemed to sense this was their last opportunity to reverse the series of conservatives elected as president. They even had TV ads on local stations in Las Vegas. I never really understood why they did this. By the time messengers arrived in Vegas, surely their minds were already made up.

I did not do a lot of traveling. I was not invited to speak at any of the state evangelist conferences. When I did speak around the convention, I preached about personal soul winning. I did little speaking about Southern Baptist issues. I really didn't mind being snubbed by state convention meetings. I was busy at First Baptist, Jacksonville. We were building parking garages. We were looking toward building a larger auditorium. There was more than enough for me to do at home.

Actually Las Vegas is a good place to have a convention. The hall was comfortable and spacious. The convention hotel was the Hilton. I was bug-eyed. I never saw anything quite like it. There were rooms with slot machines, the one-armed bandits. There were other tables where the high rollers gambled for huge sums of money.

There were eating establishments all over the place. And the meals were cheap. I think it was because they wanted people to throw their money away gambling, not spend it eating. But it was a big deal to me. We ate at a cafeteria that served delicious food. Almost like the home cooking on which I had grown up back in Carroll County! Janet enjoyed looking in the shops. But the expensive clothing and jewelry were out of our range. Someone quipped that Southern Baptists came to Las Vegas with the Ten Commandments in one pocket and a ten-dollar bill in another and never broke either one!

There was going to be a boxing match at the same time Southern Baptists were there. Sugar Ray Leonard and Thomas Hearns were going to have their second fight. They fought what became known as "The Showdown" in 1981. Leonard won. The Vegas fight was called "The War." I really wanted to go to the fight. But I thought better of it. I could just see the picture of myself in the morning news. Probably wouldn't be good for the convention. Leonard won again.

Jerry Falwell

Jerry Falwell did go to the fight. When he was introduced and stood, some in the crowd booed. Falwell didn't care. He was used to it. Jerry was there to speak at the Southern Baptist evangelists' meeting. I think this was the first SBC annual meeting he ever attended. Jerry and I became good friends. As previously noted, Jon attended Liberty on a football scholarship. I became a trustee at Liberty University, serving as chairman for five years. This didn't win me any friends among the moderates. I often talked with Jerry about becoming a Southern Baptist. He never was a part of the hard-line, legalistic, mean-spirited kind of independent Baptists. Jovial, gregarious, fun-loving, practical-joking Falwell had many friends among Southern Baptists. At that point in time, however, plans to join us were not on his radar.

Contrary to what some asserted, there never was any kind of agenda on the part of Falwell, myself, Adrian, or anyone else to take over the SBC. We just wanted the problem of liberalism to be addressed. We were drawn to Falwell because of his conservative views. And we admired his stand for morality in America. We loved his vision to build a world-class Christian university.

Prepping for the Meeting

I arrived in Las Vegas several days ahead of the meeting. There were many preconvention meetings. The most important of these was the meeting with Dr. Barry McCarty, the parliamentarian. He served in that capacity since the 1985 convention. I appointed him to be mine as well. This was the beginning of a fulfilling relationship and marvelous friendship with Barry. I have known few men as congenial, capable, and gracious as he. On numerous occasions Dr. McCarty has kept the convention from imploding. His skill in the ins and outs of parliamentary procedure is breathtaking.

I was really uptight about presiding at the largest democratic assembly in the world. I moderated in church business meetings through the years. The longest one hardly exceeded five minutes. Now I was to preside for a two-day business session! Not to worry. Dr. McCarty scripted the entire proceedings in books I still have. He let me know exactly what to expect, what my options were, and how I was to handle every possible contingency. He assured me he would be right behind me at all times. This relieved my anxiety. A tiny bit. I was still as tight as the strings on a baseball.

No Water

Tuesday morning came. I decided to get up early to go over the proceedings again. I asked for a wake-up call at 4:30 a.m. The call came. I quietly got out of bed so as not to awaken Janet. I stumbled into the bathroom to wash the sleep out of my eyes. I turned the water faucets. No water. No water! I lost it. I'm just hours away from presiding over the Southern Baptist Convention meeting! I can't stand before the messengers without bathing, shaving, combing my hair, etc.

Bill DeWitt from church was my security man for the convention. He ushered me where I needed to go. He obtained clearance from the Hilton people and convention officials to use back halls, elevators, and other means of rapid movement. I called Bill. "Bill, I don't have any water," I shouted. Long story short. Bill got the water turned back on. I was shaken but showered and shaved. I was ready to preside over the convention.

Dr. Paige Patterson is the world's greatest practical joker. He made Falwell look like an amateur. I was the victim of some of his chicanery previously. One convention he somehow got in my room. When I returned, my socks were floating in a tub full of water. But this was the mother of all practical jokes. Paige, and some others I could name, bribed people at the Hilton to get my water cut off.

Presidential Message and Election

I presided on Tuesday. Then I quickly changed gears from presiding and preached. My presidential message that year was entitled "Bringing in the Sheaves," using Psalm 126 as my Scripture passage. I hit the theme of personal witnessing. I showed them my little red book. I had asked the Lord to help me win fifty-two people to Christ that year. I led a Hilton employee, number fifty-two, to Christ in an elevator.

The sermon was ended. Now the election was just ahead. Tom Eliff nominated me for my second term. David Sapp nominated Daniel Vestal. The results didn't take as long in coming. I had received 10,754 votes (56.58 percent). Dr. Vestal received 8,248 votes (43.39 percent). I won reelection by a 2,506 vote margin.

My press conference was much tamer in Las Vegas. I stated the issue of the Bible was basically settled in Southern Baptist life. I did not mean the controversy was over. I meant that Southern Baptists, every time they had had an opportunity to do so, overwhelmingly affirmed we believe the Bible is without error. And I stated that those who say there are errors in the Bible are a distinct minority in Southern Baptist life. I announced my theme for the year would be Building Soul-Winning Churches.

Little divisiveness surfaced in the business sessions. There was an attempt to move the president's message and the convention sermon until after the election of president in future conventions. This motion had been made before and failed. The messengers rejected it again.

The Executive Committee honored my request to hold off on the recommendation to establish a religious liberty commission. This defused possible controversy. My appointments were unchallenged. When I announced them in April, I said I made them on the basis of recommendations from many people throughout our convention. I appointed the best Southern Baptists I could find. All of them were inerrantists. I also pointed out that the vast majority of them never served before on any committee in the SBC.

James Dunn was publicly relieved no effort had been made to defund the Baptist Joint Committee. When asked about this, I said: "He has no reason to feel good. The vote this morning was an affirmation of the Executive Committee and its budget procedure, not James Dunn and the Baptist Joint Committee. He's like the man who fell from the fortieth floor who remarked as he was passing the thirtieth floor, 'So far, so good.'"

It Doesn't Stay in Vegas

You have heard the well-known saying, often turned into a song: "What happens in Vegas stays in Vegas." The term is most often used to indicate something that went on in Las Vegas a person doesn't want to be heard about back home. Of course, when it comes to sinful matters, what happens in Vegas doesn't stay in Vegas, does it? The results of sin have staying power. I heard a country preacher say one time, "Sin will take you farther than you want to go. Sin will teach you more than you want to know. Sin will keep you longer than you want to stay. Sin will cost you more than you want to pay."

And when it comes to what Southern Baptists did in Vegas, it didn't stay in Vegas either. They left Vegas with me as their president for a second term. I was actually getting some accolades from the Baptist media. Bob Terry, editor of Missouri's *The Word and Way*, praised me for focusing on witnessing and evangelism.[25]

One committee on nominations change got some positive coverage. The Home Mission Board had a trustee vacancy that needed to be filled. At the suggestion of HMB president Larry Lewis, I recommended to the committee on nominations that Richard Jackson be named. They agreed to do so. "This is a wonderful move," I said. "I have great love for Richard Jackson. I want this to be a kinder, gentler Southern Baptist Convention."[26]

Something else didn't stay in Vegas. I felt two matters must be addressed. I didn't wait long. When I addressed the Executive Committee at its September meeting in Nashville, I set forth my emphasis on building strong soul-winning local churches. I was setting the stage for my presidential message at the upcoming New Orleans convention. I pointed out that the New Testament teaches both the independence and the interdependence of local churches. I indicated my agreement with what one of Southern Baptist's great leaders said many years ago: "Lord, we Southern Baptists aren't much, but we're the best You've got."

But I wasn't through. There were a couple of things I didn't want to stay in Vegas. The Peace Committee report recommended the administrations and faculties of all of our seminaries be polled to determine their theological positions. I heard no such reports from the seminaries in Las Vegas. I stated my belief that the vote of the convention mandated such accountability should be forthcoming. I said the convention should receive an update on this recommendation at the convention in New Orleans.

This didn't sit well with some of the seminary presidents. Nor did many in Baptist media like it. There were attempts to goad me into naming a liberal at one of our seminaries. I wasn't falling for it. That was what the trustees were to do. I was just concerned that the seminaries had been unresponsive to the Peace Committee report and the will of the messengers.

To this day there has been no accounting. There is really no need for it now. Since 1989 the trustees of all of our seminaries have ensured that every administrator and faculty member believe in the inerrancy of Scripture.

There was another matter that couldn't stay in Vegas. The Executive Committee had graciously agreed to defer their recommendation on establishing a religious liberty commission. The new commission was proposed so Southern Baptists would no longer be a part of the Baptist Joint Committee on Public Affairs. By deferring, we put the focus on evangelism and witnessing in Vegas. Now, I said, we must face the issue head-on. I wanted us to settle it in a clear-cut, uncomplicated way.

That was music to the Executive Committee members' ears. That same day they proposed religious matters be assigned to the Christian Life Commission where strong conservative Dr. Richard Land had replaced Foy Valentine. A funeral dirge was playing in James Dunn's ears.

Neutral Leaders Take a Stand

In the months after the Vegas Convention meeting, I made an attempt to get some clearly identified conservatives who stayed out of the fray to come out strongly for the Conservative Resurgence. Two I knew very well. The third I knew just casually. Jim Henry and I met when we were students at New Orleans Seminary. We maintained a warm friendship through the years. He was at First Baptist Church, Orlando, Florida. I talked with Jim about openly endorsing the Conservative Resurgence. In subsequent months he made some statements clearly aligning himself with the conservative cause.

I did not know Joel Gregory as well. He was the new pastor at First Baptist, Dallas, Texas. I flew to Dallas and arranged to have a breakfast meeting with him. I told him of my desire that he clearly identify himself with the Conservative Resurgence. He listened respectfully. He gave no indication he would do so.

My third contact was with John Bisagno. John and I were friends. I preached for him on one occasion. The biggest banana split I ever ate in my life was at his house the night after I preached for him. John was sitting behind me when I preached "Our Ascended Lord" at Dauphin Way in 1976. Everyone knew John was a strong conservative. For his own reasons he had not aligned himself with those of us who were in the Conservative Resurgence. I told John he could be the one who might well tip the scales and bring total resolution to the controversy.

John exceeded my fondest dreams. In February he issued a five-page release stating his conviction the Conservative Resurgence was right in its concerns. He stated his firm adherence to the theological convictions of those in the CR. Then, to the amazement of all, he announced that in

New Orleans he would nominate Morris Chapman, pastor of First Baptist Church, Wichita Falls, Texas, for president of the convention. Jim Henry, Ken Hemphill, Joel Gregory, and others who had chosen not to align themselves with the Conservative Resurgence quickly publicly endorsed Bisagno's intentions to nominate Dr. Chapman.

Morris came to Jacksonville. Our annual pastors' conference was in full swing. He would be presented to the thousands who were in attendance. Before he arrived, I was told there was no room to be found for him. The hotels were packed. I didn't know what to do. In desperation I asked my friends, Fred Wolfe and Len Turner, if Morris could stay overnight with them in their room. They graciously agreed. Morris was always known for his immaculate appearance. Rumor has it that Morris, fully dressed, slept between Fred and Len that night. There was another vicious, untrue rumor that there were rooms available and that I was channeling my inner Patterson. I will let the judgment seat provide the answer to that one.

At the Executive Committee in February, I spoke my final time as president. I told them I left them with the words of Paul, "Ye shall see my face no more" (see Acts 20:38). I was ready to finish my tenure as president. There was work for me to do in Jacksonville. There was a family to love. There were sermons to prepare and preach. Lost people needed to be won to Christ. I had been to Vegas. What happened didn't stay there. What would happen in New Orleans?

Chapter 16

Free at Last

I have often told the story of the drunk who was picked up one Saturday night. He was placed in a brand-new paddy wagon for his trip to jail. He looked at the shiny lights overhead. He stroked the fancy new leather seats. He peered down at the thick, rich carpet beneath his feet. Then he declared, "If it weren't for the honor of this thing, I'd just as soon walk!" Such was my feeling the two years I served as president of the Southern Baptist Convention. There is the honor of it all. There are the opportunities to preach all over the Southern Baptist territory. There is the wonderful experience of meeting some of the finest believers in all the world. But the burdens and responsibilities can be extremely stressful. This was especially true for those of us who were the Conservative Resurgence presidents.

Even without the added tensions of those years, the presidency of the Southern Baptist Convention could easily be considered a full-time job. Not that I, or any rational person, would ever want it! I just mean serving the SBC as president can take up all your time. Most men who are elected president are also pastors of large churches. That was certainly my situation. I had the advantage of having a co-pastor, Homer Lindsay Jr., who could hold the fort while I was away. I was usually gone several days a week. I studied for my messages on airplanes, in hotel rooms, even in committee meetings! I never neglected my pulpit responsibilities the two years I served as president. Nor did I miss a single Sunday beyond the normal three Sundays per year I missed every year.

New Orleans Approaching

As the convention in New Orleans approached, all indications were it would be a watershed convention. Bisagno's stated intention to nominate Morris Chapman was pronounced by a number of people on both sides of the aisle as an "historic breakthrough." I well remember what happened at our First Baptist, Jacksonville, Pastors' Conference. Morris was introduced and spoke briefly. A phone call from John was played live to the thirty-five hundred plus attendees who were there. John announced that he was going to nominate Morris. The place exploded.

Dan Vestal was not dissuaded. He was running full force toward New Orleans. He announced his first vice-presidential running mate. The candidate would be Carolyn Weatherford Crumpler, retired executive director of the WMU (Woman's Missionary Union).

President George H. Bush was scheduled to appear and address the convention. Before the meeting he invited leaders of homosexual and lesbian organizations to attend a bill-signing ceremony at the White House. This was unprecedented. Southern Baptists were not happy. For the first time in history, a sitting president recognized leaders of the gay rights movement. There is no clarity about whether the president even knew they were going to be present. I liked President Bush very much. He seemed to me to be a genuine and sincere man. His testimony of personal faith in Christ was convincing. I was pleased he had such a good relationship with Billy Graham. I was then, and am now, convinced President Bush is a born-again man.

Though it was difficult for me, I let it be known to the White House that I must un-invite him. The president was gracious. I was happy for him to announce that he would not be able to attend. I never viewed my decision as particularly courageous. I did get a letter from Charles Colson thanking me for my stand. President Bush sent his "warmest greetings" to the convention in session.

The Convention Sessions

My arrival in New Orleans brought a flood of memories. I graduated from the seminary there. I preached often on the streets of the French Quarter. I would not have time to visit some old familiar places. There was work to do. I met with parliamentarian Dr. Barry McCarty. We went through the agenda with a fine-tooth comb. There would be many attempts to jam the proceedings. We even received reports that Southern Seminary students were given instructions about how to disrupt the convention. Some said they were told to stomp the floor and cause general confusion. There were rumors some planned to charge the platform. I never knew if any of these reports were true. But it did increase our efforts to have a meeting run decently and in order.

In the sessions all kinds of motions and resolutions were introduced. Points of order were raised. Some of the moderate entity heads presented rather rancorous reports. Caustic statements were made. In the middle of one report, smoke was seen rising in the Superdome. This alarmed some of the messengers. Dr. Ike Reighard, chairman of the order of business committee, checked it out.

Superdome officials let him know it was not smoke but haze caused by humidity clashing with the cold air from the air-conditioning. I interrupted the report being given for a word concerning the smoke. Ike gave the messengers the explanation and then said, "He has informed me this is being caused by a bunch of hot air being pumped into the room at this exact moment and we need to cool it." The place went crazy on the conservative side; the moderates fumed. A few past presidents later rebuked Ike for it. I thought it was perhaps the funniest statement ever. I'm sure not everyone was as tickled as I was by it.

Presidential Message

The time came for my presidential message. I spent several months preparing the message to give biblical support to my theme of building soul-winning churches. Our First Baptist Jacksonville choir and orchestra, three hundred plus in number, presented the special music. The music was the kind I have always believed necessary to build a soul-winning church. Warm, biblically sound, exquisitely presented, "gospel music with a flair," as I have termed it. My message was entitled "Glory in the Church." My text was Ephesians 3:21. I preached about the church universal, the church local, and the church denominational. In the message I introduced a little guy I called "Billy Baptist." I used this imaginary character to show the importance of evangelism and the responsibility the convention had to our young preacher boys. I have used this little guy in various ways since then. Along the way many people have mentioned "Billy Baptist" to me.

The people were responsive, as they always had been. They "amened," shouted, and stood. When the message was over, the choir and orchestra sang and played, "'Tis a Glorious Church without a Spot or Wrinkle." Time for the presidential election was just a few hours away.

The Election

Some moderates predicted they would have ten messengers from three thousand churches to ensure the election of Dr. Vestal. Those kinds of predictions were made by conservatives and moderates through the years. Never did any of those grandiose predictions come to pass. There was just no way of knowing with any degree of accuracy how many messengers for either side would make it to the convention.

Dan Vestal and Morris Chapman were nominated. When the result came back, Dan Vestal received 15,753 votes or 42.32 percent. Morris Chapman received 21,471 votes or 57.68 percent. Morris Chapman was new president of the SBC. And decisively so. There was no more doubt. The Conservative Resurgence was successful. The New Orleans meeting made it apparent that, for all practical purposes, the battle was won. Conservatives won every vote during the sessions. The moderates knew it was all over.

I was pretty well worn out. In the closing hours of the last session, I looked at the sides of the Superdome. There were bright red "EXIT" signs over the tunnels. I pointed to one of them and declared to those around me on the platform: "That's what I'm getting ready to be, an ex it." And I meant it. There were still a few reports to be given. I had had it. Evangelist Junior Hill was my first vice president. I turned the chair over to him. And walked off the platform! I went back to the president's room where I watched the final proceedings. I returned to the platform just in time to gavel the session finished. Free at last, free at last!

The Gathering at Café Du Monde

On Wednesday night after the meeting was over, I was invited to attend an informal gathering with conservatives at the Cafe Du Monde in the French Quarter. I went there from time to time when a student at New Orleans Seminary. I loved the beignets. The coffee was a little too strong for me. This was the place where Judge Paul Pressler and Paige Patterson met so many years ago to discuss how to return the SBC to its conservative roots. I was weary and in need of some fellowship. I invited parliamentarian Barry McCarty to go with me. There was quite a crowd there. We fellowshipped, laughed, ate beignets, and enjoyed ourselves. Someone suggested we sing "Victory in Jesus." Evidently the only one who could lead a song was Dr. McCarty. He did. There were moderates there. They were not happy. In retrospect I was just having a good time fellowshipping with conservative brothers who were my friends. I really didn't intend to offend. As I recall, I did what I customarily do. I went around and shook every hand, not knowing who was who.

I look back on those years with appreciation for the opportunity to do what I promised the Lord, as a college student, I would do—do something to address the problems of liberalism in the Southern Baptist Convention. I was just one of thousands of pastors and laypeople who wanted our convention to be Bible believing, evangelistic, and mission minded.

The politics, meetings, controversy, proceedings of the whole affair were uncomfortable to me. From that perspective I really didn't enjoy being president of the convention. Many friends of mine were moderates. I tried to maintain my friendship with them through it all. I believe I succeeded with most of them. I never did take the controversy personally. I was never offended at anyone who ran against me. I can truthfully say I have no animosity toward anyone. There is no one I do not love or refuse to pray for. I was just involved in something I believe the Lord intended. I was a part of something that had never happened before in Christian history. A denomination drifting toward liberalism returned to its conservative roots.

I made many mistakes. They were mistakes of the head, not the heart. I can testify to all that my desire was to do what the Lord wanted me to do. I await the judgment seat of Christ where my participation in the Conservative Resurgence will be examined by the One whose eyes are a flame of fire. Whatever is wood, hay, and stubble will go up in smoke. And I will be happy for that. Whatever is gold, silver, and precious stones will remain. I will be happy to lay all of that at the feet of Jesus.

Home Where I Belong

Now it is back to the work that brings me such joy. The work of serving as pastor of my beloved First Baptist Church, Jacksonville, Florida. As I stated, I never missed a Sunday as president of the SBC beyond those I normally missed every year. I did miss a great deal of the weekly activities. I didn't get to go on our weekly visitation every week. Committee meetings and preaching responsibilities throughout the convention caused me to miss a good many weekdays. Now I could return to my weekly joy of going into the homes of lost people and witnessing to them. To see people receive Christ as their Savior in their home was what made the bells ring in my heart. To see them come forward to make it public on Sunday was the cherry on top of the Sunday!

The New Auditorium

Several building projects were completed through the years. We built additional parking garages. The two services on Sunday morning were packed and running over. We needed a new auditorium. This was a major part of my work when I returned to Jacksonville. At the suggestion of Adrian Rogers, we contacted Roe Messner and secured his services to design a building for us. He was the best-known builder of large church auditoriums in America. Bellevue Baptist's new auditorium was designed and constructed by him. Between the time the building was designed, constructed, and completed, Bellevue experienced some problems. We made the decision to go with another company for the actual construction of the building. This turned out to be a wise decision. My friend Duke Westover, who had built the auditorium in Rome, Georgia, led this construction.

The building was to seat nine thousand to ten thousand. I felt the building was too large. I preferred seven thousand. My reasoning was that we could reach fourteen thousand in two Sunday morning services easier and sooner than we could reach ten thousand in one service. I lost the debate. Some thought it should be twelve thousand! On one occasion when Dr. Wiersbe was teaching in the new auditorium, he said, "To get from one side of this building to the other you have to pass through three time zones!"

The new auditorium was completed in 1993. What a grand opening day it was. Rodney Brooks, our minister of music, and Ed Dickinson, our orchestra director, prepared a program of glorious music to make the angels proud. The auditorium was packed. The day will be forever cherished in my heart. God helped us build an auditorium costing $18 million. And we entered the edifice debt free.

Soon after the auditorium was completed, I taught a special class in the old auditorium. I led the people in a survey of all the books in the Bible. I gave an introduction, synopsis, and outline of each of the sixty-six books in forty-four studies. The average attendance was between fifteen hundred and two thousand each Sunday night. Calling it "A Journey through the Bible," I have since made it available through my ministry.

I continued to do some writing. My biggest project in those years was the trilogy on the Holy Spirit. I was concerned about the charismatic movement. I felt it was presenting an incorrect view of the Holy Spirit and His work. Broadman published *Spirit Life* in 1998, *Spirit Works* in 1999, and *Spirit Fruit* in 2001. These were combined in 2010 as *The Spirit Book*. These books seem to have helped many benefit by the person and work of the Holy Spirit while avoiding some of the unbiblical extremes.

The Pastors' Conference

Through the years we continued our yearly pastors' conference and Bible conference. Soon after I arrived at First Baptist, Homer asked me to plan such a conference. He felt the things we did to reach people for Christ and help Christians grow in their Christian life were transferrable to other churches. Any church could follow our simple methods. If First Baptist could become "The Miracle of Downtown Jacksonville," as our church was called, other churches could grow and reach the lost. Our staff members and laypeople would have seminars covering every phase of our church's life and work.

I agreed with Homer. Our first conference was planned for 1985. The attendance was not earthshaking. As I recall, 120 were present. We conducted such a conference each year until we started construction of our new auditorium. The attendance was growing a little bit each year. But the attendance was not extraordinary. We suspended the conference during the construction of the new auditorium. The conference would be resumed when it was completed.

We did restart the pastors' conference in 1994. Attendance exploded. Pastors, staff members, and laypeople from all over the country and many foreign countries began to flock to the annual conference. They jammed the seminars covering everything from the music ministry to the baptismal committee. We developed a large notebook including basic information about every area of our church's ministry. Nothing was left unexplained. Every area of the work had a strategy and process to accomplish our goal of winning the lost and growing believers in the faith.

Several special opportunities were provided for the attendees. We served meals in the dining room. Our bookstore offered discounts on the purchase of books. Jim Tatum, one of our godly laymen, provided suits at an inexpensive price. We opened the conference with a sumptuous ban-quet on Friday night, followed by a music and testimony service.

The members of our church opened up their homes to attendees who could not afford hotel accommodations. This was most gracious on their part. Lasting bonds of love were established between many of our people and the people they hosted. Our people attended the evening sessions in great numbers. Many of them took a vacation that week so they could serve in the conference. One of the reasons for the great success of the conference was the participation and involvement of our people.

I didn't forget my country preacher pals. Danny Watters brought four of them each year to the conference. All expenses were paid for them. They had a great time, glorying in the music and preaching and cutting up with one another.

Music

The music of the conference became a major drawing card. One of my greatest joys was meeting with Rodney Brooks before the conference. He put the music together. We looked at every song, where it would fit best in the presentation, and how to arrange the entire music package for maximum blessing.

By watching our televised services, we came to understand the importance of having no dead time between any part of the service. On television a ten-second gap can seem like an eternity. So the music was presented in a seamless fashion. There was not a single second's gap between the various numbers. This created an air of excitement.

One feature I suggested to Rodney was a grand finale. At the end of the final session, the musicians would give a reprise of many of the numbers that had been used during the conference. And there would be a concluding presentation depicting the resurrection, ascension of our Lord, or some such exciting scene. This became one of the most anticipated parts of the meeting.

Preaching

I prayerfully sought the finest preachers and Bible teachers in America to be featured speakers. Dr. Warren Wiersbe and Dr. John Phillips did Bible studies in the morning sessions. They were both phenomenal Bible teachers.

I used a number of evangelists. Dr. Gene Williams and my son-in-law, Tim Williams, were used. Dr. Bailey Smith spoke. The favorite became Dr. Junior Hill. So much so that I had him every year until I left Jacksonville. He has continued to be a favorite. Junior is one of my best friends. We talk on a regular basis.

I used great preachers in the Southern Baptist Convention. They are too numerous to name. Drs. Charles Stanley, Tom Elliff, Jack Graham, Bobby Welch, and Ed Young, to name a few. Dr. Adrian Rogers preached every year. He normally was the closing speaker. I brought the finest Bible scholars from our colleges, seminaries, and denominational life. Drs. Paige Patterson, Danny Akin, Al Mohler, John Sullivan, Gray Allison, David Allen, and others preached.

I used men who were not in the Southern Baptist Convention. Dr. John McArthur spoke. Dr. Jerry Falwell preached on numerous occasions. There were others who graced our pulpit. I selected speakers not because of their denominational affiliation but for their faithfulness to the Word of God.

Preacher Fellowship

There was great camaraderie between the speakers. I always had a suite in the convention hotel where the speakers would gather for food and fellowship before and after the evening sessions. We laughed and wept and prayed and preached to one another. Some classic exchanges took place.

After talking much with him about it, Jerry Falwell became a Southern Baptist. Shortly thereafter his trousers came unbuckled at an inauguration ball for Ronald Reagan. We brought him before a "Southern Baptist Court" to deal with him. We made him promise never to let that happen again and embarrass Southern Baptists. He dutifully promised.

Drs. W. A. Criswell and John McArthur were on the same program one year. Dr. Criswell sat down beside John and proceeded to give him a doctrinal quiz. John was like a little schoolboy in the presence of the patriarch.

"Lad, do you believe in salvation by grace?"

"Yes sir," John responded.

"Do you believe in baptism by immersion?"

"Yes sir."

Several other pertinent questions were asked; John replied in the affirmative. Then Dr. Criswell slapped Dr. McArthur on the leg and said, "Why Lad, you're a Southern Baptist!"

Criswell Is in the House

The most moving session of any in the conference was the night when Dr. Criswell preached. Perhaps it was the last time he ever preached a full message. He came into the building adorned in his dark suit, his wavy white hair shining. When he stood to preach, Homer and I had to help him to the pulpit. I thought, *He's not going to be able to preach.* But preach he did. He preached on "The Old-Time Religion." That dear man of God, in his nineties, got stronger and stronger as he preached. He closed by leading the congregation in singing "'Tis the old-time religion, 'Tis the old-time religion. 'Tis the old-time religion, and it's good enough for me." He left the building; it was like Moses saying good-bye to the children of Israel. To this day, with all the new, way-out stuff going on, I still sing with Dr. Criswell, "'Tis the old-time religion, it's good enough for me."

Junior Hill said something to me I believe is true. He said, "For many people the pastors' conference became an annual homecoming. They saw friends from across the country. They developed friendships with many of our laypeople. The gathering was one big, happy time when a multitude of God's people got together."

A large part of the attendance was made up of rural pastors and their people. Many of these precious men needed to come to a place where they would receive encouragement and inspiration. I always asked my speakers to seek to encourage and uplift. So many of these rural servants of God are in difficult, struggling places. We provided a setting where they would hear great old-time music. They would hear splendid Bible preaching. They would rub shoulders with some choice men of God.

The conference also became a rallying place for the Conservative Resurgence. This was not the reason for its inception. But, as the years went by, more and more people came to see it fulfilled that function. On several occasions the conservative candidate for president was presented there. This was not by plan either; it just became a natural place for that to be done.

Looking back, I consider the pastors' conference and Bible conference to be one of the greatest ministries of our First Baptist fellowship. I hear constantly from men who attended every year without fail. In later years several thousand would register. At the conclusion of my last conference, it was estimated that fourteen thousand people showed up for the final night.

I have been told by several that the annual First Baptist Jacksonville Pastors' Conference is my most significant contribution to God's work. This may be true. I will again await the final evaluation at the judgment seat of Christ.

Just around the corner was an unexpected event that would change the direction of my ministry again.

Chapter 17

Men of God and Muhammed

O
ur 2000 pastors' conference promised to be the best one ever. I secured a "who's who" of preachers and Bible teachers. Rodney prepared a smorgasbord of gospel music. Registration was at an all-time high. The opening Friday night banquet and special service always set the tone for the conference. The people gathered. The music and testimonies were outstanding. Homer's son, Homer G., was in attendance.

Homer G.

Homer G. was one of the sweetest, most delightful young men I ever knew. I remember well staying at the Lindsay's house during a revival meeting. He was just beginning tuba lessons. The sound was like a big airplane trying to take off! I told him in later years that enduring those first rehearsals gave me some stock in his orchestra performances. He stayed at our house in Rome during a revival there before our move to Jacksonville.

Homer G. was experiencing some chest pains. During the Friday evening service he went into the bathroom. He fell to the floor. An emergency vehicle rushed him to the hospital. When the service was over, I went to the hospital to be with his dad and family. Homer G. had experienced a massive heartache. He didn't survive. The family was crushed. Homer Junior had thought the doctors would pull him through. They did not.

Homer G.'s death put a gloom over the conference. Things were just not the same. I conducted the funeral. Homer was there in a wheelchair. He was obviously very sick. And brokenhearted because of the death of his only son.

In December of the previous year Homer announced to the congregation he was going to retire. I was planning to have a glorious celebration for him. He would never make it to a retirement celebration. He would go to a glorious homecoming celebration in heaven.

Homer Junior

Homer was obviously very sick. Several times I suggested that he go to MD Anderson in Houston, Texas. My friend, Dr. Ed Young, told me he would handle all the arrangements. Homer chose not to go. He lived only days after Homer G. died. Official cause of death was a cancerous mass at the base of his spine. But I believe there was an additional cause. He died of a broken heart.

On Saturday night Homer was rushed to the hospital. He would not live long. I visited him at the hospital several times. Because it was Sunday, I had to be at the church to preach and comfort the people. The last time I saw Homer in ICU, I leaned over him and said with tears, "I love you, Homer. I'm going to preach the Word now." He died later that night, February 13, 2000.

The funeral was a wonderful celebration. A large crowd attended. Preachers from all over the Southern Baptist Convention gathered. Dr. Paige Patterson delivered an evangelistic message and gave a public invitation for people to come to Christ. I spoke on the passage about Elisha in 2 Kings 4, where it was said of him, "Behold now, I perceive that this is an holy man of God, which passeth by us continually" (v. 9). I applied the words to Homer Lindsay Jr. I said, "I don't know of a Scripture that more epitomizes to me the life and ministry of Homer Lindsay Jr. than right there. . . . I'm so thankful this man of God passed by me and touched me. He passed by Jacksonville, and he has left his mark on the city of Jacksonville."

Homer was a most remarkable man. There was a simple, almost child-like quality about him. He was bold as a lion yet childlike and playful. He and I served together as a team. We didn't always agree on every decision. We did agree we wanted to reach Jacksonville for Christ. His ability to take the principles found in the New Testament and put them to work at First Baptist Church was without doubt a gift from the Lord. He is acknowledged as the greatest church builder of his generation.

Church Builder

He put together a total church program that was simple on the out-side, yet complex on the inside. He was like a championship football coach. He developed detailed processes for every area of the church's life and work. Nothing was left to chance. His organization of the church's programs was amazing. To Homer Lindsay Jr. goes the human credit for the "Miracle of Downtown Jacksonville."

His love for Jesus and the lost was his crowning characteristic. Few men I have ever known manifested such a deep, genuine love for the Lord Jesus. His goal was to teach the people of the church to have that same kind of love. Thousands will testify that Homer taught them to love the Lord Jesus Christ. He possessed a burning passion to see lost people saved. He instilled that same kind of love in the people. Thousands will declare Homer gave them the desire and the know-how to lead people to personal faith in Jesus Christ. Only in heaven will see the fruit so carefully cultivated by this "holy man of God who passed by."

Going It Alone

I was now the sole pastor of the church. When I came there in 1982, the people understood I was being called as their pastor. Now I was pastor without the benefit and blessing of my true yokefellow, Homer.

My immediate task was to lead the people through the grieving process. They must have time to mourn the loss of their beloved pastor. I did not attempt to introduce any new programs. I made only minor changes. The people needed to go through a time of mourning and healing due to their great loss. I would demonstrate continuity with the ministry that had gone on before. They needed to know they could continue to trust me as their pastor.

We did build a state-of-the-art children's building. The building had been in the planning stage many months before Homer's death. What a building it is! Some have described it as a "Disney World for Jesus." Each department had a theme. We had a Jonah's whale slide for the children. There was a Kidz Theatre where Bible events could be presented. One of the most popular was David and Goliath. Tim Tebow played the part of Goliath. The church was doing well.

2000 Baptist Faith and Message Revision

On a Southern Baptist level I still maintained a presence. I was not as actively involved as I had been before. I did serve on the Baptist Faith and Message Revision Committee of 2000. Dr. Paige Patterson, then president of the convention, asked me to serve. I was not an effective member of the committee. Homer was increasingly sick, and I stayed as close to home as possible. I was not able to give my full attention and input on the committee to the degree I otherwise would have. I was able to have a revision made in the BFM that clarified what Southern Baptists believed about the Holy Spirit. But, other than that, I looked to others on the committee to do the larger share of the work.

Although I was up to my earlobes in my work, I did publish *Pursuing God's Own Heart* in 2003. This was a treatment of the life and times of David. Broadman graciously published this work for me. Nancy Smith Bethea, a gifted member of our church, assisted me in making the transition from oral to written English. She was helpful on several volumes.

Islam and Muhammad

I was still speaking at convention events. I was privileged to speak many years at the annual SBC Pastors' Conference. I was invited to speak in the Saint Louis meeting. I prepared a message entitled "Some Silver, a Suit, and a Meal Ticket." This was a message to pastors taken from the book of Judges. My main thrust was to encourage pastors to be faithful and courageous to their calling.

The annual meeting was held in June 2002. The terrorist attack on the World Trade Center took place September 11, 2001. The attack was an act of war perpetrated by radical Muslims. At the time Islam was not widely understood in America. After the attacks there were many voices, even those at the White House, who proclaimed that Islam was a religion of peace. I knew this to be untrue. There are, of course, many, Muslims who are peace-loving people. But there is a violent strain in Islam that comes directly from their founder, Muhammad, and their book, the Quran. I was pretty fed up with all the incorrect information being disseminated.

The night of my message, I was addressing a Southern Baptist Pastors' Conference. I was not speaking on a national platform. Had I been, I would have taken a far different approach. However, in my message I was trying to contrast the differences between Christianity and Islam. I said, "Allah is not Jehovah. . . . Jehovah is not going to turn you into a terrorist who will try to bomb people and take the lives of thousands of people." Then I contrasted the founder of Christianity, Jesus Christ, and the founder of Islam, Muhammad. I said, "Christianity was founded by the virgin-born Jesus Christ" while "Islam was founded by Muhammad, a demon-possessed pedophile who had twelve wives, and his last one was a nine-year-old girl."

There was a reporter in the audience from the *Houston Chronicle*. He took my statement, put it on AP, and the story was scattered worldwide. Jerry Falwell was in the audience. He leaned over to a friend and said, "He'll hear from that."

After the service I was going to dinner with friends. My cell phone rang. My son, Jon, said, "Dad, you're on worldwide television."

"I am?" I responded.

He told me my statement was all over the news. That was when I became aware of the furor my statement had caused.

I got my information from a book by the Caner brothers, *Unveiling Islam*. In it they document that Muhammad feared he was possessed by a demon and that he consummated his marriage to Aisha when she was nine. These facts have never been challenged by knowledgeable Muslims. As I said, had I been speaking on a national platform, I would have expressed myself differently. But I made the statement at a pastors' conference.

I was totally unprepared for the firestorm. Passing through the Atlanta Airport to change planes, I saw Jerry Falwell on CNN defending me. Hundreds of people were gathered around the television, watching. They had no idea the man who started the furor was standing there watching with them.

I must address my congregation the next Sunday. I refused any comment to newspapers, telling them my people would hear from me first. The Bible teaches, "In the multitude of counsellors there is safety" (Prov. 11:14). I arranged a conference call with Paige Patterson, Al Mohler, and Jerry Falwell. They gave me good, wise counsel. I prepared a statement for my church.

Sunday came. There were all kinds of rumors. There would be thousands around the church protesting. There would be attempts on my life. Security at the church was beefed up. That morning I went about my normal routine. Janet always played hymns on the piano as I got ready for church. That morning she was playing and went into "Precious Memories."

"O Lord, is this it?" Actually, throughout the whole ordeal I had a supernatural peace. There was not one moment of fear. "Thou wilt keep him in perfect peace, whose mind is stayed on thee: because he trusteth in thee" (Isa. 26:3).

When I arrived at church, there were two signs and three protestors. One of them mistakenly thought he was there to picket for the legalization of marijuana! When I entered the auditorium, the people stood and applauded. I made my statement at the beginning of the service. I did not back down. I stood by my comments. I told the people where I got my information. I said, "If I have misread this information, I would be glad for Muslim scholars to explain their own documents to us all." At the conclusion I said, "I love Muslim people. I have found many of them to be kind, gentle, and loving people. . . . Many Muslims have come to our church to hear of the love, joy, peace, and saving grace available to all in Jesus Christ." The people gave me several standing ovations. The service continued. I preached. Many came forward making their public professions in Jesus Christ. When I went to my car, the door was opened by one of my security men—a Muslim!

The Aftermath

There were calls for meetings, appearances on TV programs, all kinds of things. I said, "I do not have much time to attend meetings, appear on TV programs, or do extensive interviews. I have no plans to speak on this matter further."

I deviated from that intention only one time. In 2003 Tom Brokaw on *NBC Nightly News* did a story on my statement. The story was a smear piece. He implied that I and First Baptist, Jacksonville, were hatemongers. I publicly challenged Brokaw or anyone else to cite one single statement I ever made that demonstrated I was hate filled. He nor anyone else ever did. I never retracted my statement. I stood by the truthfulness of what I said. No one has challenged its truthfulness.

The hate mail I received was unbelievable. There were constant threats on my life. This continued for several years. Again, let me say, there was not one moment of fear. Through it all God gave me His presence and protection and power.

Sometime later Dr. Patterson told me something encouraging about the whole matter. He said he believed my statement would result in the salvation of millions of Muslims. He felt my reference to Muhammad's marriage to a nine-year-old girl was not known to most Muslims worldwide. He believed it would cause them to search their own religious documents. They would find I spoke the truth. As a result many would turn from Islam to Christianity. I do not know. I do know that in the years after my statement there have been reports of millions of Muslims coming to faith in the Lord Jesus Christ. If my statement had any part in that, the persecutions and threats I experienced are all worth it. The joy of heaven will be increased for me if saved Muslims thank me for my statement.

There were many unusual experiences in those years when I shouldered the responsibilities of a twenty-eight thousand plus congregation without Homer. I continued to speak out on controversial issues. I always took a stand on moral issues.

The Devil and Marilyn Manson

The members of FBC, Jacksonville were accustomed to their pastor taking strong stands. Back in 1997 when shock rocker Marilyn Manson came to town for a concert, I opposed it. I went to see Mayor John Delaney. He joined me in opposition. I preached a sermon entitled "The Devil and Marilyn Manson." I didn't attack the rocker as a person. I even offered to meet with him. We couldn't keep him from coming to Jacksonville. We did greatly reduce his crowd. So much so he said in his book he would never be coming back to Jacksonville!

Paul McCormick, a Jacksonville public relations consultant, said, "First Baptist doesn't just sit on the sidelines. It engages in promoting politics and spirituality as partners."

I said: "More and more, we understand that our role as Christians is to involve ourselves in the spiritual life of the city. We don't endorse candidates, but we do set forth truth as far as moral and ethical issues."[27]

Super Bowl Halftime Show

Following the famous "wardrobe malfunction" of Janet Jackson at the Super Bowl XXXVIII, I told the people in our 2004 pastors' conference that, though I was glad to have Super Bowl XXXIX come to Jacksonville, they could "leave their filth out." I publicly announced to the city of Jacksonville and the NFL that they'd better decide then to keep their halftime program clean and not have to deal with me the entire year. Shortly after that I received a letter from NFL Commissioner Paul Tagliabue, assuring me the halftime show would not be offensive. He kept his word. The old Beatle, Paul McCartney, then in his sixties, was the halftime entertainment in 2005. I have always felt like the church should be a force for decency and morality in its community.

Adrian Rogers Flies Away to Jesus

In November 2005 I lost another close friend. Adrian Rogers went home to heaven. Adrian's illness was brief. He was taken from us rather suddenly. He retired as pastor of Bellevue Baptist Church. He was beginning to hold seminars and conferences on preaching. His Adrian Rogers Pastor Training Institute was designed to train pastors. I never understood why God took Adrian when He did. There are surely reasons He will make plain on the other side.

I was asked by Joyce to have part in the celebration service. Charles Stanley, Fred Wolfe, and I flew together to Memphis. Thousands were present for the beautifully moving service. I was honored to say a few words about my dear friend. He was the greatest preacher I ever heard. He was the perfect Christian gentleman. He never compromised; he never behaved in a less than Christian manner. I look forward to greeting him just inside heaven's pearly gates. His TV ministry *Love Worth Finding* continues until this day. I find it difficult to watch. I continue to grieve our loss but rejoice that my friend is in the presence of the Savior he so loves and so magnified when he preached.

The Perfect Fit

The people of First Baptist, Jacksonville, were a perfect fit for me. I felt completely comfortable there. They loved me, prayed for me, supported me, and followed me. I enjoyed preaching in the Jacksonville pulpit more than anywhere else on earth. I gave the best years of my life to the ministry there. I was sure I could continue as their pastor until health or death prevented further ministry.

I served as a pastor of Baptist churches since I was an eighteen-year-old boy. Fifty years in all. I served as pastor of rural churches, neighborhood churches, and city churches. I was pastor of congregations with fewer than one hundred people and congregations numbered in the thousands. Nothing brought me greater joy and fulfillment. I was soon coming to the conclusion of my pastoral years.

Chapter 18

Why Did He?

S everal years ago I heard about a pastor who resigned unexpectedly from his church. The people were surprised. Many began to inquire, "Why did he?" In explanation the wise pastor said, "I'd rather people be asking, 'Why did he?' than 'Why don't he?'"

Things were going well at First Baptist, Jacksonville. I was relatively free from Southern Baptist matters. There was a capable, dedicated staff to assist me in the work. The people seemed happy. They were taught since the days of Dr. Homer Lindsay Sr. to follow the leadership of their pastor. They were supportive of me. Christians were growing in their faith. People were steadily being saved and joining the fellowship. All the signs indicated to me I could stay as pastor of the church as long as I desired or health permitted.

The Time Has Come

Some factors caused me to think the time had come for me to step aside as pastor of my "dream church." Many years before I came to Jacksonville, the decision was made to remain downtown. The reasoning was that, regardless of how the neighborhoods around the center of the city grew or declined, the church would always be central to the population. By means of the city's bridges, people had access to the church from any of the surrounding areas. I would have concurred with the decision. The demographics made sense. Also, I felt there needed to be a strong Christian presence in the heart of the city.

But the demographics did a strange thing. Though surrounding neighborhoods did grow and decline, something else occurred. Jacksonville began to grow southward. When I first came to Jacksonville, there was little population growth south. Almost without notice, though, people began to move south. In the early years a few small churches could be seen there. In the years after the turn of the new century, the churches became larger. The population center got farther and farther away from downtown.

This population shift created some problems for us. First, the distance became greater. This had not been a problem previously. A number of members came from towns as far as fifty miles from Jacksonville. There were even a few from Georgia who made the journey to FBC, Jacksonville on Sunday. Many of them used the familiar phrase, "The difference is worth the distance." So distance wasn't a big problem on Sunday.

The distance became a problem on Wednesday night. People found it difficult, if not impossible, to get off work, gather the family, and head to downtown Jacksonville. Many families couldn't make it work. Our members recognized that our youth and children's ministries were A+ in quality. However, if they couldn't get there, they had to do something else. Churches in the south corridors with B ministries were chosen.

There was another problem. The getting-off traffic in Jacksonville was horrendous. This could lengthen and complicate the travel time on Wednesday nights. Though many families attempted to bring their families to all the activities, many did not. We were having to work hard to maintain our attendance. Attendance still exceeded three thousand on Wednesday nights. The Wednesday night program was tweaked. This helped, but there were still difficulties.

Another problem complicated things for the church. Dr. Lindsay Jr. had put together what I consider to be the finest, most comprehensive and cohesive church program ever developed. He tied the Sunday morning, Sunday evening, Wednesday evening, and other facets of the church's program together in a masterful way. I often compared it to an erector set.

Though something built with an erector set looks simple on the outside, it is actually complicated and intricate on the inside. This was the way our total church program for every member of the family was organized. Though we knew certain parts weren't functioning as well as they had, we couldn't figure out how you could tweak or change them without the entire construction collapsing.

Younger Leadership

I began to sense younger leadership was needed to best address these kinds of problems. The only solution I could see for the southward trend of the population center was to start a south campus. This would require a great deal of planning and work. A temporary meeting place would be needed. Staff would have to be assembled. Land for permanent buildings would need to be acquired. This would call for a leader younger than I. I still had a lot of energy but not that much!

I was also experiencing some minor health problems. In 2000, the morning after Homer died, I woke up with an unusual feeling in my chest. I was scheduled for my annual physical that day. In the process they discovered I was experiencing atrial fibrillation, or an irregular heartbeat. Because my father and both grandfathers died with stroke, they prescribed coumadin. This blood thinner was to lower the percentages of possible stroke.

I was also experiencing some vision issues. Reading was becoming difficult for me. I wore contacts for many years. I used reading glasses for my study. The preparation of three messages each week in a different book of the Bible required a huge amount of reading. I read forty plus hours per week. My vision difficulties made this hard.

The church was familiar and comfortable with the co-pastor model. Homers Sr. and Jr. functioned in that arrangement well. Homer Jr. and I worked together in that model for eighteen years. I thought maybe the answer was to bring in a man to minister as co-pastor alongside me. I spent many months seeking a younger pastor to come to Jacksonville. In all I talked with five men. I traveled to their place of service. I laid the proposal before them. After prayer all five men turned me down. I have chosen not to give the names of any of them. I will leave it up to them to give their names, if they so desire.

I could only take this to mean the Lord intended something else for the church. The conviction was growing in my heart that the time had come for new leadership at the church. The church must seek its next pastor.

I met privately with a small group of men who were in the inner circle of lay leadership of the church. We met in the same suite at the Omni where my pastors' conference speakers gatherings were held. These men were proven and trusted. They were godly men. They were men who knew how to lead others to Christ. They were totally involved in every activity of the church. They served on the finance committee. They loved the Lord and me, their pastor. I would have willingly gone to war with these men.

I told these men what I believed God wanted me to do. I gave the reasons I have already enumerated in this chapter. They seemed surprised but also understanding and appreciative of my reasoning. I shared with them my futile attempts to find someone to serve as co-pastor with me. I told them this convinced me the Lord wanted the church to choose its next pastor. According to the church's bylaws the chairmen of the deacons and finance committee were to appoint a pulpit committee (now routinely called a search committee). Nelson Sturgill and David Bristowe were respective chairmen at that time. The men understood the process. I suggested a six-month period of time before my retirement was final. They asked me to extend it to nine months to give adequate time to find a new pastor. I agreed to do so.

The Announcement

On May 1, 2005, I announced to the congregation my plans to retire. I would continue on until the last night of the annual pastors' conference in February 2006. In a written statement I said: "I want you to make this not a sad time but a time of recommitment to the Lord. My prayer is that these months ahead will be the greatest months in the history of our church." I explained the secrecy surrounding my plans and the sudden announcement. But I wanted the congregation to hear the news from me rather than getting it through the media. Then I said, "This has been kind of a hard day." After the closing prayer I walked through the congregation as I left the building. I spoke briefly to the media after the service.

I guess some were sad; perhaps others were glad! Many questions were asked. "Why did he?" Now it was time for me to use the phrase I borrowed from someone else: "I'd rather people ask, 'Why did he?' than 'Why don't he?'" I watched some athletes play past their prime. I watched some great men stay too long at their churches. I tried to learn from their mistakes. I have felt comfortable from that day to this. I know I did what the Lord intended for me to do.

I did get one letter of rebuke from another pastor. I never heard of the man before. He wrote to me that I was out of the will of God. He said nowhere in the Bible does it say a pastor was to retire. The dear man didn't understand. I wasn't retiring from the ministry. I was retiring as a pastor. I was retiring for a new ministry. I intended to keep on rolling for Jesus!

Pulpit Committee

Something historic was happening to the church. For the first time in over sixty-five years there was a pulpit committee to prayerfully find the next pastor of FBC, Jacksonville. I explained to the people the process for forming such a committee as stated in the bylaws. I then announced the committee that had been chosen by the deacon chairman and finance chairman: Jud Whorton, chairman; Guinell Freeman; Robert Harrison; David Hodges; James Ingoldsby; David Kay; Tom Stimler; and Ricky Wallace.

I never tried to steer the committee toward anyone, contrary to what some thought. I met with the committee one time. I told them everything I knew about the responsibilities and work of a pulpit committee. I gave them all the warnings I could. I gave them all the encouragements I could. After about an hour and a half, I told the committee I would be praying for them. If they wanted any further counsel from me, they would have to ask.

I gave myself in the closing months of my ministry at First Baptist to preaching and encouraging the people. I sought to get them ready for the next man. I encouraged them to pray for the committee and the man God was preparing for them.

Preaching through the Bible

Something meaningful happened in my preaching in those closing months. During the almost twenty-four years of my pastorate there, I went systematically through books of the Bible. I did then, and do now, believe this is the best preaching a pastor can do. There were certain books I preached through several times like Philippians, Genesis, 1 Thessalonians, etc. I also moved on to books not previously expounded. The only pastor I knew who preached a series through every book of the Bible was my great hero and mentor, Dr. W. A. Criswell. I didn't set out to emulate him; it's just what happened through the years of my pulpit ministry in Jacksonville.

When I came to my final months, there was only one book remaining: the book of Deuteronomy. As I prepared and preached messages through Deuteronomy, I saw it is a series of farewell messages from Moses to the children of Israel! Perfect! What better way to complete preaching through the Bible than that. I was able to give the people counsel and encouragement by means of Moses' farewell sermons.

Through the years I marveled at how the Lord led me into particular books of the Bible at just the right time in the life of the church. Sometimes the book would address problems I didn't even know would surface at that time. There are many reasons I know the Bible is God's inerrant Word. To see the leading of the Holy Spirit in preaching its truths to the people is one of the most convincing ones.

I strongly encourage young pastors to prayerfully consider preaching books of the Bible. Certainly other ways can be effective. But there is nothing so effective as systematically expounding to the people what God has to say, book by book.

Retirement Celebrations

I asked Rodney Brooks to plan and arrange the retirement activities. No one can plan programs better than Rodney. He outdid himself. There were special events. For the staff there was a formal dinner at one of the exclusive clubs in the city. The staff was so kind and gracious to me and Janet. They gave us lovely gifts. My favorite was the gift of season tickets to the Alabama Crimson Tide football games! I am not going to name all of my staff members at Jacksonville. I'm afraid I might leave someone out! At the time of my retirement, I believed it was the most dedicated, effective staff to assist me in my entire ministry.

There was a special time of celebration with the deacons and wives. Joe Kines, then defensive coordinator for the Alabama football team, was the featured speaker. I was Joe's pastor back in Cedartown, you may recall. He really turned the people on! What a sweet time it was. They gave me lovely chairs for my study. Every time I see them I am reminded of the wonderful, faithful men who served as deacons through the years.

Sometime after our delightful banquet together, I attended my final deacons' meeting. In my almost twenty-four years there, the deacons' meetings were special times of prayer, rejoicing, and blessing. Not one time in those years did I encounter a negative vote, an unkind word, or a disrespectful act toward me. That night we laughed, wept, hugged, and prayed together. Then I got in my car and drove home from my final deacons' meeting. I was not alone in the car. I carried them and all the deacons I knew through the years with me in my car and in my heart and in my memories

A lovely luncheon was planned for Janet. She invited ladies who were a special blessing to her. From her hairdresser to ladies in the church! They showered her with lovely gifts and sweet words of encouragement.

There was a special time with the support staff at the church. I was grateful for my two superior assistants, Shirley Cannon and Jacki Raulerson. Both approached their work as a ministry, not just a job. I always appreciated the secretaries and those who did the most menial tasks. The housekeepers were some of our finest workers. They helped keep things moving forward. The last time I spent with them was most special.

Elaborate plans were made for my retirement to coincide with the pastors' conference. Rodney built it around the theme "A Faithful Soldier." A special devotional book by that name was prepared. The book contained devotionals from family members, church members, and pastor friends from all over the country. A brief historical sketch was also included. Pictures were in the book as well. I treasure that book.

I want to reiterate, there is no way I can mention all of the faithful staff members who assisted me in the ministry at First Baptist, Jacksonville. They know who they are. They never served to get their name in my book in the first place! Their names are on the roll of the faithful; they will receive proper recognition and reward at the judgment seat of Christ.

My Final Pastors' Conference

The days of the final pastors' conference were like heaven on earth to me. My best preacher friends from all over the nation were there. Each night after the sessions, special gatherings were held. Good friends like Paige Patterson and O. S. Hawkins roasted me. None can do it any better than Paige and O. S.! What a happy, hilarious time we had.

The sessions of the conference were electric. On Friday night they devoted the entire time to my retirement. The music was designed around my favorite numbers. The choir and orchestra never sounded better. This was just the prelude to the music and preaching for my final conference as pastor of First Baptist Church, Jacksonville.

I was to preach the closing message of the conference. The Lord led me to preach my message "Glimpses of Glory." I preached it several times through the years in conferences and other settings. I preached a series on glory at Jacksonville but not one single message on the subject. As I always do, I studied through the Bible passages again. I sought new and fresh illustrations. I brought the message up-to-date in terms of what was going on in the culture and in the churches. I was ready to preach the message.

But there was one remaining detail. How would I end message? I really did not have a clue. The Lord didn't let me know how to conclude until that Tuesday afternoon. Perfect. That's exactly how I would do it.

The final session came Tuesday night. I was told that fourteen thousand plus showed up for the service. There were several overflow rooms. People lined the walls. The music package was presented. I preached the message. The people were attentive and responsive. I came to the conclusion of the message. And, just as the Lord led me to do, I walked off the pulpit preaching. I walked up the aisle preaching. I thanked the people for glimpsing the glory with me for almost twenty-four years preaching. Then I walked out of the building preaching.

I always wanted to see the grand finale from the balcony. That's where I went. I sat up there and through tear-filled eyes witnessed my last grand finale as the pastor of FBC, Jacksonville.

After the service, as was my custom, I gathered with some special friends at Ruth's Chris for a good steak dinner. I went home to bed. I was no longer a pastor. Precious memories were flooding my heart. A long list of friends slowly passed through my soul. Some already there; some still here. Friends, you know, are forever, if the Lord's the Lord of them.

So, where shall this ex-pastor live?

Chapter 19

Georgia on My Mind

Georgia, Georgia, The whole day through. Just an old sweet song keeps Georgia on my mind. . . . Other arms reach out to me. Other eyes smile tenderly. Still in peaceful dreams I see, the road leads back to you." So sang Georgia native, Ray Charles. Ironically, the song was written by Hoagy Carmichael and Stuart Gorrell, both Indiana natives. Perhaps they wrote about it with secondhand information. Willie Nelson and others also recorded it. None sang it with such poignancy and longing as did Ray Charles.

Where to Live

I was something of a schizophrenic when it came to my place to live during my retirement years. I well remember my pastor saying to me when I was planning to go to a college out of state, "Do you want to preach and pastor in Georgia?" Never did it occur to me the Lord would want me to preach anywhere else! Turns out I was pastor in three states: Alabama, Florida, and Georgia. And through the years I have preached in most of the states of the Union and in several foreign countries. My pastoral ministry was confined to those three states.

I love all three states where I served as pastor. My years in Alabama were blessed. I look back on them with more mature eyes and now know the Lord gave me some of my best messages there. He taught me ministry lessons about being a pastor and life lessons about the Christian life that have served me well all through these years.

My years in Florida were the best years of my ministry. For almost a quarter of a century I preached, witnessed, served, and lived in the fellowship of a church that was the closest to the New Testament pattern I have ever seen. The blessed attachments I developed in First Baptist and the city of Jacksonville itself would not be easy to sever.

My football loyalties pretty much illustrate my state schizophrenia. I was an Alabama fan from Georgia living in Florida! How did that happen? When I was pastor at West Rome Baptist in Georgia, a fine young person named David Watkins was a member and star high school football player. David played defensive end at Alabama when Bear Bryant was the coach. I used to go over to see him play. Alabama was winning big. The atmosphere was southern class at its finest. In those years you could see ladies in their mink coats and their husbands in their overcoats, with their houndstooth hats. I was impressed. So I became an Alabama fan.

Tim Tebow was brought up in our church in Jacksonville. His dad, Bob, served as chaplain of Jon's high school team. I saw Tim play football at Neese High School. There was no question in my mind Tim would become a superstar. My jogging buddy was a retired FBI man from Pittsburgh. He told me a friend of his watched Joe Namath play in high school. "This Tebow kid will be as good as Namath or better."

Tim was highly recruited. Alabama wanted him bad. Joe Kines often talked with me about it. Alabama's head coach, Mike Shula, pursued Tim. I never put pressure on Tim. I just told him to do what the Lord wanted him to do. On signing day Joe called and told me Coach Shula wanted me to tell him what I thought Tim would do. I told him both of Tim's parents were Florida graduates. Tim was a huge a Florida fan; I predicted Florida. That day he committed to play for the Florida Gators. At my last pastors' conference Tim gave his testimony. We both joked a little about the Florida-Alabama thing. After he spoke, I said, "I hope you win the Heisman Trophy, Tim." Turns out my statement was prophetic!

Tim made it really hard on me for four years. I wanted him to do well. I also pulled for Alabama in their classic matchups with Florida. I just told people I hoped Tim threw for four hundred yards, ran for two hundred yards, passed for four touchdowns and ran for two. And that Alabama won by one point!

Seriously, I have been proud of Tim's tremendous testimony through the years of his career. Since his high school days he has been faithful to the Lord Jesus Christ. Football is a game. I enjoy it. But the real game is the game of life. Tim has demonstrated how to win in the game of life. He is a fabulous role model for young people.

Now back to our return to Georgia. Our roots were deep in Jacksonville. Scores of friends would be left behind, should we move away. We were close to so many, in and out of the fellowship of First Baptist Church. We could have happily retired and lived out our lives in Jacksonville. We did seriously consider doing just that. I even looked at some places where we might build a retirement home. But there were compelling reasons that made it clear to me the Lord wanted us to move back to our home state of Georgia.

New Pastor Mac Brunson

The church would have a new pastor. The pulpit committee presented Dr. Mac Brunson to the congregation. Dr. Brunson, pastor of First Baptist Church, Dallas, Texas, was to be the next pastor. We left in February; Dr. Brunson and his family came to Jacksonville in April 2006. Dr. Brunson was now the pastor of the church, not I.

I believed it was best for him that I not be in the city and the church. I am aware others choose to remain where they served as pastor. Each retiring pastor must make that decision for himself.

For me, I didn't think he needed me to be around. My friend, O. S. Hawkins, told me something I have never forgotten; and it's very true. He said, "A pastor's tenure at a church is a snapshot in time." My ministry at First Baptist, Jacksonville, is now over. The snapshot has been taken. The next pastor will have his snapshot in time.

I have heard and seen the horror stories of retiring pastors who can't take their hands off the reins of leadership. This has caused a great deal of heartache and sorrow for many pastors and churches. I determined I was going to gracefully step away from the church. The best way for me to do that was to move back to Georgia.

I am no longer pastor of the church. I am no longer responsible so I am no longer accountable. My role is to pray for the church and my successor. I faithfully pray for the church and Dr. Brunson. Every Sunday morning I send him an e-mail or text message. I assure him of my prayers for him as he preaches the Word that day.

Dr. Brunson is most kind and gracious to me. Soon after his arrival he announced I was pastor emeritus of the church. I appreciated this so much. He has me return annually to preach at the pastors' conference. Every retiring pastor should have a successor with the kind of respect and spirit Dr. Brunson has demonstrated to me.

Getting Family Matters Arranged

One pressure made the move more difficult. Jodi, our special-needs daughter, wanted to remain in Jacksonville. All of her friends and relationships are there. She is assisted in her living arrangements by an excellent program provided by the state of Florida. Those who assist Jodi told us it would be better for everything to be set up for her while Janet and I are alive. This would be preferable than it being done after our deaths. We felt better about it. Things have worked out beautifully. Jodi has her own apartment. She has a job. She is active in the choir. She has scores of friends. She is constantly on the go. We talk with her on the phone virtually every day. Our fears about leaving her there were unfounded.

Totsi, my father, Clarence Vines, died in 2005. He was eighty-eight. My mother, Ruby, died in 2008. She was ninety-four. I spoke at both funerals. I gave tribute to both of them for the Christian home they provided and their prayers and support for my ministry. My sister, Brenda, was a fabulous caregiver. I lived in Florida for their declining years. When they were no longer able to care for themselves, we helped them move into a fine assisted-living facility. I handled the financial arrangements. Brenda was there to give them hands-on service. No brother could have a finer sister; no parents could have a finer daughter.

First Baptist, Woodstock, Georgia

Sometime before my retirement Johnny Hunt asked me to have lunch with him when I was in Atlanta. He told me when I retired he would like for me to consider moving up near his church, First Baptist, Woodstock. He would assist us in getting a home built. He asked me to consider doing some preaching on Sunday night for him. At the time he was unaware just how close I was to announcing my retirement. I told him I would pray about it.

I preached at First Baptist, Woodstock, on many occasions through the years. When I preached there, I was thrilled to see how close it was to the kind of ministry we had in Jacksonville. I was blessed by the glorious evangelistic, gospel music. The people were warm and responsive, very much like FBC, Jacksonville.

After prayer I came to the definite conclusion this is what the Lord wanted us to do. I agreed to preach a number of Sunday nights at Woodstock. There was a clear understanding this was my one and only responsibility. I was not a member of the staff. I would not attend any meetings. I was to preach some on Sunday nights.

Janet and I made several visits to the Woodstock area. Johnny and his Janet graciously hosted us in their home. Members of First Baptist Woodstock assisted us in locating the lot, building the house, and furnishing it. I will always be grateful and thankful for Johnny's graciousness and helpfulness.

A Painless Move

Janet and I moved quite a few times during the years. I often say, "If you and your wife can move without getting a divorce, you have a pretty solid marriage!" This time, however, I wanted the move to be as easy as possible.

Pat Makepeace, a member of FBC, Jacksonville and one of Janet's friends, offered to pack, move, unpack, and arrange everything for us when the move was made. She is one of those amazing individuals who likes to do those kinds of things! We agreed with her to do this and to pay her for it. When the time came to leave Jacksonville, Janet and I walked out of the house. Pat took care of the rest. She came to Georgia and stayed ten days with us. Before she and Glenda Pumphrey were through, the house was in perfect order, down to the clothing folded and placed in the drawers!

This was it. We would be leaving the city where we lived for almost a quarter of a century. I drove around a bit. I went to the church. I looked at the buildings. I reflected on the wonderful services and events I experienced there. I shed some tears of joy for the blessings and some of sadness at my departure.

Soul-Winning Memories

As I drove around the city, special memories flooded my heart. I reflected on the many Tuesday nights I visited in the homes of lost people. As I passed certain streets, I recalled people who came to Christ. Matt and Sandi came to mind. They started visiting our church. They requested I come to visit them. When I got there, a marriage was about to be torn apart. I shared the Roman Road with them. I led them in a sinner's prayer. Both were saved. Every year upon my return to First Baptist, they greet me and thank me for leading them to the Lord.

Mr. Lance lived just off Beach Boulevard. I remember well the night I witnessed to him. He said, "It sounds too easy."

I asked him if he had grandchildren. He had a grandson, who was the apple of his eye. "Suppose there was something in the kitchen you wanted him to have? Would you barricade the kitchen door, hide it in the kitchen, and make it difficult for him to get it?"

"Oh, no," he replied, "I would put it on the table and tell him to come get it."

I told him God had done the hard part. He sent His Son to die on the cross for his sins. All he had to do was receive Christ as His personal Savior. Tears filled his eyes. Then he said, "Well, it just sounds too good to be true." But it is true. And he found the gift of salvation that night.

I could write several books about my experiences in the homes of lost people in the rural, village, town, and city homes where I visited through the years. I look back on these witnessing experiences with great joy. I can't say with Paul, "I continue unto this day, witnessing both to small and great" (Acts 26:22). I missed too many opportunities. I did not witness as faithfully as I should have.

One failure still haunts me. Many times when I would finish my studying for the day and head to church, I would stop for a diet drink at a convenience store near the house. There was a young lady in the store at the cash register who had a thumb that looked reconstructed. You couldn't miss it. On several occasions I sensed I needed to talk to her. I was busy, often running rather tight on the way to a meeting. I didn't say anything to her. Soon thereafter she was no longer at the store.

Several months later I was on my way home from church. The winter day was cold. When it got cold in Jacksonville, it was cold! I stopped at a red light. Standing alongside the road was a Moonie selling roses. I looked and saw the thumb. The girl I failed to tell about Jesus. A great sense of shame overwhelmed me. I should have led her to the Son; they led her to the Moon.

Just One More Soul

I asked the Lord to help me lead someone to Christ before we left Jacksonville. Our next-door neighbors were wonderful people. Both husband and wife were police officers. We learned to love Tom and Sandi. During the days of death threats because of the Muhammad statement, Tom assured us we could call on them anytime.

Sandi was not saved. I tried to witness to her from time to time. She was respectful but made clear she was not interested. The night before we were leaving, Sandi called Janet and asked her what time we would be leaving. Janet told her we planned to leave at 8:30 the next morning. Sandi said she was working the night shift but would be over to see us at 8:15. She was right on time. I became keenly aware of the reason she wanted to be there. "Are you ready to receive Jesus as your personal Savior, Sandi?" Tears rolled down her cheeks. She nodded yes. I led her in a sinner's prayer. Sandi received Jesus as her personal Savior.

Talk about a glimpse of glory! Janet got in her car. I got in mine. We left where we had lived our lives the last twenty-three years and seven months. I rejoiced. We left our subdivision. I praised the Lord. We passed our beloved church. I wept. We got on I-10 to head to Georgia. I shouted, "Good-bye, dear Jacksonville." You can get the boy out of Georgia, but you can't get Georgia out of the boy. Georgia on my mind.

Three quarters of ministry were now completed. The game was rough but exciting. The game was being won. Still more game left to play. The final outcome would be determined in the remaining minutes. I still had on my pads and helmet. There were some scars from the fierceness of the contest. Time to raise four fingers in the air. Toward this final quarter I had been headed all my ministry. The fourth quarter was just ahead.

Chapter 20

The Fourth Quarter

Jerry Falwell frequently talked about the latter part of a man's ministry. He called it "the fourth quarter" ministry. That always appealed to me. Being an avid college football fan, I know the importance of the fourth quarter. Very often this is when the game is won or lost. All the training, planning, strategy, and effort pay off in the final fifteen minutes of the game.

The worst possible thing that can happen is for a team to blow a big lead and lose the game in the final minutes. Likewise, a ministry can be lost or hopelessly stained in the final years. What comes to your mind when you think of David? Perhaps his victory over Goliath? Or his failure in the Bathsheba affair? I have seen more than one ministry marred by foolish, sinful behavior toward its conclusion.

My constant prayer through the years is to finish well. God is gracious to me. There is no scandal or moral failure to mar my ministry. I am keenly aware, however, that the game is not over. I pray daily, as I have through the years, that He will keep me clean. I do not want to bring any reproach on the name of my Lord and Savior, Jesus Christ. Nor do I want it to be said, "The name of God is blasphemed among the Gentiles through you" (Rom. 2:24).

Actually, though, the outcome of the game itself is not in doubt. We are promised we can be thankful to "God, which always causes us to triumph in Christ" (2 Cor. 2:14). I often tell congregations about my fourth-quarter ministry: the game is not in doubt. The game is already won. I'm just putting points on the board. I'm just running up the score! I want to stay faithful and productive until the final gun is sounded.

I didn't know exactly how the game plan would unfold in my fourth-quarter ministry. I planned to continue preaching, of course. I envisioned continuing writing. I hoped to have conferences to assist preachers in the preparation and delivery of their sermons. I just hadn't put it all together in my mind.

Jerry Vines Ministries, Inc.

Two of my fine young deacons asked me to have lunch with them. David Hodges and Tom Stimler were great friends and faithful to the work of the Lord at First Baptist, Jacksonville. Over lunch they asked me about my plans. I shared the general outline of what I hoped to do. Then they challenged me. They asked me to make it a full-time ministry, much more extensive than I intended. The forward-reaching ideas they shared for my ministry inspired me. They expressed their willingness to help me not only in prayer but financially.

I liked their ideas. Many years before I set up a 501c3 nonprofit ministry. The name would be changed to Jerry Vines Ministries, Inc. Someone should be secured to direct it for me. My son, Jon, was a whiz at computers, the Internet, and the operation of ministries. After graduation from Liberty University, he had worked for a number of ministries. One of them was the online division of Liberty. I asked him to be my chief operations officer. He was willing. We held some meetings with individuals who were interested in my ministry and were willing to provide financial support. The Jerry Davises, R. C. Mills, and many others were helpful with their financial gifts. The Mills also graciously provided their lovely condo where I stay when I am in the Jacksonville area. Jerry Vines Ministries was underway!

I quickly filled my speaking schedule. A number of pastor friends asked me to come to their churches. I received numerous invitations to speak at conferences in various states. God is good to provide these opportunities for me. Each year's schedule filled up quickly. I met some new pastor friends. There are some wonderful, dedicated pastors in churches of all sizes. I never felt there are big and little churches. That may be true as to numbers, but it need not be true in vision and ministry. All across this country are pastors who love the Lord and are leading their churches to reach the lost. A church little in size can be BIG in its work.

I did something else. I set up a schedule of study. During most of my years as a pastor, I gave my mornings to God in study, my afternoons to the work of the church, my evenings to my family. Upon retirement I set up a study plan. If a preacher doesn't continue to study, he will dry up intellectually and spiritually. I assigned myself further studies in the biblical languages, Old Testament and New Testament, church history and theology, and homiletics. My studies in these retirement years are sufficient to earn several more graduate degrees. My purpose was not that, however. I just wanted to continue to learn. I wanted to be the sharpest instrument possible to place into the hands of the Lord for His use.

I was able to do more writing and book publishing than previously was possible. I republished some books. I also published a book on the days of creation versus evolution. Titled *24/7*, this book was done in 2005; 2007 saw the publication of *Immortal Kombat*, a brief treatment of the book of Job. In 2008 I put out the little book based on the book of Ruth entitled *It Happened in a Bethlehem Field*. I built the book around the Christmas story. I was happy to complete *A Journey through the Bible, Old Testament* and *A Journey through the Bible, New Testament* in 2011. These books are based on the survey of every book of the Bible I did during Church Training at Jacksonville. For some time I had been wanting to do a daily devotional book. This came to fruition in 2012 with the publication of *All the Days: Daily Devotions for Busy Believers*. This may become my most widely distributed book; 2012 saw the publication of a small booklet on church music entitled *Bring Me a Minstrel*. Also, *Whosoever: Revealing the Riches of John 3:16* was published.

The Falwell Funeral

Jerry Falwell also talked about his own death. He was making fifty-year plans! His dream was for Liberty's football team to play Notre Dame. He said, "One day in a wheelchair, I plan to be at the fifty-yard line in South Bend when we whip Notre Dame." I heard him say several times, "If you read some day soon that 'Jerry Falwell has died,' be assured that I was greatly surprised."

The day came sooner than any of us expected. I knew Jerry was struggling with some health problems, but he seemed bigger than life to me. In May 2007 I heard the news on television that Jerry had been rushed to the hospital. I called his associate, my friend Duke Westover. He confirmed Jerry was dead. The news spread worldwide.

Jerry Falwell will go down as one of our greatest Christian visionaries. God used him to build a great church and a great university. His impact on national politics will be written about for years to come.

I was asked to conduct his funeral. Franklin Graham and Elmer Towns assisted me. Jerry and Judy Davis flew us to the funeral service. The crowd was unbelievably huge. Men from all walks of life, religious and secular, were present. I applied Paul's words about David to Jerry: "After he had served his own generation by the will of God, fell on sleep" (Acts 13:36). I told the people Jerry made plain to me he didn't want a lengthy funeral. If it went over forty-five minutes, he was getting out of the casket and walking out! I took a cautious glance at the casket. I pointed out that, like David, Dr. Falwell had three special anointings: (1) as a pastor, (2) as a founder of a great Christian university, and (3) as a national statesman. He indeed served his own generation by the will of God.

I spoke at the funeral services of three of God's greatest men: Jess Hendley, Adrian Rogers, and Jerry Falwell. I miss these men greatly. They were very wise. I find myself to this day wanting to pick up the phone and ask their opinion about a matter. I said at Jerry's funeral that he told many people I was his best friend in the ministry. I also said, when he said that, a thousand preachers were stunned. They all thought they were! Jerry was that kind of man. As was Adrian. My life is richer because of having known and served the Lord with them.

Darrell Gilyard

For several years our family has celebrated Christmas in Pigeon Forge, Tennessee. The hot Christmases in Jacksonville just weren't conducive to a white Christmas. We go there with the entire family. The children and grandchildren have a large cabin. Janet, now Mema to the grandchildren, and I (I'm Poppy) have our own cabin. You learn some things along the way! After having a fun time with family, Mema and Poppy head to the quietness of our own cabin.

In December 2008, Christmastime, I received a phone call. Darrell Gilyard called and told me he had done something stupid. The call was a harbinger of things to come. I first met Darrell in the late 1980s when he was in our singles' ministry in Jacksonville. He was very active. Sometimes in the Tuesday night visitation testimony time he would give his testimony. He obviously was a gifted speaker. On an occasion I asked him if he ever considered he might be called to preach. He said he had and believed he was. Homer and I were so thrilled. We followed an open-door policy at the church. We were truly a "whosoever will" church. I was told at one time our church had the largest African-American membership of any predominantly white church in the Southern Baptist Convention. I don't know how anyone ever came to that conclusion. Such might be the case. But we didn't keep membership records of the racial identity of our members.

I called Dr. Paige Patterson, then president of the Criswell College. He arranged for Darrell to receive a free education at the school. Darrell moved to Dallas. His remarkable abilities quickly manifested themselves. He was soon serving as an assistant in a local church. From there he moved on to a church in Oklahoma.

There were rumors. Accusations of moral improprieties began to surface. All of them were denied by Darrell. Dr. Patterson checked them out as best he could. There were inconsistencies and contradictions in the stories. Some were made by church people who had moral failings themselves. One accuser was a member of the KKK. As it turns out, all the rumors were true. A young person in our FBC, Jacksonville church met with me about a matter of impropriety as well.

Darrell returned to Dallas to be pastor of Victory Baptist Church. The church was multiracial. The growth of the church was phenomenal. Soon more rumors. Though denied, they turned out to be true also. Dr. Patterson demanded to Darrell that he resign as pastor of the church. He did so. Dr. Patterson did everything a man could do to help in the situation. He is responsible for Darrell leaving the church. Amazingly, some of the members wanted him to stay! He was married at the time. His wife left him with their small son. After a period of time, Darrell came back to Jacksonville in 1993 to become pastor of Shiloh Metropolitan Baptist Church. I did not see him for ten years. I heard Homer went to see him. I do not know this to be true. Homer never mentioned it to me.

Jerry Falwell used Darrell and widely distributed a DVD of one of his sermons. Turns out much of his personal story was not true. Several years after Darrell returned to Jacksonville, Dr. Falwell visited Darrell and saw his church. He led the church to build a four thousand-seat auditorium. Falwell asked me to visit with Darrell. I wasn't sure.

I arranged a meeting with the father/son co-pastorate of the Rudolph McKissicks at Bethel Baptist Institutional Church. Bethel is the most influential African-American congregation in Jacksonville. I asked for their counsel. They encouraged me to make the visit. I felt I should. Not to go would have opened me up to accusations of racism.

I met with Darrell. He went through his story. He admitted his moral failings, apologized, and asked for my forgiveness. He assured me he had been clean since coming back to Jacksonville.

I had no other option but to forgive him. I felt he disqualified himself to ever be a pastor again. But I did not call him; the church did. Perhaps I could be helpful to him and to the church. I met with him from time to time. I was often concerned by the obvious materialism. I warned him about it. I was naive and never even thought he might be continuing immoral activities. After my retirement I preached for him on two occasions. There were thirty-five professions of faith the first time. Perhaps I should not have done so. At the time I just felt I could be helpful.

The phone call in the mountains was the first sign I had been misled. I will not go into all the matters that transpired. He pled guilty to charges for sex crimes against minors and served three years in prison.

I was severely criticized by some. I am amazed at how there were those who would accuse me of covering up Gilyard's immorality. When the time for the trial came, I made this statement to the *Florida Times-Union*: "I extended forgiveness and mercy to him, and evidently he trampled upon them. No minister, if guilty of sexual improprieties, especially with underage children, should ever be allowed to stand behind the sacred desk again. Let the truth be found and let justice be done."[28] Conveniently, those who criticized me, never quoted this statement.

I have been helped to understand the whole matter by a book written by Watchman Nee, *The Latent Power of the Soul*. The soul and the spirit are so close together only the Word of God can distinguish between the two (Heb. 4:12). Talents emanating from a man's soulish nature can easily be mistaken for spiritual power. I leave the whole matter to the Lord. He will make it all clear to us one day.

Conferences

Meanwhile, my fourth-quarter ministry was doing far better than I ever imagined. I was holding some Power in the Pulpit Conferences. I brought in men who are gifted in sermon preparation and delivery. They assisted me in the conferences. We held them at First Baptist, Woodstock, Pigeon Forge, and other places. These conferences are well received by preachers. Many have thanked me for having them. I believe they serve a useful purpose. I do not have them every year. I try to conduct them from time to time. This is one of the most enjoyable aspects of my fourth quarter.

Worship Wars

I am vitally interested in the role of music in the ministry of the local church. I mentioned that I served as an interim minister of music my first year in Mercer. My dad was my minister of music on one occasion. I stayed close to the ministers of music in my churches. I think I understand just how vital music is in a church worship service. In the booklet I mentioned, *Bring Me a Minstrel*, I state my views on a lot of matters relative to the current worship wars. I am saddened when I see what is intended to bless the people become such a source of conflict and heartache.

Several matters trouble me. I do not make it a big deal, but I feel it is incorrect to refer to the person who leads the music as the worship leader. As I understand the New Testament, the pastor is to lead every aspect of a church's ministry. Properly understood, the pastor is the worship leader. For a pastor to be less than that is to abdicate his responsibility as the spiritual leader of the congregation. Most ministers of music I know welcome input and support from their pastor.

Also, too often in our churches today the music is viewed as the worship time in the service. Sometimes when I am preaching in a church, after the music it will be said, "Hasn't the worship been great today?" Music is only a part of the worship. The preaching of the Word is the central feature of the worship service. When people come to Christ, there is worship (Rom. 15:16). And, ultimately, we really haven't worshipped until we present our bodies to God, which is our "reasonable service or worship" (Rom. 12:1–2).

I am also troubled when young people and children aren't taught the great hymns of the faith. These hymns have stood the test of time. They minister to God's people in special ways and at times of crisis in life. To rob the young of them is a great tragedy. Congregations can be taught to sing the great hymns. Great congregational singing is one of the church's most powerful evangelistic tools. If we aren't careful, congregational singing will be lost in our churches.

I am not against contemporary music. To take such a position would be to oppose any new music being written. Some great songs are being composed today. I am blessed by many of them. Some modern lyrics, however, aren't very deep. Compare "Yes, Lord, yes, yes, Lord" with "Alas! and did my Savior bleed, and did my Sovereign die."

I believe the pendulum will swing back toward a more balanced music ministry in the future. There isn't much further the music can go in the current direction.

Five-Point Calvinism

Five-point Calvinism is nothing new. The history of Calvinist theology is well documented. Many of my lifetime friends are five-point Calvinists. I have preached for them; they have preached for me. Though we engage in friendly discussions about where we differ, there is never any breach in fellowship. But something new is on the scene. On more than one occasion, I stated the problem currently creating havoc in the SBC is not classic Calvinism but a new Calvinism. I describe it as "hostile, aggressive and militant."

I was asked to speak on Calvinism on a Sunday night at First Baptist, Woodstock. I did so. This lecture is on my CD series *Baptist Battles.* My presentation was irenic and kind. I just tried to honestly present my views concerning the theology of five-point Calvinism and the controversy that was developing because of it. Whatever our view on the subject, we have the right and the responsibility to set forth what we believe.

I also sponsored my first John 3:16 Conference. The conference was held at First Baptist, Woodstock, in 2008. Approximately eight hundred people attended. I brought the opening address, using John 3:16 as my text. The speakers, all Southern Baptist scholars, gave a critique of one of the five points of Calvinism, commonly called TULIP. As a review of the taped messages will reveal, a respectful, Christlike spirit was reflected in each of the presentations. These lectures became the substance of a book published by B&H Publishing Group entitled *Whosoever Will: A Biblical-Theological Critique of Five-Point Calvinism*, edited by David Allen and Steve Lemke. The book is an academic best seller.

As a result of my message and the John 3:16 Conference, I was attacked by many new Calvinists. I really wasn't surprised. What surprised me was how some of my own brethren distanced themselves from me. I guess I should not have been.

I learned an important lesson at junior high camp many years ago. My cabin was supervised by a guy in his twenties. We campers were all twelve to fourteen. He was a bully who made our week miserable. Each night we huddled together and grumbled about him.

One night someone said, "Hey, there are a lot more of us. We can take him."

"Yea," we all agreed.

We decided to confront him the last morning of the camp. There was a prearranged signal. D-Day came. We circled him and told him we were tired of his bullying. The signal to charge was given. I charged. I was the only one who did! The scene wasn't pretty after that. I learned an important lesson. Many talk a good game. When the time comes to take a stand, you may be the only one to do so. To paraphrase Vance Havner: Too many are known for caution under cover, not courage under fire!

The lack of courage on the part of many today is a concern. But I care not what others may do. I will take my stand for what I believe is right, regardless. This is what I did in the Conservative Resurgence. I am grateful there were many leaders and pastors who were courageous enough to take the same stand. I can truthfully say I hold no grudges against those who have not stood with me through the years on whatever issue.

I sponsored another John 3:16 Conference in 2013. The attendance was not as strong as the first one. I did not expect it to be. The subjects were more academic in content. There are also more and more conferences for people to attend. I was pleased with the attendance. I plan to do additional conferences as I perceive the need.

I speak as lovingly as I know how on this issue. Those of us who do not subscribe to five-point Calvinism have as much right to set forth our views as those who do. To so do is not to be combative, divisive, or a disturber of unity. I am responding to a theological system with which I disagree. I am not attacking individuals who hold to the five points of Calvinism.

Calvinism is rather difficult to engage. So many different shades, nuances, and views held by people, it is difficult to pin down. When you address one form of the theology, you hear, "That's not what we believe; quit representing our theology." Then the same thing happens when you speak to another facet of the theology.

I view all systematic theologies as man-made attempts to systematize the unsystematizable (is that a new word?!). We should attempt to do it. But we must realize all of our systems are man-made. There is no way we can squeeze the infinite mind of God into our finite systems. To overemphasize one area of biblical truth to the exclusion of another is to miss the beautiful balance we find in Scripture.

The most problematic part of "TULIP" for me is limited atonement. I might add it is also problematic for a number of Calvinists as well. I believe in a "whosoever will" gospel. I believe anyone, anywhere may believe on the Lord Jesus Christ and be saved. I do not believe Jesus died ONLY for the elect. I find nowhere in Scripture Jesus died ONLY for the elect. I view such as a truncated gospel. He did die for the elect, to be sure. But not ONLY for the elect. I believe He died for all of the sins of all of the people of the world. John 3:16 and 1 John 2:2 settle it for me. I believe the overwhelming majority of Southern Baptist people believe this as well. For a preacher to come into a church "under the radar" without stating clearly his position on the atonement is dishonest and unethical. This is tearing churches asunder throughout the convention.

I signed a statement with others who are now referred to as traditionalists. I signed it because it articulated my belief that Christ died for the sins of every person in the whole world. As I stated at the time, I find myself in general agreement with the statement. This does not mean I subscribe to every detail therein. However, I do not want to be called a traditionalist. I certainly do not want to be accused of being a heretic or inane because I signed it. To be called an anti-Calvinist is certainly offensive to me. I am not against people who are Calvinists. If you believe disagreement means a lack of love, I hope you aren't married! I am most certainly not an Arminian. I refuse to allow any other person's label to define me. I am sure many from other viewpoints would say what I am going to say. I just want to be known as a Bible-believing Baptist Christian.

Five-point Calvinism can have a devastating effect on the Southern Baptist Convention. Evangelism and missions, the core of the convention's life, will not be helped but be hindered in my opinion. I reiterate what I have previously said: There are five-point Calvinists who are evangelistic. But they are in spite of their Calvinism, not because of it. To say Jesus Christ died on the cross for only the sins of the elect is certainly not good news to all the people of the world.

What will be the outcome? Only God knows. I am perfectly comfortable resting in His providence. I do not fret and worry about it. God is far bigger than the Southern Baptist Convention. I am actually rather optimistic. Calvinism carries within itself the seeds of its own demise. Whatever the outcome of the Calvinist debate, He will accomplish His purposes. Contrary to what some may think, I do believe in His sovereignty! I wrote a book on John 3:16 entitled *Whosoever: Revealing the Riches of John 3:16*. This small book gives the essence of what I believe about the matter. I do not plan to dwell on the issue. I have a limited amount of game time. I must maximize what I am able to do for the Lord as the game draws toward its conclusion.

Total Abstinence

Another concern of mine is the alcohol issue. I am aware many sweet, wonderful people use alcohol in a social setting. What follows is not intended to offend them in any way. I'm just going to state my own position as kindly and lovingly as I know how.

I have never tasted an intoxicating beverage. I am glad I was brought up in a church that counseled against alcohol. The first study course I conducted in my first church was *Shadow over America*, a Southern Baptist study course book taking a total abstinence position relative to alcohol. I led all my churches to take strong stands against the sale and use of alcohol.

I am proud to be part of a denomination that has consistently taken a strong antialcohol stand. In more resolutions than I can number, Southern Baptists always take a firm stance against it. Imagine then, my shock, when a routine resolution against alcohol was opposed by young men at a Southern Baptist Convention meeting. This was my first indication that all was not well.

I guess I just didn't keep up with where things were headed. I have since learned that some young pastors teach moderation and drink themselves. In light of the tremendous damage it does in our culture—the broken homes, little children's lives scarred and personal destruction of millions—how can this be wise? Proverbs 20:1 says, "Wine is a mocker, strong drink is raging: and whosoever is deceived is not wise." I have a lecture setting forth my views about what Scripture teaches on the use and abuse of alcohol. This is in my CD series Baptist Battles. The first step to the abuse of alcohol is its use. The first step to addiction is moderation. If you never use it, you will never abuse it. If you never use it in moderation, you will never abuse it in addiction. I can guarantee this: if you never drink, you will never be an alcoholic. So I just plead with you to consider what is wise relative to the use of alcohol.

To those of you who take a different view, don't allow my blunt language to offend you. Take it as coming from the heart of an older preacher who loves you and is trying to spare you great miseries down the road.

Technology

I am discovering some wonderful tools to use in my work for the Lord. The computer, iPhones, iPads, social media, etc. are all opening new avenues of study and service for me. I was born fifty years too soon.

Three surgeries have greatly helped my eyesight. The use of the iPad, however, has made my reading much easier. I am able to adjust the font to a size that makes reading easier. Before, I read about one book a week. Now I am reading two. I have hundreds of commentaries, language tools, etc. available to me. I can do instant research. I can type out my sermon outlines and download them to my iPad. Wow, what a day!

I'm just now learning to use social media. Jon is helpful to me in this. I don't care for blogs too much. A lot of negative blogging brings an ugliness and divisiveness to the Christian community. I suppose it is like every other form of communication; you can use it for positive or negative purposes. I just see it abused so often, I guess. I especially like Twitter. I primarily use it for encouragement. And for fun. I am in a new day of opportunity because of the technology available to me. I am learning how to use the newest technology in my ministry. I can write articles, send out e-mails, and literally touch the world through my website. What a glorious day to be a servant of the Lord!

Full Schedule

I am amazed at how the Lord keeps filling up my schedule. As I write, I am full for the next year and a half. The Lord keeps opening up marvelous doors for preaching and writing. I am continuing to write books. I am producing CD sermon series. I am producing a Sunday school curriculum based on my sermon notes through the Bible. The five-year New Testament curriculum is finished and available for churches. I am almost halfway through the five-year Old Testament curriculum. Many churches are finding this curriculum helpful. I am grateful Jerry Vines Ministries is making this available.

I am making big plans for the future. The book you are currently reading is my most current one. I have plans to take me to my one hundredth birthday! I hope to produce devotional commentaries on every book of the Bible. I may not live long enough to get them all published. No problem. The material is available. Just editorial work needs to be done. I would hope it would be said of me as it was said of Abel, "He being dead yet speaketh" (Heb. 11:4).

Early in my life I saw you can go through life in one of two ways. You can be miserable or happy. I decided to take the happy route. I am now in the fourth quarter. I pray constantly that the Lord will help me not to become a bitter old man. I can truthfully say I am filled with blessedness, not bitterness. Why should I be bitter? My heart is filled with love for everybody. And, "I wouldn't take nothing for my journey now!"

A great joy to my life is the grandchildren. I look forward to being with them for our Christmas in the Smoky's each year. Brittney, Ashlyn, Jay, Caroline, Catherine, Jack, and Carson are special to their Mema and Poppy.

I love the fourth quarter. The final seconds are ticking away. The outcome of the game is not in doubt. We are now in the victory formation. I'm about to take a knee. The final whistle will soon blow. Now, "Thanks be to God, which giveth us the victory through our Lord Jesus Christ" (1 Cor. 15:57). The celebration is just ahead!

Epilogue

I'm going to close with the account of my death. I know, I really can't do that. Scholars have raised concerns about Moses' account of his death as found in the last chapter of Deuteronomy. If Moses is the human author, as most conservative scholars believe, how could he give the account of his own death? Before the fact? Of course, we would have to say God could have revealed Moses' death to him before the fact. But there is another option. There is no problem in believing that someone else, perhaps Joshua, added this conclusion to the book. This is not unheard of in literature. Gleason Archer considers the account of Moses' death a "kind of obituary notice that is added to the main text of the book."[29] But, I reiterate, God could have revealed the details of Moses' death to him ahead of time.

I prefer to write my own obituary. Oh, not the time, nor the cause, or even if it occurs at all. Jesus may come before I die, you know. When I was a young preacher, I used to say I couldn't decide if I would rather be dead when Jesus returns or alive. If dead, on resurrection day I would like to experience the kick when I come through the grave clods. If alive, at the rapture I would like to feel the thrill when I am caught up. The older I have become, the more attractive rapture is to me! "Oh, joy! oh, delight! should we go without dying, No sickness, no sadness, no dread and no crying. Caught up through the clouds with our Lord into glory, When Jesus receives 'His own.'"[30]

But, If I die before Jesus returns, I can tell you a lot about it. One moment I will be here; the next I will be there. This Billy Baptist and his Bible will walk through the gates of pearl onto streets of gold. I look forward to seeing my mother and father, Totsi and Ruby, who preceded me. I will be excited to see Poppa Johnson and other family members again. What a happy reunion. I will see Adrian Rogers and Jerry Falwell. "What took you so long, Dr. Kudzu," Adrian will probably say. Falwell will be grinning from ear to ear. Friends and mentors will greet me. Then I will go to see our ascended Lord. O what a moment! I shall see His face. No more glimpses of glory; I will gaze upon the glory revealed in the face of my Savior, the Lord Jesus Christ! Then, I will take a knee. And I will say, "Thou art worthy, O Lord, to receive glory and honour and power" (Rev. 4:11).

I pray He will be able to say to me, "Well done, thou good and faithful servant." If so, that will be heaven enough for me.

Appendix: Chronology

1825 — Indian treaty ceding land including Carroll County, Georgia to U.S. government.

1825, May 30—Chief Williams McIntosh murdered.

1826 — Carroll County, Georgia, chartered.

1829 — Carrollton, Georgia, incorporated.

1899 — Central Baptist Church constituted.

1914, June—Tabernacle Baptist building completed.

1936, September 19—Clarence Vines and Ruby Johnson married.

1937, September 22—My birth.

1947, March 16—Conversion experience.

1955 — Graduation from Carrollton, Georgia, High School.

1956 — Ordained to the gospel ministry, Tabernacle Baptist Church, Carrollton, Georgia.
Pastor, Centralhatchee Baptist Church, Centralhatchee, Georgia.

1957 — Pastor, Bethesda Baptist Church, Carroll County, Georgia.

1959 — Graduation from Mercer University, BA.

1960, December 17—Married to Janet Denney.

1961 — Pastor, Second Baptist Church, Cedartown, Georgia.

1964 — Pastor, Eureka Baptist Church, Carrollton, Georgia.

1965 — Pastor, Second Baptist Church, Cedartown, Georgia.

1966 — Graduation from New Orleans Baptist Theological Seminary, BD.
       Pastor, First Baptist Church, Fort Oglethorpe, Georgia.

1968 — Pastor, West Rome Baptist Church, Rome, Georgia.

1974 — Graduation from Luther Rice Seminary, Th.D.

1974 — Pastor, Dauphin Way Baptist Church, Mobile, Alabama.

1976 — Elected president, Alabama Baptist Pastors' Conference.

1976 — Elected president, Southern Baptist Pastors' Conference.

1976 — Lost in election for Alabama Baptist Convention president.

1977 — Lost in runoff, Southern Baptist Convention president.

1979 — Pastor, West Rome Baptist Church, Rome, Georgia.

1982 — Pastor, First Baptist Church, Jacksonville, Florida.

1986 — Served on Southern Baptist Convention Peace Committee.

1988 — Elected president, Southern Baptist Convention.

1989 — Reelected president, Southern Baptist Convention.

1999 — Served on BFM Revision Committee.

2006 — Retired as pastor of First Baptist Convention, Jacksonville,
       Florida.

Appendix: Books Published

1975 — *Family Fellowship* (Epistles of John)
      God Speaks Today (1 Corinthians)

1977 — *Fire In The Pulpit*
      I Shall Return—Jesus

1979 — *Great Events in the Life of Christ*

1981 — *Interviews with Jesus*

1982 — *Acts Alive* (Evangelism)

1985 — *A Practical Guide to Sermon Preparation*

1986 — *A Guide to Effective Sermon Delivery*

1989 — *Exploring the Epistles of John* (formerly *Family Fellowship*)
      Wanted: Soulwinners

1990 — *Wanted: Church Growers*

1990 — *Exploring Daniel*

1992 — *Exploring Mark*
      Basic Bible Sermons on the Ten Commandments

1993 — *Believer's Guide to Hebrews*

1998 — *Spirit Life*

1999 — *Spirit Works*
Power in the Pulpit (How to Prepare and Deliver Expository Sermons)

2000 — *Spirit Fruit*

2003 — *Pursuing God's Own Heart* (Lessons from the Life of David)

2004 — *24/7* (The Genesis Account of Creation)

2006 — *God's Perfect 10* (Previously *Basic Bible Sermons on the Ten Commandments*)

2007 — *Immortal Kombat* (A Study of the Book of Job)

2008 — *It Happened at Bethlehem* (Lessons from the Book of Ruth)
Sermon Outlines (Matthew and Mark)

2006 — *The Corinthian Confusion* (Formerly *God Speaks Today*)

2009 — *People Who Met Jesus* (Formerly *Interviews with Jesus*)

2010 — *The Spirit Book* (Formerly *Spirit Life, Spirit Works, Spirit Fruit*)

2011 — *A Journey through the Bible: Old Testament*
A Journey through the Bible: New Testament

2012 — *All the Days: Daily Devotions for Busy Believers*

2013 — *Bring Me a Minstrel: Building Blocks for a New Testament Music Ministry*
Whosoever: Revealing the Riches of John 3:16

2014 — *VINES: My Life And Ministry*

Notes

1. James C. Bonner, *Georgia's Last Frontier: The Development of Carroll County* (Athens, GA: University of Georgia Press, 1971).

2. George Chapman, *Chief William McIntosh: A Man of Two Worlds* (Atlanta: Cherokee Publishing Company, 1988), 157.

3. Ibid., 76.

4. Bonner, *Georgia's Last Frontier*, 22.

5. "History of the Baptist Denomination in Georgia," *The Christian Index*, (1881), 161.

6. Bonner, *Georgia's Last Frontier*, 149.

7. Much of the material in this chapter is taken from my Th.D. dissertation entitled "A History of Tabernacle Baptist Church, Carrollton, Georgia, 1899–1973," presented to Luther Rice Seminary, May 1974.

8. Ibid., 6–8.

9. Ibid., 33.

10. Ibid., 34.

11. Ibid., 35.

12. Vines, "A History of Tabernacle Baptist Church," 58.

13. Jefferson Hascall, "Oh, Come, Angel Band," public domain.

14. Emil Brunner, *Faith, Hope and Love* (Philadelphia: Westminster, 1956), 47.

15. B. B. McKinney, "I Know the Bible Is True," © Broadman Press.

16. George Atkins, "Brethren, We Have Met to Worship," public domain.

17. George A. Young, "God Leads Us Along," public domain.

18. Edward H. Joy, "All Your Anxiety," © Salvationist Publishing & Supplies Ltd., 1953.

19. *Baptist Press*, January 23, 1969.

20. John W. Peterson, © John W. Peterson Music Company, 1948, 1976.

21. Minutes, SBC meeting, Dallas, Texas, 1985.

22. SBC Minutes, Saint Louis, 1987.

23. Carl L. Kell and L. Raymond Camp, *In the Name of the Father* (Carbondale: Southern Illinois University Press, 1999), 56.

24. Adrian Rogers, "Foreword," in Jerry Vines, *A Baptist and His Bible* (Jacksonville: First Baptist Church, 1987).

25. Bob Terry, "Encouraging Signs from the SBC," *Word and Way*, June 22, 1989.

26. Jim Hefley, *The Truth in Crisis: The Winning Edge*, vol. 5 of The Controversy in the Southern Baptist Convention (Garland, TX: Hannibal Books, 1991), 79.

27. *Florida Times-Union*, August 26, 2001.

28. *Florida Times-Union*, January 15, 2008.

29. Gleason L. Archer, *Bible Difficulties* (Grand Rapids: Zondervan, 1982), 154.

30. H. L. Turner, "Christ Returneth," public domain.

Classic Messages.
Timeless Stories.

You can find resources like these, plus much more at
jerryvines.com

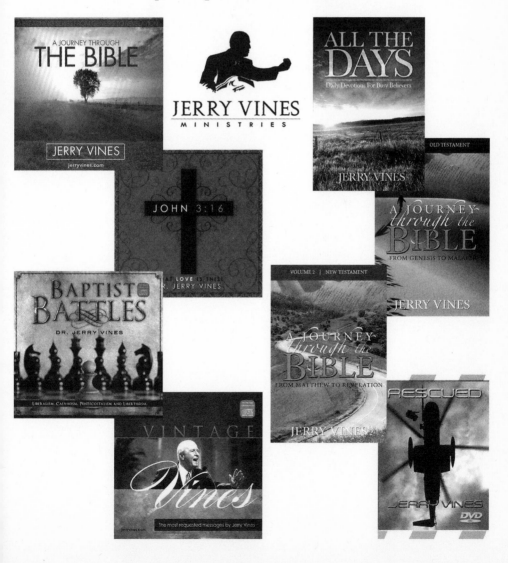

Chief William McIntosh who
signed treaty ceding Creek
Indians' land to U.S. that
became Carroll County.

Chief William McIntosh's grave
at his home place.

Adamson Square, center of Carrollton,
Georgia, economic, social life.

Dad's basketball team. He is third from the right.

Oldest picture, under lock
and key—two years old.

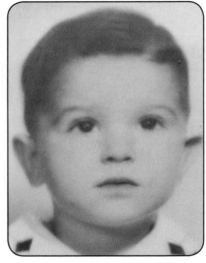

I was probably around
four years old.

My parents and I in
St. Petersburg, Florida.

I attended College Street
Grammar School.

About the time I met the Lord
at Tabernacle Baptist Church.

Mother and I.

Grandfather Johnson who
greatly influenced me.

Tabernacle Baptist Church,
Carrollton, Georgia, my spiritual
birthplace.

I attended Carrollton High School
in Carrollton, Georgia.

I played end, offense and
defense on football team.

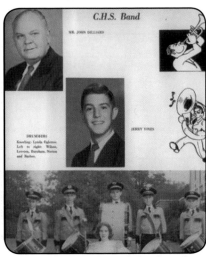

I was captain of the band in
high school.

I was associate editor of the high
school paper, The Gold and
Black.

My sister Brenda in high school.

I graduated from high
school in 1955.

My first church:
Centralhatchee Baptist
Church.

My country preacher buddies:
Seated: Carl Tapley; Standing left
to right: Danny Watters, Charles
Williams, Roop Caswell, and
Horace Wilson. I love old preachers!

Our wedding day.

Bethesda Baptist Church,
where I fell off Jacob's Ladder.

Cutting the wedding cake.

Leaving the wedding ceremony.

Janet (above) and I (left) standing outside our trailer in New Orleans. Did I mention no air-conditioning?

Standing in front of Cedartown Second Baptist Church.

Joe Kines, outstanding College Football Defensive-Coordinator. He was brought up at Cedartown Second Baptist Church.

Breaking ground for new West Rome Baptist Auditorium. Duke Westover, longtime friend and construction manager.

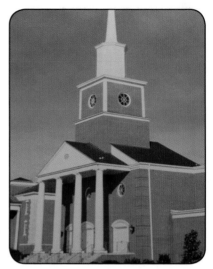

West Rome Baptist Church.

Our family in Mobile, Alabama.

Presiding at 1977 Kansas City Southern Baptist Convention Pastors' Conference.

Paige Patterson, theologian of the Conservative Resurgence and a wild game hunter.

Judge Paul Pressler, strategist of the Conservative Resurgence.

Adrian Rogers and I on the famous "Cruise of the Cardinals."

Homer Lindsay Jr. and I.

Family picture at First Baptist Church, Jacksonville.

Janet and I at First Baptist Church, Jacksonville.

Preaching in the new First Baptist Church, Jacksonville auditorium.

Janet and I in our
Jacksonville backyard.

Jerry Falwell and I became
great friends.

Talking with James
Hefley, author of *The
Truth in Crisis*.

Watching a boxing match at Jerry
Falwell's house with Ed Young,
Charlie Thompson, Richard Lee,
Freddie Gage, and Jack Graham.

Preaching at the Southern
Baptist Convention Pastors'
Conference before election in
San Antonio.

Jerry Falwell,
Liberty
University
Trustees, with
Billy and Ruth
Graham. I was
chairman of
trustees for five
years.

Janet and I after I was elected
president of SBC in San Antonio.

My press conference after
being elected president of the
SBC in San Antonio.

Meeting my political hero,
President Ronald Reagan.

Janet and President Reagan.

Janet and I with President
George H. Bush.

Homer and I with
W. A. Criswell.

Janet and I at Christmas.

O. S. Hawkins and I at 2012
SBC in Houston.

Paige Patterson, David Allen, and I.

Charles Stanley and I.

Bailey Smith and I.

Jr. Hill and I.

Janet and I at Billy Graham's house.

Janet and I visiting Billy Graham.

Janet and I visiting George Bev Shea.

Gov. Mike Huckabee paying me a 40+ year "debt!"

Gerald Wolfe, one of my favorite musicians.

Tim Tebow and I
at retirement.

Franklin Graham and I.

Preaching "Glimpses of Glory"
sermon.

Saying good-bye.

Preaching at First Baptist Church, Jacksonville.

Returning to First Baptist
Church, Jacksonville.

Preaching at Southwestern Baptist
Theological Seminary.

Preaching at First Baptist
Church, Jacksonville
Pastors' Conference, 2012.

SBC President Fred Luter and I.

Preaching for good friend, Dr.
Kevin Cosby, pastor of St. Stephens
Church, Louisville, Kentucky.

Our daughter Jodi doing
Bible study in her apartment.

Carson and Jack having fun in
the mountains at Christmas.

Mema and Poppy with grandchildren in the Smokies.

Grandchildren at the mountain cabin in the Smokies.

Joy, Ashlyn, Brittney, and Tim at Atlanta Braves baseball game.

Jay makes the Tennessee All-State track team.

Jon teaching Carson how to hit a baseball.

Leslie, Caroline, Jay, Jack, Catherine, and Jim at Jay's high school graduation.

Janet and I at our home.

Family picture in the Smoky Mountains.